Highland Scrambles North

Iain Thow

First published in 2022 by
Scottish Mountaineering Press.

Copyright © The Scottish
Mountaineering Club.

All rights reserved. No part of this publication
may be reproduced, stored in or introduced
into a retrieval system, or transmitted, in any
form or by any means (electronic, mechanical,
photocopying, recording or otherwise),
without the prior written permission of
the publisher.

Second Edition 2022.

ISBN 978-1-907233-44-9

A catalogue record for this book is available
from the British Library.

Descriptions of scrambles and climbs in
this guide, their grades and any references
to in situ or natural protection are made in
good faith, based on past or first ascent
descriptions, and are checked and
substantiated where possible by the author.
However, routes lose holds and are altered
by rockfall, the sea and the elements.
Rock can become dirty and loose. In situ
protection or abseil equipment deteriorates.
Even minor alterations can have a dramatic
effect on a route's grade or seriousness. It is
essential that scramblers and climbers judge
the condition of any route for themselves,
before they start.

The authors, editors, friends and assistants
involved in the publication of this guide,
the Scottish Mountaineering Club, the
Scottish Mountaineering Press, the
Scottish Mountaineering Trust and Scottish
Mountaineering Trust (Publications) Ltd,
can therefore accept no liability whatever
for damage to property, nor for personal
injury or death, arising directly or indirectly
from the use of this publication.

Series Editor Noel Williams.
Series design by Gino Di Meo Studio.
Layouts & typesetting by Noel Williams.
Diagram and map graphics by Noel Williams.
Cover artwork, *Liathach* by
Christopher Smith-Duque.
Printed & bound in China by Latitude Press Ltd.

Maps are derived from Ordnance
Survey OpenData™
© Crown copyright and database right 2021

Distributed by Cordee www.cordee.co.uk.
For details of other SMC guidebooks
visit www.smc.org.uk/publications

Highland Scrambles North

Iain Thow

Scottish Mountaineering Club
Scramblers' Guides

Contents

List of Maps & Diagrams	10
Icon Key	13
Acknowledgements	16
Introduction	17
Environment, Safety & Technical Notes	18
Amenities	24
Geology *by Noel Williams*	28
Human History	40
Wildlife *by Ro Scott*	46
Weather	56
Mountaineering History *by Noel Williams*	62

The Great Glen to Knoydart — 70

The Loch Lochy Hills — 72

Meall na Teanga — 73
Central Buttress, Meall Dubh — 74
Right-Hand Buttress, Meall Dubh — 74

Sròn a' Choire Ghairbh — 76
South Face, Sean Mheall — 77

Glenfinnan Area — 78

Sgùrr nan Coireachan — 79
Riabhaich Slabs — 80

Sgùrr Mhuidhe — 83
North-East Flank — 83

Beinn Gharbh — 83
Ursainn Slabs — 84
North-West Face — 85

Morar — 86

Cnoc a' Bhac Fhalaichte — 88
Tarbet Slabs — 88

Sgùrr an Eilein Ghiubhais — 89
Right-Hand Rib — 90

The Rough Bounds — 92

Garbh Chìoch Mhòr — 92
Coire nan Gall Slabs — 93

Beinn an Aodainn (Ben Aden) — 93
South Face — 94
East-North-East Ridge — 95

Knoydart — 97

Beinn na Caillich — 97
South-East Slabs — 97

Ladhar Bheinn — 99
An Dìollaid — 99

Stob a' Chearcaill — 100
North-East Ridge — 100

An Caisteal — 102
South Face — 103

Meall nan Eun — 104
Cannonade — 107

Kintail — 108

Beinn a' Chapuill — 110
East Slabs — 110

The Saddle — 111
Forcan Ridge — 112

Sgùrr na Sgine — 113
North-East Ridge — 113

Aonach air Chrith — 114
North Ridge — 114

Sgùrr nan Conbhairean — 115
North-East Spur — 115

A' Chràileag — 116
Allt Choire a' Chait — 116

Mullach Fraoch-Choire — 117
South Ridge — 117

Sgùrr nan Spainteach — 117
North Buttress — 118

Sgùrr na Ciste Duibhe — 118
North Buttress — 118

Sgùrr an t-Searraich — 119
South Ribs — 121

Beinn Fhada — 121
Bealach an t-Sealgaire (Hunters' Pass) — 122

A' Ghlas-Bheinn — 122
Allt Loch a' Chleirich — 122

Càrnan Cruithneachd — 123
South-West Shoulder — 124

Biod an Fhithich — 126
Ankle Ridge — 127

Glen Affric to Strath Carron — 128

Toll Creagach — 130
Toll Creagach Slab — 130

Càrn Eighe — 130
Càrn Eighe Pinnacles — 131

Sgùrr na Lapaich — 131
East Ridge — 131

Beinn na Muice — 132
South-West Slabs — 133

Càrn Eiteige — 133
Creag a' Chaobh — 133

Creag Ghlas — 135
East Buttress — 136

Bidean a' Choire Sheasgaich — 136
North Face — 136

Lurg Mhòr — 138
Meall Mor Ridge — 138

Bidean an Eòin Deirg — 139
North-East Ridge — 139

Applecross & Coulin — 140

Meall Gorm — 142
Long Buttress — 142

Sgùrr a' Chaorachain	**143**
Cioch Indirect	144
Beinn Bhàn	**144**
A' Chìoch	145
Beinn Damh	**147**
North-East Spur	148
An Ruadh-stac	**149**
Allt Loch Mòine a' Chriathair	150
Eastern Slabs	150
North-West Shoulder	151
Maol Chean-dearg	**151**
Ketchil Buttress	152
East Shoulder	154
North Flank	156
Fuar Tholl	**156**
South Flank	157
Leth Chreag	159
Spare Rib	159
Summit Rib	160
Sgorr Ruadh	**161**
Academy Ridge, Lower Slabs	162
Raeburn's Buttress	163
Beinn Liath Mhòr	**163**
Lochview Slabs	163
Apex Buttress	165
South-East Rib	165
Sgùrr Dubh	**166**
North-West Slabs	167
Sgùrr Dubh Gorge	168

Torridon — 170

Meall Ceann na Creige	**172**
West Spur	172
Beinn Alligin	**175**
Na Fasreidhnean, Tom na Gruagaich	175
Horns of Alligin	175
Backfire Ridge	176
Beinn Dearg	**178**
South-West Face	178
North Ridge, Càrn na Feola	179
Liathach	**180**
South Ridge, Mullach an Rathain	180
Am Fasarinen Traverse	183
East Buttress, Am Fasarinen	185
East Ridge, Stùc a' Choire Dhuibh Bhig	187
North Ridge, Spidean a' Choire Leith	187
PC Buttress	187
Northern Pinnacles	188
Beinn Eighe	**190**
Lawson, Ling & Glover's	191
Ceum Grannda	192
East Buttress, Coire Mhic Fhearchair	193
East Ridge, Stùc Coire an Laoigh	194
North Ridge, Spidean Coire nan Clach	194
Toll Bàn Headwall	195
The Black Carls	196
Ruadh-stac Beag	**197**
Long Stroll Slab	197
Overlooking Rib	199
Beinn a' Mhùinidh	**199**
Bonnaidh Donn, Route One	200
Slioch	**201**
North-West Buttress	202

Gairloch & Loch Maree — 204

Baosbheinn	**206**
Oidhche Spur	206
Meall Aundrary	**207**
North-West Buttress	207
Sìthean Mòr	**210**
North Face	211

An Groban	**211**
North-West Face	212
Humpback Buttress	213
Right-Hand Slabs	214
Creag Mhòr Thollaidh	**215**
North-West Rib	217

Carnmore 218

Beinn a' Chàisgein Mòr	**220**
Grey Ridge	220
Sgùrr na Laocainn Right-Hand	222
Càrnan Bàn	**223**
Pocket Slab	223
South-East Face	224
Cakewalk (Maiden Buttress)	225
Doddle	226
A' Mhaighdean	**226**
Bivouac Rib	227
North-West Ridge	227
Red Slab	228
Kids' Ridge	229
Beinn Tharsuinn Chaol	**230**
Gorm Loch Mòr Spur	231
Beinn Làir	**231**
Tower Ridge	231
North Summit Buttress	233
Left Wing, Butterfly Buttress	233
Meall Mhèinnidh	**234**
North-East Face	234
Beinn Àirigh Charr	**235**
Square Buttress	235
Bell's Route	237

Fisherfield & the Fannaichs 240

Mullach Coire Mhic Fhearchair	**242**
East Ridge	242
Beinn Dearg Mòr	**244**
South-East Ridge	244
East Buttress	245
An Teallach	**246**
Allt a' Ghiubhsachain	246
Ghiubhsachain Slabs	248
Corrag Bhuidhe Traverse	248
Sgùrr Ruadh	252
Beinn nam Bàn	**252**
Windy Ridge	252
Sgùrr nan Clach Geala	**253**
Slanting Buttress	253
Sgùrr Mòr	**255**
North Spur	255

Inverlael & Easter Ross 256

The Ullapool Gorges	**258**
Ardcharnich Gorge	258
Allt a' Gharbhain	258
Allt a' Bhraighe	258
Allt na h-Ighine	259
Allt Leacachain	259
Am Faochagach	**260**
Cnoc na h-Iolaire	260
Cona' Mheall	**262**
Twisted Rib	263
South Ridge	263
North-East Slab	264
Cnap Coire Loch Tuath	**265**
South Face	265
Meall nan Ceapraichean	**266**
West Face	267
Seana Bhraigh	**268**
An Sgùrr Ridge	268
Corriemulzie Rib	269

Coigach & Assynt — 270

Ben More Coigach — 272
West Ridge Direct — 272
Isle Martin Buttress — 273

Beinn an Eòin — 275
South-West Flank, Sgòrr Deas — 275
South-West Ridge, Sgòrr Tuath — 277

Stac Pollaidh — 277
East-West Traverse — 278

Cùl Beag — 281
Lurgainn Edge — 283

Cùl Mòr — 283
Table Rib — 284
Pinnacle Ridge — 285

Suilven — 287
Ridge Traverse — 287

Conival — 290
South Ridge — 290

Ben More Assynt — 291
South Ridge — 292
South Slabs, Sail an Ruathair — 292
South-East Slabs, Sail an Ruathair — 293
East Flank, Sail an Ruathair — 294

Quinag — 294
East Buttress, Sàil Gharbh — 294

The Far North — 296

North-West Sutherland — 298

Ben Stack — 299
North Flank — 299

Ben Screavie — 301
Allt Screavie — 302

Arkle — 302
South Rib — 302

Foinaven — 304
Second Dionard Buttress — 304
Upper Slabs, Creag Urbhard — 305
Twin Caves Ridge, A' Chèir Ghorm — 306
North Face, Cnoc Duail — 308
Coire Duail Slabs — 308
Ganu Mor Slabs — 311

Cranstackie — 315
Dionard Rib — 316

Ben Hope — 316
Brown's (Myles's) Ridge — 317
Petticoat Ridge — 318

Ben Loyal — 318
Sgor a' Chleirich Ridge — 319
Sgor Chaonasaid Spine — 319

Caithness — 321

Maiden Pap — 322
North Flank — 322

Morven — 323
North-East Ribs — 323

Rùm — 324

Barkeval — 326
North-West Flank — 326
Broad Buttress — 327
Narnia Arête — 327
Honeycomb Arête — 331
Descent Spur — 331

Askival — 332
North Ridge via Askival Pinnacle — 332
North Ridge, Easy Route — 333
East Ridge — 333
South Ridge — 334
West Ridge — 334

Trollabhal	**335**
East Ridge	335
South Flank	336
South Slabs	337
West Ridge	338
Ainshval	**338**
Forgotten Ridge	338
North Ridge	339
Harris Face	340
Sgùrr nan Gillean	**341**
Dibidil Face	342
Traverse of the Rùm Cuillin	**342**
Main Ridge Traverse	342

The Outer Hebrides 344

South Uist 346

Beinn Mhòr	**347**
North-East Ridge	347
Beinn Choradail	**347**
North-West Ridge	347
Hecla (Thacla)	**349**
Laire Rib	349

North Uist 352

Eaval (Eabhal)	**352**
The Route of all Eaval	353

Harris 354

Roineabhal	**355**
Left-Hand Slabs	355
Central Slabs	357
Right Edge	357
Sandpaper Rib	357
Uamascleit	**358**
North-East Face	359
Beinn na Teanga	**359**
Lingeadail Slabs	359
Gillaval Dubh	**360**
A Buttress	361
C Buttress	361
D Buttress	362
An Cliseam (Clisham)	**363**
Coire Dubh Slabs	364
Huiseabhal Mòr	**366**
Cravadale Rib	366

West Lewis 368

Griomabhal	**369**
Tealasdail Rib	369
Teinneasabhal	**370**
North Buttress	370
Tathabhal	**372**
South-West Shoulder	372
North-West Rib	374
Mealaisbhal	**375**
East Buttress	375
Suaineabhal	**378**
West Slabs	378

Maps & Diagrams

Geology
Geological Map	30
Section through the North-West Highlands	32

The Great Glen to Knoydart
Overview map	70

The Loch Lochy Hills
Overview map	72
Meall na Teanga, Meall Dubh	73
Sròn a' Choire Ghairbh, Sean Mheall	76

Glenfinnan Area
Overview map	78
Sgurr nan Coireachan, Riabhaich Slabs	79
Beinn Gharbh, Ursainn Slabs	84

Morar
Overview map	86
Sgùrr an Eilein Ghiubhais, Right-Hand Rib	89

The Rough Bounds
Overview map	86
Garbh Chìoch Mhòr, Coire nan Gall Slabs	92
Beinn an Aodainn (Ben Aden),	
– South Face	94
– East-North-East Ridge	96

Knoydart
Overview map	86
Beinn na Caillich, South-East Slabs	98
Ladhar Bheinn, An Dìollaid	99
An Caisteal, South Face	102
Meall nan Eun, Cannonade	104

Kintail
Oveview map	108
Beinn a' Chapuill, East Slabs	110
The Saddle, Forcan Ridge	111
Sgùrr na Sgine, North-East Ridge	113
Sgùrr nan Conbhairean, North-East Spur	115
Sgùrr an t-Searraich, South Ribs	119
Càrnan Cruithneachd, South-West Shoulder	124
Biod an Fhithich, Ankle Ridge	126

Glen Affric to Strath Carron
Overview map	128
Beinn na Muice, South-West Slabs	132
Càrn Eiteige, Creag a' Chaobh	134
Creag Ghlas, East Buttress	135
Bidean a' Choire Sheasgaich, North Face	137

Applecross & Coulin
Overview map	140
Meall Gorm, Long Buttress	142
Sgùrr a' Chaorachain, Cioch Indirect	143
Beinn Bhàn, A' Chìoch	145
Beinn Damh, North-East Spur	148
An Ruadh-stac, Eastern Slabs	149
Maol Chean-dearg,	
– Ketchil Buttress	152
– East Shoulder	154
Fuar Tholl,	
– South Flank	157
– Spare Rib	160
– Summit Rib	161
Sgorr Ruadh, North-East Face	162
Beinn Liath Mhòr,	
– South Flank	164
– South-East Rib	166
Sgùrr Dubh, North-West Flank	167

Torridon
Overview map	170

Meall Ceann na Creige,	
– West Spur	172
– Crux	173
Beinn Alligin, Backfire Ridge	176
Beinn Dearg,	178
South-West Face	
Liathach,	
– South Flank	180
– Am Fasarinen Traverse	183
– Coire na Caime	188
Beinn Eighe,	
– Lawson, Ling & Glover's Route	191
– Triple Buttresses	192
– North Ridge, Spidean Coire nan Clach	195
– Toll Bàn & Black Carls	196
Ruadh-stac Beag, North-East Flank	197
Beinn a' Mhùinidh, Bonnaidh Donn, Route One	200
Sloch, North-West Buttress	202

Gairloch & Loch Maree

Overview map	204
Baosbheinn, Oidhche Spur	206
Meall Aundrary, North-West Buttress	208
Sìthean Mòr, North Face	210
An Groban, South-West Face	212
Creag Mhòr Thollaidh, North-West Rib	215

Carnmore

Overview map	218
Beinn a' Chàisgein Mòr,	
– South-West Flank	220
– Grey Ridge	221
– Sgùrr na Laocainn Right-Hand	222
Càrnan Bàn, Pocket Slab	223
Càrnan Bàn, South-East Face & Maiden Buttress	224
A' Mhaighdean,	
– Bivouac Ridge	226
– Red Slab	228
– Kids' Ridge	230
Beinn Làir, North-East Face	232

Meall Mhèinnidh, North-East Face	234
Beinn Àirigh Charr, North-East Face	236

Fisherfield & the Fannaichs

Overview map	240
Mullach Coire Mhic Fhearchair, East Ridge	242
Beinn Dearg Mòr, East Buttress	245
An Teallach, Ghiubhsachain Slabs	248
Sgùrr nan Clach Geala, Slanting Buttress	253

Inverlael & Easter Ross

Overview map	256
Cona' Mheall,	
– South-West Face	262
– North-East Slab	264
Cnap Coire Loch Tuath, South Face	266
Meall nan Ceapraichean, West Face	267
Seana Bhraigh, West Face of An Sgùrr	268

Coigach & Assynt

Overview map	270
Ben More Coigach,	
– West Ridge Direct	272
– Isle Martin Buttress	274
Beinn an Eòin, South-West Flank, Sgòrr Deas	275
Stac Pollaidh, South Flank	277
Cùl Beag, Lurgainn Edge	281
Cùl Mòr, Table Rib	284
Suilven,	
– West Flank	287
– Meall Mheadhonach	288
– Meall Beag	289
Ben More Assynt,	
– South Ridge	291
– Sail an Ruathair, South Flank	293
Quinag, Sàil Gharbh, East Buttress	295

The Far North
Overview map — 296

North-West Sutherland
Overview map	298
Ben Stack, North Flank	299
Ben Screavie, Allt Screavie	301
Arkle, South Rib	303
Foinaven,	
– Creag Urbhard	305
– A' Chèir Ghorm	306
– North Face, Cnoc Duail	307
– Coire Duail Slabs	309
– Ganu Mor Slabs	311
Cranstackie, Dionard Rib	315
Ben Hope, North-West Face	317

Caithness
Overview map	321
Maiden Pap, North Flank	322

Rùm
Overview map	324
Barkeval, South Face	326
Askival, North Ridge	332
Trollabhal, South Flank	335
Ainshval,	
– North-East Face	339
– North-West Face	340
Sgùrr nan Gillean, Dibidil Face	341
Askival & Hallival from the south	343

The Outer Hebrides
Overview map — 344

South Uist
Overview map	346
Beinn Choradail, North-West Ridge	349
Hecla (Thacla), Laire Rib	350

North Uist
Overview map	352
Eaval (Eabhal), The Route of all Eaval	353

Harris
Overview map	354
Roineabhal, east side of Coire Roineabhail	355
Uamascleit, North-East Face	358
Gillaval Dubh, North Face	360
An Cliseam (Clisham), Coire Dubh Slabs	363
Huiseabhal Mòr, Cravadale Rib	366

West Lewis
Overview map	368
Griomabhal, Tealasdail Rib	369
Teinneasabhal, North Buttress	371
Tathabhal,	
– North-West Face	372
– South-West Shoulder	373
– North-West Rib	374
Mealaisbhal, East Buttress	376
Suaineabhal, West Slabs	378

Icon Key

Hazards

 Nesting birds

 Loose rock

 Midges

 Tidal

Route type

 Scramble

 Climb

Crag/mountain features

- ⊕ Map page number
- ◁ OS/Harvey map
- ↔ Aspect
- ⌂ Rock type

Route features

 Grid reference

 Approach time

 Route character

 Height gain

Diagram Key

Scrambling route

Climbing route

ooooooooo
Route hidden

▭▭▭▭▭▭
Approach route

Map Key

- ▲ Munro
- △ Munro Top
- ● Corbett
- ○ Corbett Top
- ◆ Graham
- ◇ Graham Top
- ✪ Marilyn
- ⊗ Other peak
- Ferry
- ✈ Airport

13

Pinnacle Ridge, Cùl Mòr.
© Hamish Frost

'this frieze of mountains, filed on the blue air –'

Norman MacCaig, A Man in Assynt

Acknowledgements

The original version of this guide sourced about half of its routes from SMC District Guides and Northern Highlands Climbing Guides (and the outdoor world's 'hive mind'), but many were found through the time-honoured expedient of just walking past and thinking 'that looks good'. For this second edition the additional routes were largely found the same way, but Dave Allan, Scott Muir and the late Ben Lowe all made excellent suggestions that have been included. Feedback from many people, either personally or in places such as UK Climbing and *MARHOFN* magazine, has been incorporated and has (hopefully!) improved various lines, gradings or descriptions.

My thanks again go to Noel Williams for doing the desktop publishing work, drawing the maps and diagrams, much work on the photographs, and writing the geology and mountaineering history sections, and to Ro Scott for writing the wildlife section. Also to Gino Di Meo for his design work and to Rob Lovell for holding it all together and for pushing things along.

Thanks for company on the routes and for posing for photographs go to Davie Austin, Paul Buchanan, Robin Chalmers, Pete Duggan, John Fleetwood, Simon Fraser, Nicky Gear, Jamie Hageman, Doug Hall, Keith Hoole, Marco de Man, Peter McLeod, Richard Merryfield, Gary Mooney, Jo Roberts, Gordon Rothero, George Sawicki, Lucy Williams and Noel Williams. Thanks for supplying photographs go to Nick Bramhall, Paul Buchanan, Adrian Camm, Chris Eilbeck, Peter Elford, Kinley Farmer, John Fleetwood, Hamish Frost, Al Halewood, Jason Hoffman, Vicky Hunter, Scott Muir, Grahame Nicoll, Mark Robson, Mike Watson, Finlay Wild, Noel Williams and Peter Woolnough. My apologies to anyone I have inadvertently omitted.

The North-West Highlands is an amazing place and I have thoroughly enjoyed revisiting old haunts and exploring new ones. I hope others will get as much fun out of these routes as I have.

Iain Thow
March 2022

Introduction

The North-West Highlands contains some of the best scrambling anywhere in Scotland. If you enjoy unfrequented rock on wild rugged peaks then this is the place for you. The area is huge and as a result the routes are widely scattered and sometimes quite remote. Despite this, most routes can be done from a road in a reasonable day (with the exception of some routes around Carnmore and a few in the Knoydart backlands). At one extreme Lurg Mhòr and Seana Bhraigh involve long days, while at the other there are routes suitable for an evening trip, especially around Gairloch. The vast majority are mountain routes with all that implies in the way of weather conditions, the possibility of some loose rock and the need to be able to navigate safely and competently. It is essential that anyone doing these routes carries and can use a map and compass.

This book describes both scrambles and lower grade rock climbs, and is aimed at both experienced climbers on an off day and adventurous walkers looking for some added excitement. Most types of scrambling are represented here: there are towering buttresses, narrow ridges, huge slabs and tumbling streams. Some routes find the easiest way up a big face, others look for difficulty on outcrop-scattered hillsides. One thing that many of them have in common is length – these are big hills, and the valley floors are often close to sea level. The start of one route can't be reached at high tide!

In most cases descents have not been described, as virtually all the scrambles here finish on summits or hillsides from which there is an easy way off. This may be rough or pathless and it may be quite a long way, but the skills brought into play are those of navigation and map reading rather than scrambling.

The remoteness of some of the routes gives them an added seriousness, especially in the event of an accident or drastic change in the weather (not an unknown occurrence in these parts!). Some routes involve river crossings which can be tricky or impossible in bad conditions, while in some places snow may linger late into June or arrive quite early in October. On the other hand the sheer size of the area means that at any given time weather conditions vary across the region, so it should be possible to find good conditions somewhere. It should always be remembered, however, that ALL SCRAMBLING IS POTENTIALLY DANGEROUS – MOVING UNROPED IN EXPOSED SITUATIONS CALLS FOR EXTREME CARE AND SHOULD NOT BE TAKEN LIGHTLY. Even the easier routes can take you into impressive and committing positions. Allow a wide margin for error and always be prepared to retreat or traverse off if necessary. However, don't lose sight of the fact that scrambling should be fun!

Environment

Access
Part 1 of the Land Reform (Scotland) Act 2003 gives you the right to be on most land for recreation, providing you act responsibly. This includes climbing, hillwalking, cycling and wild camping. These access rights and responsibilities are explained in the Scottish Outdoor Access Code.

The key elements are:
- Take personal responsibility for your own actions and act safely.
- Respect people's privacy and peace of mind.
- Help land managers and others to work safely and effectively.
- Care for the environment and take your litter home.
- Keep your dog under proper control.
- Take extra care if you're organising an event or running a business.

Stalking, Shooting & Lambing
- **Deer Stalking**: The stag stalking season is from 1 July to 20 October (although few estates start at the beginning of the season): the main period is from mid-September to mid-October. Hinds continue to be culled until 15 February. There is no stalking on Sundays.
- **Grouse Shooting**: The grouse shooting season is from 12 August until 10 December, although the end of the season is less used.
- **Lambing**: It is important to avoid disturbing sheep during the lambing season, from March to May. Dogs should be kept on a lead near livestock throughout the year.

Fauna & Flora
Don't disturb nesting birds, especially the rarer species which are found on crags (such as Golden Eagle and Peregrine Falcon) between 1 February and the end of July. Wilful disturbance of nesting birds is a criminal offence. For more information see www.mountaineering.scot/access/birds-and-nesting.

When cleaning routes in summer take care not to remove rare flora.

Footpath Erosion
To ensure the enjoyment of future climbers it is our responsibility to minimise any erosion we cause in the outdoors. Part of the revenue from the sale of Scottish Mountaineering Club books is granted by the Scottish Mountaineering Trust as financial assistance towards the repair and maintenance of hill paths in Scotland.

Camping, Litter & Pollution
Responsible wild camping is permitted under the new access legislation; don't camp near houses or in cultivated fields. When camping, do not cause pollution, take a shovel and bury human waste carefully out of sight and far away from any habitation or watercourse. Avoid burying rubbish as this may also pollute the environment. Take everything home that you brought and dispose of it properly. Leave as little trace of your stay as possible.

Car & Bicycle Use
Do not drive along private roads without permission and, when parking, avoid blocking access to private roads and land or causing any hazard to other road users. The use of bicycles is covered by access legislation. Bicycles can cause severe erosion when used 'off road' on footpaths and open hillsides and are best used on vehicular or forest tracks.

Mountaineering Scotland
Mountaineering Scotland is the representative body for climbers and walkers in Scotland. One of its primary concerns is the continued free access to the hills and crags. Information about bird restrictions, stalking and general access issues can be obtained from Mountaineering Scotland.

If you encounter problems regarding access you should contact Mountaineering Scotland, whose address is:
The Old Granary, West Mill Street, Perth PHI 5QP. T: 01738 493942, www.mountaineering.scot, email info@mountaineering.scot.

Safety

Participating
Scrambling, climbing and mountaineering are activities with a danger of personal injury or death. Participants in these activities should be aware of and accept these risks and be responsible for their own actions and involvement.

It is up to the individual climber to assess the reliability of bolts, pegs, belay stakes, slings or old nuts, which may be in place. Falls sometimes occur due to holds breaking. A number of routes in this guide have had few repeats so holds and blocks should be treated with caution, especially after a hard winter. You are responsible for your own actions and should not hold landowners liable for an accident, even if it happens while climbing over a fence or dyke.

Remember, this guide is only a guide, conditions in the mountains are constantly changing. Take a progressive approach and don't be afraid to turn back if you feel uncomfortable with the situation. Wherever possible avoid climbing directly below other scramblers.

Mountain Rescue
Phone 999, Mountain Rescue or Coastguard may be called out, depending on the location. Give concise information about the location and injuries of the casualty and any assistance available at the accident site. It is better to stay with the casualty, but in a party of two, it may be necessary to leave to summon help. Leave the casualty warm and comfortable in a sheltered, well-marked place.

Equipment and Planning
Good equipment, clothing, forward planning and navigation skills in the mountains can all help reduce the chance of an accident. While mobile

phones and GPS can help in communications and locating your position, consider that the former do not work in many places in the Scottish hills and both rely on batteries and electronics which can fail or be easily damaged. Consequently, they can never be a substitute for competent use of a map and compass. In recent years the general carrying of mobile phones has made getting help easier (although there are still many hill areas where there is no coverage). This has unfortunately led to an increase in frivolous calls – in many cases self rescue is both quicker and preferable and an element of self reliance is no bad thing.

Two-thirds of accidents are the result of a lengthy fall, either due to a 'simple slip', holds breaking or rockfall. About one-third are the result of planning errors – being too ambitious (trying a route that's too hard) or simply failing to judge how long a route will take and becoming benighted.

Tides

Tide details can be found on a number of websites. For example www.bbc.co.uk/weather/coast, www.sea/tide_tables and www.tidetimes.org.uk.

Midges & Ticks

Midges can be plentiful in the summer months, so try to keep to areas that are exposed to wind and sun, and avoid damp sheltered, vegetated places. Midges are at the worst from evening to morning, so only the hardy will camp in the west in mid-summer. Be prepared with repellent and midge net for belayers. Ticks may carry Lyme disease. It is worth wearing long trousers with elasticated ankles to stop ticks, or apply insect repellent. Check for ticks at the end of the day and remove any found. An early indication of Lyme disease is a circular outwardly expanding skin rash round the site of the bite. If you see this, or feel unwell after a tick bite, go to a doctor as soon as possible.

Technical

Unroped scrambling is potentially one of the most hazardous of mountain activities. A simple slip or a hold breaking may have fatal consequences.

Classification of Routes

This guide includes both scrambles and easy rock climbs. The climbs have mainly been chosen because they are not sustained at their grade and usually include lengthy sections of scrambling. In order to make it obvious which type of outing is involved, a logo is shown at the start of each route description. **All the routes are graded for dry, summer conditions. They will become much harder when it is damp or snowy.** In winter they are much more serious undertakings, and appropriate winter mountaineering skills and equipment will be required.

Use of the rope

Whether to use a rope comes down to personal choice, but if there are inexperienced or nervous members in the party then a rope should be carried, and it should come out of the rucksack sooner rather than later. A rope might well prove useful in the event of retreat, and the ability to abseil using a sling and a karabiner could also be invaluable.

It goes without saying that a rope will only increase safety if at least one member of the party knows how to use it properly, and if it is put to use as soon as anybody needs it. Many parties will also decide to carry harnesses and a rack of gear for Difficult climbs.

Scrambles

Scrambling covers the intermediate area between walking and rock climbing. The lower boundary is easy to define – once the hands are needed for progress, you are scrambling – but the upper one is more problematic. One approach is to say that scrambling covers rock too easy for most rock climbers to need a rope, another is to say that scrambling becomes rock climbing once the interest of the moves become greater than the interest of the situation. There is also a difference in approach, with climbs often tackling challenges directly, while scrambles usually look for the easiest way up a feature. Routes such as Lurgainn Edge on Cùl Beag are definitely rock climbs if climbed direct but make good scrambles if a little deviousness is employed.

A simple numerical grading system (1–3) is used to indicate the difficulty of a scramble. For those unfamiliar with scrambling, a rough guide might be to say that fit and agile hillwalkers should be fairly happy to tackle Grade 1 scrambles. However, those without climbing experience may well find that Grade 3 scrambles are too difficult or too frightening for them.

- **Grade 1:** Most hillwalkers should find scrambles of this grade reasonably straight-forward. The hands will occasionally be required for progress, but the holds will normally be large, so the moves themselves will not be difficult. There may be some exposure, but usually it will not be too daunting.
- **Grade 2:** Routes of this grade will normally require the hands to be used for more sustained sections. There may be considerable exposure. Some routes may have short technically difficult sections, while others may be easier but hard to escape from. Retreat may be quite difficult.
- **Grade 3:** This grade of scramble may involve making thought-provoking moves on steep rock in exposed situations. All but experienced climbers might prefer the reassurance of a rope in some places. In which case, a few slings, nuts and karabiners may prove useful for setting up belays. The route might be hard to escape from, and the ability to abseil could be useful if a retreat has to be made.

Rock Climbs

The rock climbs described in this guide are graded according to the standard adjectival system for summer climbs. Only routes in the two lowest grades are described. (The Easy grade is not recognised here.) Climbs are graded for their hardest move irrespective of length. Such routes will normally be climbed using standard rock climbing equipment.

- **Moderate:** Climbs of this grade will normally make use of fairly obvious holds. However, there may be tricky moves in exposed positions. The route could be serious or sustained (but probably not both at the same time). It overlaps with the Grade 3(S) used in some scrambling guides.
- **Difficult:** Technical climbing skills are required here. There could be long exposed sections and hard moves in airy and serious situations. Most will want a rope and retreat could be tricky.

Choosing a Route

Rock type, position and weather/season are the major factors here. Some considerations should be obvious: north-facing routes dry more slowly, while higher routes are more likely to hold late snow. Others are slightly less so: high routes are more exposed to weathering and so more likely to have some loose rock, especially the ridges. Popularity can make surprisingly little difference. Stac Pollaidh, for example, is the busiest route in this book but has no shortage of loose rock, while the gneiss slabs on Foinaven get hardly any ascents but are as clean and sound as you could wish. By far the biggest influence is rock type, so the following pointers may be useful.

- **Schist:** Poor friction if wet and its strong grain means that flakes can break off easily. It supports more vegetation than most of the rocks here so can be quite slow drying. Holds tend to be plentiful and positive.
- **Psammite (metamorphosed sandstone):** Coarser grained than the schist so better friction and more solid, often forms clean slabs or juggy steps but grassy ledges between them tend to weep after heavy rain.
- **Quartzite:** Slabs are usually solid but their friction if wet is appalling. Steeper ground tends to break up into angular blocks, so has lots of big holds but is frequently very loose. Very clean so dries quickly and routes are often easier than they look.
- **Torridonian Sandstone:** Much coarser than the neighbouring quartzite so good friction if clean, even when wet. Breaks into blocks easily so steeper routes and ridges can be quite loose. The ridges tend to be clean but north-facing routes can get quite greasy and lichenous. Usually has rounded holds and is often more difficult than it looks.
- **Gneiss:** Lots of holds and usually good friction, although more affected by being wet than the sandstone. Where it's slabby the quality is usually superb, but flakes on steeper ground can often be suspect. Generally dries fast after showers but as it supports more vegetation than sandstone or quartzite it can weep for a while after more prolonged rain.

- **Left and Right:** The terms left and right are used when facing the direction being described, i.e. facing a crag in ascent, and facing out in descent.

- **Crag Diagrams:** Most of the routes are shown on diagrams close to the relevant text. The route numbers on the diagrams correspond to the route numbers shown in the text. Some approaches or linking sections of walking are shown by a white dashed line. Scrambles are shown as orange lines, whilst climbs are shown as blue lines. See key on page 13. Where a route has both scrambling and climbing options, the activity icon (scramble or climb) indicates the option most commonly chosen.

- **Descent Routes:** Advice on descent routes is not generally given, so some thought may need to be given to the best way off. Many routes finish on high mountain summits and the subsequent descent may entail difficult navigation in bad visibility.

- **Recommended Routes:** A three star system has been used to indicate the 'quality' of a route. The stars generally refer to the quality of the activity itself. Various aspects of the route may also contribute to the overall quality rating. These include soundness of the rock, the situation, how sustained a route is and how natural a line it follows.

  ***   Among the best routes of their grade in Scotland.
  **   A good route, but lacking one or more of the features that make it top class.
  *   A worthy outing which may lack line, situation, or balance.

Even routes with no stars can make very enjoyable outings. They may be in wild and beautiful country.

Maps

Various symbols are used on the sketch maps in this guide to indicate different categories of summit. See key on page 13. Munros are 3,000ft high and above. Corbetts are 2,500–2,999ft high. Grahams are 2,000–2,499ft high. There are different criteria (or not!) for the various tops. Two main sources of map are available for the areas in this guide.

- **Ordnance Survey:** maps cover the whole country and are available at both 1:50,000 scale (Landranger) and 1:25,000 scale (Explorer).
- **Harvey Maps:** available for all the more popular areas. They are also available in a variety of scales.
  - **British Mountain Maps:** Waterproof maps at 1:40,000 scale are available for Assynt; Knoydart, Kintail & Glen Affric; Torridon & Fisherfield.
  - **Superwalker™ Maps:** at 1:25,000 scale are available for An Teallach; Fannichs, Seana Bhraigh & Wyvis; Knoydart, Kintail & Glen Shiel; Suilven; Torridon and Rùm.
  - **Summit Maps:** at 1:12,500 scale is also available for Beinn Alligin.

Amenities

Travel

The Traveline Scotland website is useful for route planning, travelinescotland.com, while the Traffic Scotland website gives information on current incidents and roadworks, trafficscotland.org. Travel information for the Outer Hebrides is given in that chapter.

🚆 Trains
Scotrail operates trains up the east coast, from Inverness across to Kyle of Lochalsh, as well as from Glasgow to Mallaig via Fort William. The stations at Achnashellach, Strathcarron and Glenfinnan are convenient for routes included here.
T: 0344 811 0141, scotrail.co.uk

🚌 Coaches
bustimes.org is a useful source of timetables.

Citilink Coaches run from Inverness to Ullapool (twice daily), and to Kyle of Lochalsh from both Inverness and Glasgow (twice daily).
citylink.co.uk

Stagecoach run buses up the east coast from Inverness, and also from Muir of Ord to Cannich (Tue, Wed & Sat).
stagecoachbus.com

Rapsons run from Ullapool to Lochinver, Mon-Sat.
T: 01463 482893
georgerapsontravel.com

The Durness Bus runs on Satudays from Inverness to Durness via Lairg.
thedurnessbus.com

Westerbus run from Inverness to Gairloch (Tue & Sat) and from Gairloch to Ullapool (Fri only).
T: 01445 712255
mackenziemaclennan.co.uk

DMK Motors run daily from Strathcarron to Shieldaig.
T: 01520 722682

🚢 Ferries
Ferries operated by Caledonian MacBrayne run to Rùm from Mallaig; Mull from Oban, Lochaline and Kilchoan; Islay and Colonsay from Kennacraig and Arran from Ardrossan.
T: 0800 066 5000, calmac.co.uk

Arisaig Marine also run a ferry to Rùm from Arisaig.
T: 01687 450224, arisaig.co.uk

Western Isles Cruises run from Mallaig to Inverie (Knoydart), and occasionally Tarbet.
T: 01687 462233
westernislescruises.co.uk

There is also a local charter boat, Calanna, based in Inverie.
T: 01687 462844 or 07766 082757
E: calannaboat@knoydart.org

🚗 Road
The infrequency of these services, however, means that most people will arrive by car, most of the roads these days being fast and, although the popularity of the North Coast 500 has made the roads busier, they are still quiet relative to further south. There are petrol stations at Lairg, Tongue, Durness, Kinlochbervie, Scourie, Lochinver, Ullapool, Contin, Laide, Gairloch, Kinlochewe, Lochcarron, Kyle of Lochalsh, Inverinate and Shiel Bridge. On the Outer Hebrides there are useful petrol stations

at Stornoway, Timsgearraidh, Ardhasaig, Tarbert and Leverburgh, all closed on Sundays.

Accommodation

There are numerous hotels and B&Bs scattered around the area. Most of the former offer bar meals. Booking accommodation ahead can be done through Visit Scotland T: 0845 2255121 (9am to 5pm) www.visitscotland.com/accommodation, or through local Tourist Information Centres at Inverness, Ullapool and Stornoway. Most of the small villages have a shop, and there are supermarkets in Ullapool, Kyle of Lochalsh, Fort William, Mallaig and Stornoway. There are small climbing shops in Ullapool and Scourie and larger ones in Inverness and Fort William.

⛺ Camp Sites

Dunbeath, Inver Caravan Park (ND 165 299).
T: 01593 731441
inver-caravan-park.co.uk

Tongue (NC 586 585).
T: 01847 611789
tonguehostelandholidaypark.co.uk

Talmine (NC 585 627).
Cheap, friendly and a nice beach.

Durness, Sango Sands (NC 406 679).
Fine clifftop position.
sangosands.com

Sheigra (NC 182 601).
No facilities but gorgeous setting.

Scourie (NC 154 447).
Good setting and handy bar.
T: 07899 736840
scouriecampsitesutherland.com

Clachtoll (NC 040 274).
Close to beach.
T: 01571 855377
clachtollbeachcampsite.com

Achmelvich (NC 054 248).
Superb beach & bouldering.
shorecaravansite.yolasite.com

Altandhu (NB 986 124).
Handy for the cragging at Reiff.
T: 01854 622440, portabhaigh.co.uk

Ardmair (NH 108 984).
Excellent view, ardmair.com

Ullapool (NH 125 938).
Town site handy for pubs etc.
T: 01854 612020, broomfieldhp.com

Contin (NH 457 561).
Handy shop and often better weather than further west.
T: 01463 513599
lochness-chalets.co.uk

Badrallach (NG 065 916).
Quiet scenic spot.
T: 07719 536870, badrallach.com

Laide (NG 904 919). Seashore site.
T: 01445 731556, gruinardbay.co.uk

Poolewe (NG 861 811).
Lochshore site in village.
T: 01445 781249
campingandcaravanningclub.co.uk

Gairloch (NG 797 774).
Village site, all facilities.
T: 01445 712373
gairlochcampsite.co.uk

Sands (NG 759 785).
Expensive but good beach & facilities.
T: 01445 712152
sandscaravanandcamping.co.uk

Taagan (NH 013 637). Basic free site.

Torridon (NG 905 558).
Basic site with nearby bouldering.
T: 01445 712345

Shieldaig (NG 816 542).
Basic village site near to pub.
T: 01520 755224
shieldaigcampingandcabins.co.uk

Applecross (NG 711 444).
Peaceful setting with
community-run facilities.
T: 01520 744268
visitapplecross.com

Lochcarron (NG 906 401).
Small sheltered village site.
T: 07876 642355

Cannich (NH 342 313). Good value village site with all facilities.
T: 01456 415364
highlandcamping.co.uk

Morvich (NG 961 212). All facilities.
T: 01599 511354, caravanclub.co.uk

Shiel Bridge (NG 938 186).
Shop and nearby pub.
T: 01599 511221
glenshielcampsite.co.uk

Invergarry (NH 287 018).
Quiet friendly site.
T: 01809 501314
campsite.faichemard.scot

Barrisdale, Knoydart
(NG 872 002). Basic wild site.
barrisdaleestate.com

Morar (NG 664 918).
T: 01687 450221, camusdarach.co.uk
and Silver Sands (NG 653 896).
T: 01687 450269.
Both next to superb beaches.

Kinloch, Rùm. Basic site.
See also Rùm Bunkhouse.
pitchup.com

Cairinish, North Uist (NF 835 599).
Quiet site handy for Eaval.
T: 01876 580305
moorcroftholidays.co.uk

Balranald, North Uist (NF 707 707). On machair in RSB reserve.
T: 01876 510304
balranaldhebrideanholidays.com

Horgabost, Harris (NG 049 969).
Basic site by beach.
T: 01859 550386

Seilebost, Harris. (NG 064 973).
Basic community-run site
by beach.
T: 01859 503901
westharristrust.org

Drinishader, Harris (NG 177 941).
Craggy setting.
T: 01859 511207

Uig Sands (NB 049 329).
Basic site by huge beach.

Climbing Huts
Naismith Hut (NC 216 118).
SMC, on loop road at north end of Elphin.

The Smiddy, Dundonnell (NH 094 878). JMCS Edinburgh section.

Ling Hut (NG 957 563). SMC.
In Glen Torridon, 300m along path from Coire Dubh car park.

Glen Lichd House (NH 005 173).
Edinburgh University MC.

Independent Hostels
hostel-scotland.co.uk and
www.independenthostels.co.uk

Glenfinnan Sleeping Car.
T: 01397 722295
E: glenfinnanstationmuseum
    @gmail.com

Mallaig Backpackers Lodge
(NM 675 971).
T: 01687 462764
mallaigbackpackers.co.uk

Barrisdale, Knoydart.
barrisdaleestate.com

Saddle Mountain Hostel, Invergarry.
T: 01809 501412
saddlemountainhostel.scot

Kintail Lodge Hotel Bunkhouse
(NG 938 197). All year.
T: 01599 511275
kintaillodgehotel.co.uk

Gerry's Hostel, Craig (NH 038 492).
T: 01520 766232 and 07894 984294
gerryshostel.com

Ledgowan Bunkhouse (NH 158 579).
T: 01445 720252
ledgowanlodge.co.uk

Hartfield House, Applecross
(NG 722 467).
T: 01520 744333
hartfieldhouse.org.uk

Kinlochewe Hotel Bunkhouse
(NH 029 619).
T: 01445 760253
kinlochewehotel.co.uk

Badrallach Bothy (NH 065 915).
All year.
T: 07719 536870, badrallach.com

Forest Way, Inverlael (NH 195 797).
T: 07912 177419
www.forestway.co.uk

Acheninver (NC 042 056).
T: 07783 305776
acheninverhostel.com

Inchnadamph Lodge (NC 252 219).
01571 822218
inchnadamph.co.uk

Lazy Crofter, Durness.
(NC 402 675). All year.
T: 01971 511202
visitdurness.com

Tongue Hostel (NC 586 585).
T: 01847 611789
tonguehostelandholidaypark.co.uk

Helmsdale Hostel (ND 028 155).
helmsdalehostel.co.uk

Rùm Bunkhouse.
T: 01687 460318
rumbunkhouse.com

Howmore, South Uist
(NF 757 364). No advance booking.

No 5, Drinishader, Harris
(NG 172 949).
T: 01859 511255, 5drinishader.co.uk

Backpackers Stop, Tarbert,
Harris (NB 155 001). All year.
T: 07708 746745
backpackers-stop.co.uk.

Rhenigadail, Harris (NB 229 018).
No advance booking.

Gearranan, Lewis (NB 190 450).
T: 01851 643416, gearrannan.com.

🔺 SYHA Hostels
hostellingscotland.org.uk.

There is a central booking number
for these.
T: 0345 293 7373
E: reservations@
  hostellingscotland.org.uk.

Durness Smoo (NC 417 672).
Achmelvich (NC 058 247).
Ullapool (NH 129 940).
Gairloch Sands (NG 763 776).
Torridon (NG 904 558).
Glen Affric (NH 080 202).
Ratagan (NG 919 199).

Geology

Bodaich Dubh, Sgùrr nan Fhir Duibhe, Beinn Eighe. © Noel Williams

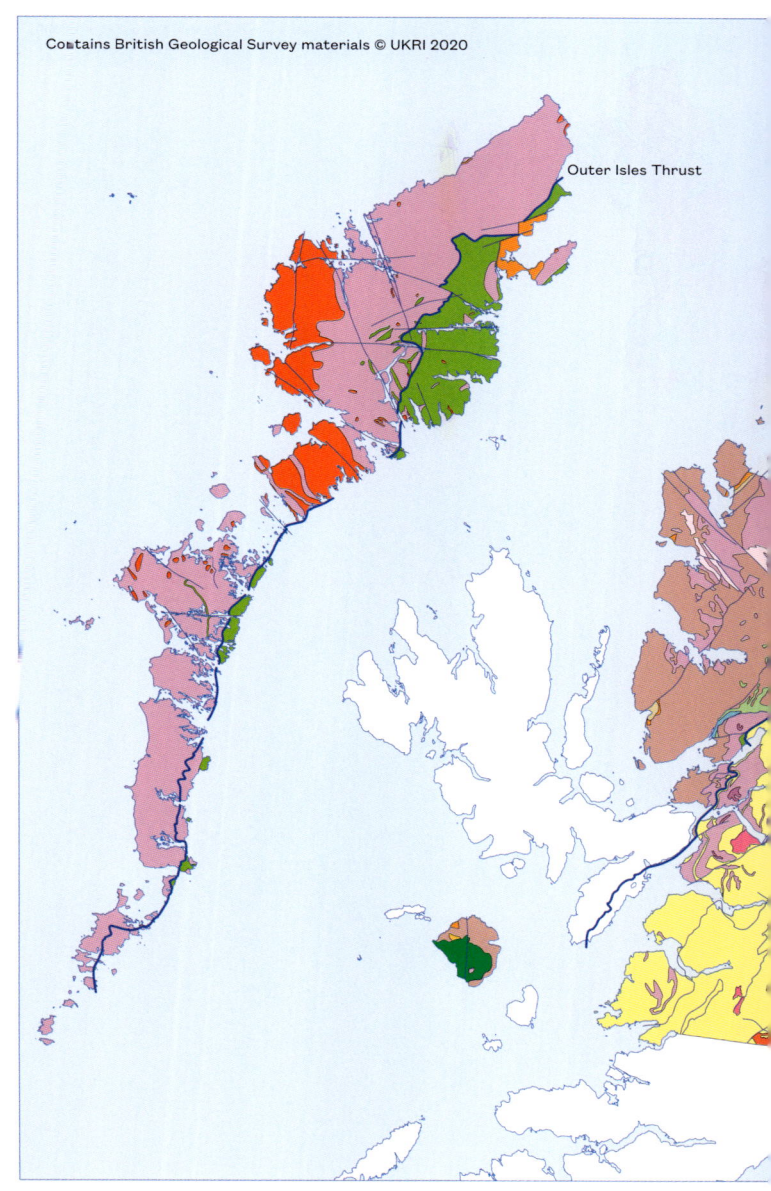

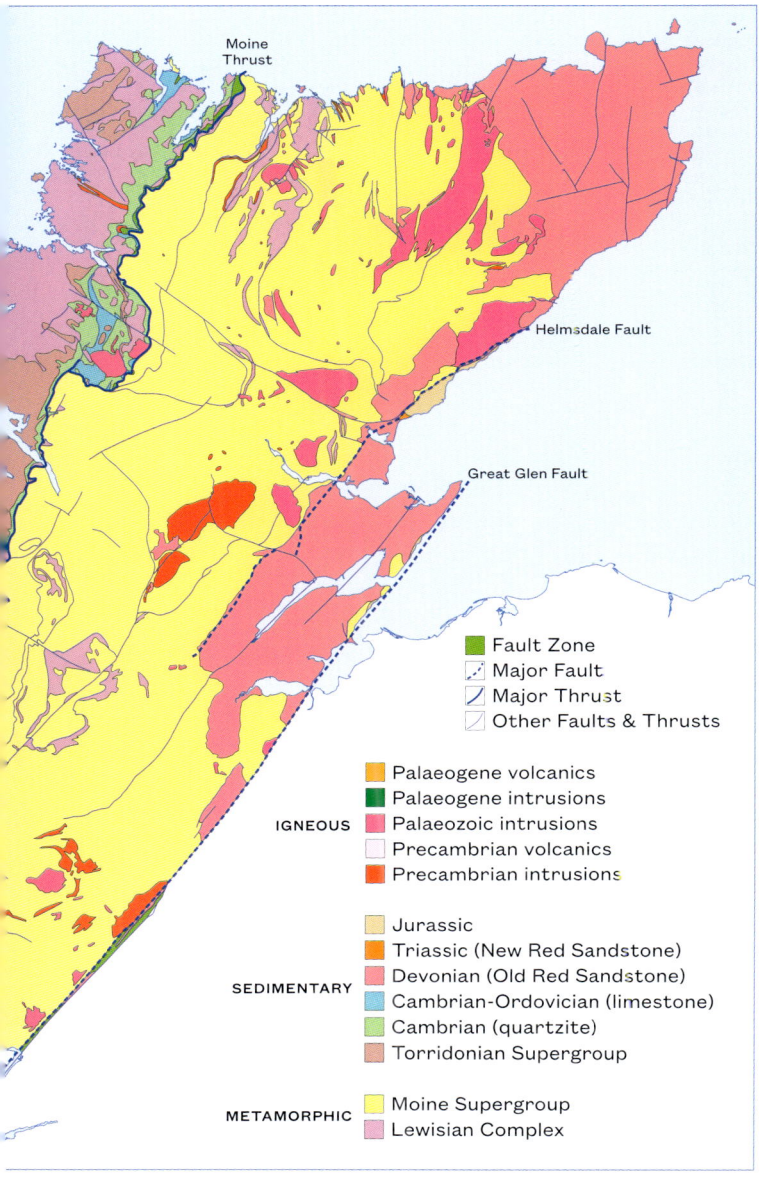

The area covered by this guide has a complex but fascinating geology. A glance at the geological map (see overleaf) allows a simple interpretation to be made – older rocks in the west pass into younger rocks in the east, but with a great swathe of Moinian metamorphic rocks in the middle. However, there is one important complication. A major structure called the Moine Thrust runs all the way down through the North-West Highlands.

Most of the best scrambles in this guide are situated to the west of the Moine Thrust on rocks which comprise the Hebridean terrane or 'foreland' area. The unique character of this part of the Highlands is largely due to its distinctive rocks. The geology of the region is so special that in 2004 an area comprising much of Sutherland and part of Wester Ross was recognised as a European Geopark – the first area in Scotland to be awarded this status.

Section through the North-West Highlands

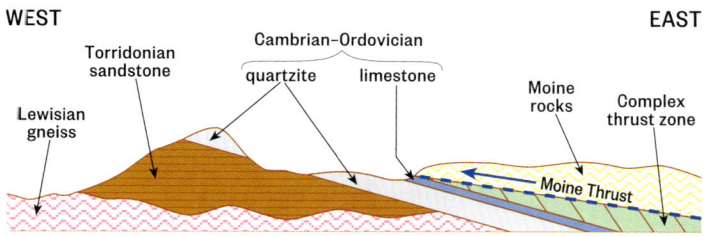

The structure of the North-West Highlands is summarised by the simplified cross-section shown above. The various rocks identified in this section will now be described in more detail, starting with the more westerly rocks of the foreland.

Lewisian
The oldest rock, found at the bottom of the pile, is a coarsely crystalline metamorphic rock known as Lewisian gneiss. It is some 3,000 million years old and one of the oldest rocks in Europe. The gneiss has pale/dark banding and is permeated by countless basic dykes, granite sheets and pegmatite veins which themselves have been metamorphosed to varying degrees.

Research is still unravelling the complex history behind this set of rocks, but three different metamorphic episodes are currently recognised. These are named after localities in Sutherland. The Scourian event dates from around 2,600 million years ago, the Inverian around 2,450 million years ago, and the Laxfordian around 1,800 million years ago. There then followed a long period of gradual uplift and erosion.

The Outer Hebrides are built almost entirely from Lewisian rocks – hence the name. On low ground, being crystalline and impervious, the gneiss tends to form rugged, lochan-peppered moorland. Where it forms high ground it gives magnificent scrambling, among the best in this guide. In the Outer Hebrides the hills of Uig and North Harris give superb outings, as do the hills around Gairloch and Carnmore on the mainland. All of Ben Stack and the northern end of Foinaven are also built of this rock.

Torridonian
The basement of Lewisian gneiss was deeply eroded before the Torridonian sediments were laid on top. A pile of sandstones and conglomerates, at least 7km thick, was subsequently deposited on what was a very irregular land surface. On the slopes of Slioch above Loch Maree, for example, the Torridonian sandstone is seen to infill a deep valley in the Lewisian gneiss.

The Torridonian sediments were laid down some 1,200–1,000 million years ago, probably as extensive alluvial fans, and in wide channels of braided rivers. The rocks are too old to contain recognisable fossils, but microscopic traces of primitive life forms have been extracted from some beds. Despite its great age, the Torridonian sandstone to the west of the Moine Thrust zone has survived largely unchanged since it first formed. In other words, it has not been metamorphosed and so must have remained outwith any mountain building areas.

The Torridonian rock strata are mainly horizontal or gently inclined, and are cut by numerous vertical joints. They weather to produce terraced cliffs with steep chimneys and gullies, as well as rounded bastions and pinnacled ridges. Extensive outcrops of Torridonian sand-

Lewisian rocks exposed in a road cutting near Scourie – showing grey gneiss cut by black dykes, both of which are cut by younger pink granite veins.

stone occur throughout the North-West Highlands, making it the best exposed sedimentary formation in Britain. Being red in colour and well stratified, it contrasts starkly with the contorted crystalline gneiss on which it rests. The extraordinary difference in character between these two rocks has been emphasised by erosion, and has produced some of the most dramatic mountain scenery in the country.

Suilven, though by no means the highest, is perhaps the best known and certainly one of the most spectacular of the peaks in the north-west. It consists of an isolated remnant of flat-lying Torridonian sandstone resting on a platform of Lewisian gneiss. The normal access route to the bealach on the summit ridge (see Route 137, p287) follows the line of a vertical fault. The main summit lies on the downthrown side of this fault.

Among the other peaks of Torridonian sandstone situated north of Ullapool are Cùl Beag, Stac Pollaidh and Ben More Coigach. Several other peaks in that area (notably Quinag, Canisp and Cùl Mòr) are built of Torridonian strata with a capping of Cambrian quartzite. Farther south, mighty An Teallach is built largely of Torridonian sandstone. In Torridon itself, Beinn Alligin is built entirely from this rock, whilst Liathach and Beinn Eighe have minor and major caps of quartzite respectively. The Applecross hills are also carved from rocks of Torridonian age.

Although the coarse-grained sandstone gives good friction, the bigger faces tend to be unsuitable for scrambling or rock climbing because the thicker beds of sandstone are lacking in features and can prove surprisingly difficult to climb. The most common type of scramble on this rock is along ridge crests or easier angled buttresses, such as on An Teallach. On the south-east side of Fuar Tholl the Torridonian strata are inclined at a steeper angle than usual and so there give pleasant scrambling on delightful slabs.

Around 600 million years ago the Lewisian and Torridonian rocks were tilted north-westwards and eroded to a flat surface (peneplain) before the next group of rocks were deposited.

Cambrian and Ordovician

About 540 million years ago the sea began to transgress across the land, and eventually some 1,000m of marine sandstones and limestones were laid down on an almost level platform of Lewisian and Torridonian rocks. These new sediments were deposited along the southern margin of 'Laurentia' (North America and Greenland) in a broad shallow shelf environment.

Quartzites: The earliest deposits consist mainly of white, and sometimes pink, siliceous sandstones called quartzites. The upper part of the group includes a distinctive type of quartzite known as Pipe Rock. This contains numerous vertical tubes or pipes (10–20cm long) thought to represent the sand-filled burrows of worm-like organisms living in a beach environment.

Quartzite is a hard, well-jointed rock which breaks up readily into sharp-edged blocks. These blocks remain angular even after prolonged weathering and consequently are awkward to walk on. The rock is often badly shattered by freeze-thaw action and some impressive scree slopes flank

A vertical section through Pipe Rock showing the white pipes or burrows created by worm-like creatures that lived in quartz beach sand in Cambrian times.

the ridges of Foinaven for example, but where crags of sounder rock occur there is fine scrambling, notably on Creag Urbhard and Ruadh-stac Beag.

Foinaven and Arkle in the north of Sutherland are perhaps the best examples of mountains composed mainly of Cambrian quartzite. There the quartzite rests directly on Lewisian gneiss. However, for the most part the quartzite forms a cap or top tier to what are largely Torridonian sandstone mountains. The junction between sandstone and quartzite is easily seen, for example, running across the triple buttresses of Coire Mhic Fhearchair.

Limestones: As time went by the sandy sediments gave way to limestones and dolomites. These rocks are generally pale to dark grey in colour, although some beds weather to a creamy yellow colour. Limestone tends to produce a greener sort of scenery with a more varied flora of great interest to botanists.

Although these beds are not extensive enough to form significant hills, around Inchnadamph and Elphin numerous caves have been created by streams sinking into the limestone – the longest over 2km in length. A very spectacular cave, Smoo Cave, lies on the north coast just east of Durness.

Fossils such as trilobites and brachiopods present in these Cambrian and Ordovician rocks can be matched with fossils found in Newfoundland and East Greenland. These are very different from the species found in the rest of Britain because 'Avalonia' (England, Wales and southern Ireland) at that time lay further south on the opposite side of the Iapetus Ocean.

Some time after they were deposited the Cambrian and Ordovician strata were tilted gently to the south-east. This caused the underlying Torridonian sandstone to return to a more or less horizontal position.

Moinian

At roughly the same time as the Torridonian sediments were being deposited in rift valleys on land, a thick sequence of sands, silts and muds began to accumulate offshore (1,000–870 million years ago). These sediments were later caught up in a number of mountain building episodes caused by plate collisions, and were squeezed, folded and heated on a massive scale. The resulting group of rocks consist mainly of psammites (metamorphosed sandstones) and pelites (metamorphosed mudstones and shales) and are referred to as Moine rocks – named after the peninsula of A' Mhoine (the Peat Bog) in northern Sutherland. These rocks form much of the Northern Highlands, but because they attract vegetation and generally form rather rounded hills they tend not to lend themselves to good scrambles or climbs. The Forcan Ridge of the Saddle is a notable exception.

In places the Moine and some of the foreland rocks were intruded by molten material, which cooled to form sills, dykes and stocks of various igneous rocks including syenite. Some of the intrusions have a distinctive porphyritic texture i.e. they contain prominent crystals (usually feldspar) set in a finer groundmass. Conspicuous sheets or sills can be seen within the Torridonian sandstone strata on the north-west side of Canisp and around Suilven's eastern top, Meall Beag. Much of Ben Loyal is formed from a syenite pluton.

The Moine rocks we see today represent the eroded root of part of the once mighty Caledonian Mountain Chain, remnants of which can be traced from Spitzbergen down through Scandinavia, across the British Isles to Newfoundland and eastern North America. The Caledonian

The classic exposure of the Moine Thrust at Knockan Crag, near Elphin.
Dark Moinian rocks have been thrust over younger cream-coloured limestones.

mountains, which at one time were probably comparable in character to the present day Hindu Kush and western Himalaya, were deeply eroded prior to the deposition of the next group of rocks belonging to the Devonian period.

The Moine Thrust Zone

A thrust is a low angled fault. The Moine Thrust itself is the highest of a series of thrusts which lie within a narrow belt of dislocated rocks known as the Moine Thrust Zone. The plane of the Moine Thrust slopes up gently towards the west-north-west. During the Caledonian mountain building episode about 430 million years ago, Moine metamorphic rocks were pushed a total of at least 100 kilometres west-north-westwards up onto the younger Cambrian and Ordovician quartzites and limestones. As a result of this large scale displacement, the rocks immediately above the thrust plane were 'rolled out' and changed into a new rock called mylonite. Numerous 'chopped up' slices of quartzite and other foreland rocks are present within the thrust zone. In some localities (notably Glencoul) large slices of Lewisian gneiss were also brought up and thrust on top of younger quartzites.

Much controversy accompanied the early study of the rock sequence in the North-West Highlands, and some very eminent geologists – notably Murchison and Geikie – tried to insist that the Moine rocks were in normal stratigraphical sequence with the underlying Cambrian and Ordovician strata. However, a teacher with an amateur interest in geology, Charles Lapworth, thought the Moine rocks were older. Careful mapping by members of the British Geological Survey in the 1880s, however, demonstrated convincingly that older rocks had indeed been translated several tens of kilometres over younger rocks. This work culminated with the publication of an important memoir to the area in 1907. Such was the importance of these discoveries that in subsequent years geologists came from around the world to attend field excursions at Inchnadamph organised by Peach and Horne – two of the principal geologists who mapped the thrust structure for the Geological Survey.

Anyone interested in understanding the landscape of the North-West Highlands is referred to two well-illustrated publications: *Northwest Highlands: a Landscape Fashioned by Geology* (NatureScot) and *Exploring the Landscape of Assynt* (BGS). Both have been produced very much with the non-specialist in mind. The trail at Knockan Crag near Elphin, which visits a classic exposure of the Moine Thrust, is also strongly recommended.

Mention should also be made of two other important structures present in the area. The first is the eastward-dipping Outer Isles Thrust, which runs the full length of the Outer Hebrides, and manifests itself most clearly in the Uists as a line of hills with a west-facing scarp. The second is the Great Glen Fault – a tear fault most active around 430–400 million years ago – which forms the eastern boundary of the Northern Highlands area.

Devonian (and Mesozoic)

Following the Caledonian mountain building episode, the only significant deposits which survive in the Highlands are the conglomerates and flagstones of Devonian age (about 410–370 million years old), which outcrop extensively in the north and east.

Fossil fish, found at numerous localities from John o' Groats to the Black Isle, suggest that many of these sediments were laid down in a huge body of freshwater – the Orcadian Lake. The rocks generally form fairly featureless moorland, with Morven in Caithness being the most significant summit. However, the sandstone seacliffs around the north-east coast are especially scenic.

A narrow strip of much younger sedimentary rocks (of Jurassic age) outcrops on the south side of the Helmsdale Fault between Brora and Helmsdale. A metre-thick seam of coal was worked at Brora for many years.

Palaeocene Igneous Activity
Prior to the opening up of the North Atlantic, Europe was still joined to Greenland. Around 55 million years ago there was a burst of igneous activity which extended down the west coast of Scotland and into Northern Ireland (Antrim). Large volcanic centres developed on Rùm, as well as Skye, Ardnamurchan, Mull and Arran. Basalt lavas covered much of Rùm initially, and these were followed by the formation of a collapse structure called a caldera. Next granite was intruded in western Rùm, before cone sheets and dykes developed. These were followed by the formation of the Rùm Layered Centre (peridotites and gabbros).

Quaternary
The mountains we see in the North-West Highlands today were created by uplift which took place during the rifting process associated with the opening of the North Atlantic around 50 million years ago. However, the final moulding of these mountains was brought about mainly by the action of the huge ice sheets and glaciers which built up and melted away many times during the last two million years. Large quantities of rock were scooped out of the corries and glens. At times of maximum glaciation the area was completely covered by ice, but at other times the higher summits in the west remained exposed as nunataks.

During the most recent minor glacial episode 12,000 years ago (the Loch Lomond Stadial), ice built up principally where precipitation was greatest, i.e. over western hills. A large ice cap extended from the Trossachs in the south to Torridon in the north. Further north many of the major peaks developed glaciers in their northern corries. A very obvious example of a terminal moraine can be seen, for example, below the north-eastern corrie of Beinn Dearg Mòr – this is especially obvious when viewed in the right light from Sàil Liath on An Teallach.

Freeze-thaw action occurred on summits exposed above the ice, and on ground surrounding glacial areas. Such periglacial conditions produced shattered bedrock (blockfield), scree, stone stripes and polygons, as well as debris showing signs of downslope movement or solifluction. For example, the frost-shattered quartzite ridge between Conival and Ben More Assynt points to these peaks being nunataks during the last major glaciation.

Remains found in the Bone Caves near Inchnadamph indicate that during milder inter-glacial episodes brown bear, Arctic fox, lynx, reindeer and wolf were roaming this part of Scotland. Other remains tell of the presence of polar bear during colder spells.

Where glaciers stagnated and melted away in places they left behind extensive hummocky moraines. One of the best examples of this sort of terrain can be seen in the glen behind the Ling Hut in Torridon. Its name, Coire a' Cheud-chnoic, means Corrie of a Hundred Hills.

Numerous straight troughs eroded in bedrock by moving ice called 'mega-grooves' have been identified in the North-West Highlands in recent years from satellite imagery and digital elevation models. Several fine examples of these features can be easily viewed looking west from a large layby in Ephin (NC 2118 1058).

In early postglacial times numerous large rock slope failures occurred where steep hillsides were no longer supported by valley glaciers. A superb example (best viewed from Sgùrr nan Saighead) lies on the south-western flank of Beinn Fhada above Gleann Lichd, where an area of more than 3km² has moved downslope. Three uphill-facing scarps (or anti-scarps) up to 5m high extend for 700m across the hillside.

Looking up Narnia Arête, Barkeval, Rùm. Harker described the rock (peridotite) as 'Perhaps the best rock in the world for climbing.'

Human History

The Callanish Stones, Calanais, Lewis.
© Noel Williams

Human History

With the exception of a narrow strip along the east coast the North-West Highlands are rough and rocky, ideal scrambling country but poor farming land – less than 10% of it has ever been used for crops. Thin acid soils mean that it has never been heavily settled, although there are scattered sites going back as far as the Mesolithic – there are shell middens on Uist and at the mouth of Strathnaver, for example, as well as a village site at Kinloch on Rùm and house foundations at Crabhadail on Harris. Bloodstone from the northern cliffs of Rùm was widely used as a substitute for flint in the making of stone tools. By 2000 BC there were enough people in the area for the construction of the stone circles around Callanish in Lewis, the main circle being one of the most impressive prehistoric sites in the country, aligned to the extreme rising and setting points of the moon. In the Late Bronze Age the climate became colder and wetter, making farming even harder, and the arrival of Celtic-speaking people with iron weapons meant more people chasing less cultivable land, leading to the construction of many small forts as people tried to protect what they had. The most spectacular of these are the brochs, tall tapering drystone towers unique to Northern Scotland. Dun Dornaigil below Ben Hope, Dun Carloway in Lewis and the two near Glenelg are good examples.

The rugged and indented coastline of the North-West means that until recently the sea was always the best highway, and while Lowland Britain was under Roman control tribes from the north of Ireland known as Scotti sailed across and settled here, bringing the Gaelic language.

Dun Carloway (Dùn Chàrlabhaigh) on Lewis. This broch was probably constructed about 200 BC. © Iain Thow

By the early 6th century they had set up a kingdom known as Dalriada with its heartland in modern Argyll but stretching much farther north. The bulk of the North-West was probably part of the Kingdom of the Northern Picts, centred on Inverness, although only half a dozen Pictish carvings have survived away from the east coast.

In 563 an Irish monk named Columba was exiled from Ireland and set up a community on the tiny island of Iona, close to Mull. This became the religious centre from which Scotland was converted to Christianity. Most of its early kings are buried there and it still exudes a sense of quiet peace and holiness today. Columba and contemporaries such as Maelrubha set up monasteries all over Scotland, and after the Scots King Kenneth MacAlpin took over the Pictish throne in 843 it is likely that their influence was important in enabling the Scots to absorb the much larger and more populous Pictish kingdom (although the wiping out of much of the Pictish nobility by the Vikings in 839 must have helped!).

The joint kingdom prospered and expanded southwards, but in doing so lost control of the west and north to the Vikings. The Isles were officially ceded to the wonderfully-named Norwegian king Magnus Barelegs in 1098. The Western Isles became Norse territory, ruled either from the Isle of Man, by the Earls of Orkney or by the Norwegian kings themselves. Place names such as Durness (deer headland) and Suainaval (pigs hill) are the result, with Norse/Gaelic hybrids such as Suilven (pillar mountain) reflecting a bilingual society. In 1156 a half Norse, half Gaelic chieftain named Somerled won a sea battle over the Norse King of Man (his brother-in-law) and gained control of the Inner Hebrides and the West coast. Somerled was killed in 1164, but from him descended the MacDonalds and MacDougalls who ruled the area for the next three centuries. Feuding continued with the Macleods, the descendants of the Vikings who still controlled Lewis, Harris and parts of Skye.

The last Viking Earl of Orkney died in 1231, then in 1263 the Norwegian king Haakon failed to make it back to Norway after raiding the West Coast. The succeeding Norwegian king sold his rights over the area to the Scottish King Alexander II, but he died in an attempt to enforce them, and his successors were preoccupied with the threat from England. In the resulting power vacuum, the descendants of Somerled styled themselves Lords of the Isles and presided over a sea-based empire with wide trading links and a thriving cultural life. They were effectively independent princes with their own court and laws, building castles such as Ardtornish and Dunscaith to emphasise their authority. A dispute over the Earldom of Ross led to an invasion of the east and a bloody defeat at Harlaw in Aberdeenshire in 1411, but it was not until John of the Isles signed an independent treaty with England that the Stewart kings decided to turn their theoretical overlordship into reality, and the Lordship was forfeited in 1494.

For the next 300 years it was the policy of the Scottish (and later British) Crown to neutralise the MacDonalds by building up the power of the Campbells in Argyllshire and the Mackenzies in Ross. They were aided in this by Clan Donald's talent for backing lost causes, notably those of the later Stuart kings, Charles I, James II and the Jacobite pretenders.

The ruins of Ardvreck Castle, originally built about 1590. © Noel Williams

The area did see the occasional pitched battle during this chaotic period, notably at Carbisdale on the east coast, where the royalist Duke of Montrose was defeated and fled across to Ardvreck Castle, home of Macleod of Assynt, an ally. Unfortunately for him, old Macleod had died and his son decided to change sides, locked Montrose up and sold him to the Cromwellian government to be executed. In revenge, Charles II allowed the Mackenzies to evict the Macleods and seize the area.

Further south, Spanish troops were landed in Kintail in 1719 and defeated in Glenshiel, the Spanish retreating up the hillside until forced to surrender at the top of Sgùrr nan Spainteach. A few years later Bonnie Prince Charlie mustered his troops at Glenfinnan and, after Culloden was pursued over the southern part of the region after Culloden being sheltered around Arisaig, above Glen Doe and on South Uist.

Throughout all these upheavals it is likely that for most people most of the time life was dominated by more domestic considerations. They lived in small settlements of a few families, raised cattle, grew oats and barley, fished, wove cloth and cut peat for fuel. The land was divided into strips, which were allocated to tenants on a yearly basis by lot (the runrig system), then the cattle were allowed onto the fields once the crops were harvested. In the summer the animals were grazed high on the hills, looked after from temporary shelters known as shielings, the remains of which can be seen in numerous places. In the autumn cattle which couldn't be fed over the winter were driven south to the markets at Crieff (and later Falkirk) and sold to provide a small monetary income in order to buy the things the communities couldn't make themselves. The droving trade reached its height in the 18th century, when tens of thousands of animals were sold every year. The introduction of the potato in the 18th century caused an increase in population, and the small raised potato beds known as lazybeds are still very prominent all over the west coast and islands.

The failure of the Jacobite rising of 1745 led to drastic consequences for the Highlands, initially due to the brutal reprisals carried out by the Duke of Cumberland, but more permanently as successive governments made a concerted attempt to eradicate Highland culture. Ironically they were aided in this by many of the chiefs themselves. Up to this time these had managed their land so as to maintain as many fighting men as possible, but once the Highlands were disarmed after Culloden their power depended on having money and influence in Edinburgh and London rather than men. The easiest way to obtain this was to evict the people, now an encumbrance, and let the land for sheep to Lowland shepherds, who could pay ten times the rent. In the century after Culloden tens of thousands were evicted and shipped, more or less unwillingly, to Canada and Australia, while many more went to swell the populations of Glasgow, Edinburgh, Dundee and Paisley. Popular myth (backed by the notorious case of Sutherland) has it that this was done by the English, but in most cases it was the clan chiefs themselves who carried out the Clearances, leaving large swathes of the Highlands an empty land. By the end of the 19th century the sheep had largely gone too, replaced by herds of deer managed for shooting, leaving even fewer people.

The decline of the Gaelic language followed from the evictions, and now there are only around 70,000 native speakers, mainly in Skye and the Outer Isles. It is having something of a revival at present though, centred around Gaelic music, which has led to many younger people continuing to use the language after childhood. The building of new roads has made the area far more accessible, and tourism is by far the biggest employer, although fishing and crofting are still important and there are a few large employers, mostly on the east coast. The biggest changes of the last century are the damming of many lochs for hydro-electric schemes and the introduction of large scale forestry, especially in the eastern part of the area. At first most plantations were of imported Sitka spruce, which grows far faster than the native Scots pine, but the last few years have seen a promising trend for the planting of native species, notably in Glen Affric and Kintail. Despite its sad history, most of the North-West remains unspoiled wild mountain country, breathtakingly beautiful, and as aloof from the turbulent activities of man as it has ever been.

Wildlife

A springtime display on the machair, North Uist. © Iain Thow

This chapter gives an introduction to the varied plant and animal life which may be encountered whilst tackling these scrambles in north-west Scotland. Because the scrambles are widely spread across the north-west mainland and the Western Isles, it is not possible to give a detailed guide to each locality – so this is more of a general introduction to the whole area. Also, the rocks most suitable for scrambling tend to be hard and stable, which makes them less conducive to plant growth than softer, more friable rocks. So, whilst a limited range of plant species will be encountered on the routes themselves, the approach to and descent from the scrambles offers a greater opportunity to observe some of the diverse plant and animal life for which the area is famous. The references listed under 'further reading' (see endflap) should be consulted for more detail on individual localities.

Different plant species are variously equipped to cope with the challenges of geology, climate and topography. The nature of the vegetation found at any particular place depends on the chemical composition and physical characteristics of the substrate, degree of exposure to wind, annual rainfall, duration of snow-lie and also the land management history. Biogeography also plays a part, with some common mainland species being completely absent from the Western Isles and Rùm. We will start at sea level and work upwards through the major habitat types.

Coastal Areas

In north-west Scotland the coast is never far away, and sea views add greatly to the enjoyment of a day on the hill. Several plants of coastal habitats – thrift (or sea-pink), sea plantain, scurvy grass and sea campion, are also found in the mountains. Other cliff plants – the celery-ike Scots lovage, and the leathery sea spleenwort fern – are more strictly maritime. Conversely, because of the extreme severity of the climate, some plants found only at high altitudes in the south and east of the country (for example, the yellow saxifrage and mountain avens) descend to sea level in the north-west. These two species are not found at all in the Western Isles, but are both present on Rùm.

The cliffs of the north-west mainland and Lewis, with their spectacular offshore islands and stacks, form summer tenements for colonies of seabirds – guillemots, razorbills, kittiwakes and fulmars. These birds spend most of their lives at sea, only making landfall to breed. Peregrine falcons exploit this seasonal bounty, hunting along the cliffs to feed their own broods. Forty years after their initial re-introduction to Rùm, white-tailed sea eagles are recolonising their old west-coast haunts. On the north Sutherland coast, short cliff-top turf is studded in spring with the bluebell-like flowers of spring squill and, in a few places, the tiny Scottish primrose. The sea-lochs which indent rocky coastlines on either side of the Minch, with their thick fringe of brown sea-weeds, skerries, small salt-marshes and yellow iris beds, provide ideal sheltered habitat for otters and common seals. Further offshore harbour porpoises and grey seals are more likely. When travelling out to the islands, you may be lucky enough to spot a minke whale or a pod of common or bottlenose dolphins, or even orca.

Sandy bays, as at Sandwood, Oldshoremore and Clachtoll on the

A pair of white-tailed sea eagles resting on the shoreline. © Peter Elford

mainland, and the western seaboard of the Uists, support crofting landscapes with colourful displays of flower-rich machair (grassland on blown shell-sand) in summer. The Western Isles machairs support important populations of ground-nesting waders such as lapwing curlew, oystercatcher and redshank. Introduced predators such as hedgehogs and American mink pose a threat to these birds, and have been subject to recent control programmes. Burrowing animals such as moles (not in the Western Isles or Rùm) and rabbits are restricted to these drier grassland areas. Both of these species are preyed upon by the buzzard, which is the commonest large bird of prey at lower altitudes. Another common bird of agricultural and moorland landscapes is the hooded ('hoodie') crow – a two-tone version of the more southerly carrion crow. The short, steep river systems of the western seaboard are generally low in nutrients and support species, such as the freshwater pearl mussel and dipper, which require clear, sediment-free water, as do the commercially-important populations of Atlantic salmon and sea trout.

Woodlands
Native woodlands are generally sparse in the North-West Highlands, and practically absent from the Western Isles. Their occurrence is limited by the restricted extent of mineral soils, extreme oceanic climate and long history of burning and grazing. This deficit has historically been addressed by extensive planting of native trees, as on Rùm. More recently rewilding projects, aiming for natural regeneration, have commenced on several landholdings in the north. Oak is a southern species which reaches its northern geographical limit in Assynt, where its growth is severely limited by the wind. These damp north-western oakwoods, as at Letterewe, are remarkable for their profusion non-flow-

Scots pine by Loch Quoich. © Noel Williams

ering plants – lichens, mosses, liverworts and filmy ferns, which thrive on the high humidity. Typical birds here are the redstart and wood warbler. Scots pine is more at home on the colder north-facing slopes of Torridon, the west side of Loch Maree and Glen Barrisdale in Knoydart. These western pinewoods lack some of the 'typical' pinewood plant and bird species found further east, but the tinkling calls of tiny goldcrests may still be heard as they seek out insects among the foliage. Woods of ash and hazel are restricted to the calcareous soils of the Durness limestones, as at Kishorn. These woods have a rich ground flora, with bluebell, dogs' mercury, sanicle and in a few places the scarce dark red helleborine orchid.

In the extreme north, only the resilient birch forms extensive woodlands, such as those at Loch Stack. The rowan is equally resilient, but usually grows scattered amongst trees of other species, or clinging to the side of a sheltered gully high on the hill. Eared willow prefers the damper ground on lower slopes or in valley bottoms, where the banks of rivers and burns are lined with alder. Of the woodland mammals, pine martens have made a tremendous comeback, spreading out from their refuge in the North-West Highlands, where they evaded 19th century persecution, to recolonise most of the Highland mainland. The wildcat has not fared so well because of its propensity to interbreed with the domestic cat, and is now considered functionally extinct in its pure form. Roe deer are widespread but wary, most often seen as a white rump bouncing away into the undergrowth, accompanied by a gruff bark of alarm. In recent years a population of wild boar has arisen from escaped animals and is now spreading through the woodlands along the Great Glen.

Bogs

The combination of high rainfall and acidic rocks makes north-western Scotland ideal for the growth of bogs, and the approach to many of the scrambles will involve a somewhat soggy walk-in. The colourful Sphagnum mosses which carpet the bog surface are also essential to its formation. Their growing-point is at the top, and as the lower parts die, the acidic water which they hold prevents decomposition, so that peat slowly accumulates. The oldest Lewisian rocks, found in the Western Isles and the mainland west of the Moine Thrust, present a knobbly low-relief topography, with bogs and lochans occupying the hollows between bald rocky knolls. Here, familiar plants such as heather and deer-grass grow in combination with bog specialists which are well adapted to the nutrient-poor, acidic and wet conditions. The carnivorous sundews and butterworts, which trap insects on their rosettes of sticky leaves, are found on bare peat and along the margins of pools and lochans. Below the water, bladderworts also pursue a carnivorous lifestyle, ensnaring small aquatic creatures in their tiny traps. Unfortunately, the combined efforts of all these carnivorous plants still fail to make much of a dent in the midge population! Bog bean and bottle sedge are 'emergent' plants – rooting on the loch floor but with leaves and flowers above the surface. These watery boglands provide excellent habitat for damselflies and dragonflies, including the spectacular azure hawker, which has its stronghold in the north-western Highlands. Among the birds, the greenshank is similarly concentrated in the north-west, including the Western Isles, during the breeding season. The golden plover is more widespread, inhabiting drier moorlands and mountain tops as well as the bogs. Both species winter in coastal habitats. Red-throated divers nest on islands in the smaller peatland lochans, whereas their black-throated cousins prefer larger lochs. Some of the larger mainland lochs, such as Loch Sionascaig (Inverpolly), are home to the Arctic charr, a non-migratory member of the salmon family.

Intermediate between bog and moorland, wet heaths cover extensive areas in the north-west. Sphagnum mosses are still present, but occupy a smaller proportion of the surface. Heather and cross-leaved heath are the dominant dwarf shrubs, accompanied by deer-grass, purple moor-grass, common cottongrass, bog asphodel and lousewort. The aromatic bog myrtle prefers to grow where there is lateral water movement through the peat.

Moorlands

Where drainage is better and peat thinner, drier moorlands dominated by heather, blaeberry (bilberry) and bell-heather are found. Beneath the taller shrubs creep stems of tormentil, with its four-petalled yellow flower and heath bedstraw, bedecked with clusters of tiny white stars.

Flowers of the heath milkwort may be white, blue or purple. Smaller evergreen shrubs such as the confusingly-named crowberry, cowberry and bearberry occur more sporadically. The upright branched stems of the fir clubmoss conceal spore-producing parts among their topmost leaves, whereas the creeping stag's-horn clubmoss produces conspicuous twin cones on a separate stalk. Under leggy heather, the tiny lesser twayblade orchid, with its paired leaves, may be found. More conspicuous flowers include those of the common spotted orchid, which can occur in a range of colours from almost pure white to dark blotched purple and, later in summer, the pale blue devil's-bit scabious. On drier knolls, low-growing dwarf juniper, Arctic bearberry and mountain everlasting are characteristic.

Red deer range over most of the moorlands in the north-west and the Western Isles, and deer stalking is an important part of the local economy. The red deer population of Rùm has been the subject of pioneering long-term research. Rùm also has a population of feral goats, as do the areas around An Teallach and the hills of Kintail. These shaggy beasts are the descendants of domestic goats allowed to run free in centuries past. Their exact antiquity is disputed. Of the smaller animals, mountain hare, common lizard, common frog, adder, and slow worm can be found on the mainland moors, although all are absent from the Western Isles and all but the common lizard from Rùm. A variety of impressively large moths and butterflies inhabit the moorlands and bogs. For much of the year, the hairy caterpillars and papery pupal cases are the most conspicuous evidence of the northern eggar moth. The velvety-brown adults take wing in May and June. Emperor moth caterpillars are well-camouflaged on their food-plant, heather, being green with a line of small pink dots resembling flower-buds. The adult moths have spectacular eyespots on both pairs of wings. In July the dark

Feral Goat, An Teallach. © Iain Thow

Emperor moth caterpillar. © Iain Thow

green fritillary butterfly is a powerful flyer across the drier moorlands, where its larvae feed on violets. The large heath is less conspicuous and, since cotton-grasses are its larval food-plant, tends to be found in boggier areas. Perhaps the commonest moorland bird is the meadow pipit, whose ground-level nest is a favourite target of the cuckoo. The stonechat and whinchat nest among shrubby vegetation, whereas the wheatear chooses rocky or stony places. These small songbirds provide food for the merlin, our smallest moorland bird of prey. The hen harrier, which prefers lower, rolling moorlands as in the Uists, also takes larger prey items. Populations of field voles, although at lower densities than in grassland habitats, support mammal-eating predators such as the short-eared owl. Both species are absent from Lewis, Harris and Rùm.

Geological Influence
The sudden appearance of a green patch, in a predominantly brown moorland landscape, indicates an outcrop of base-rich rock. These are more frequent as small intrusions among the Lewisian rocks of the western seaboard and Western Isles than in the Torridonian and Moine rocks of the mainland interior. Along the Durness limestone outcrops which follow the Moine Thrust northwards from Kishorn to Durness, more extensive species-rich calcareous grasslands occur. These present a colourful spectacle in early summer, with a proliferation of orchids, common birds-foot-trefoil, eyebrights, wild thyme and fairy flax in their short turf. Later in the season, the flowers of frog orchid and grass of Parnassus will appear, along with fertile fronds of the tiny fern, moonwort. Montane species such as mountain avens, whortle-leaved willow, Alpine bistort, Alpine meadow-rue and Alpine cinquefoil may be seen at relatively low altitudes on the limestone, most notably at Inchnadamph. Here, and at Kishorn and Durness, areas of bare limestone

'pavement' occur, where grazing-sensitive plants such as wild garlic and holly fern are able to survive in the shelter of deep cracks, or grykes, where water has dissolved away the rock. Seepages of alkaline water across the ground surface form calcareous 'flushes', where plants such as the Scottish asphodel (a smaller, paler relative of the bog asphodel), black bog-rush, yellow saxifrage and the worm-like hooked scorpion-moss may be found. The limestone streams of Assynt provide a habitat for the water vole, now endangered in many places by the spread of introduced American mink. The alkaline lochs of Assynt and Durness support plants such as mare's-tail, blue water-speedwell and stoneworts, which cannot tolerate acid water.

On more acid soils, grasslands composed of bents and fescues may be poorer in flowers, but provide favoured grazings for red deer and domestic stock far up onto the hill. Viviparous fescue, which produces ready-made plantlets in place of seeds, shows adaptation to the harsh mountain conditions. The appearance of Alpine lady's mantle, dwarf cornel and Alpine clubmoss, signal that you are gaining altitude.

Crags and Corries

The plants most likely to be encountered on the scrambles themselves are either those with long taproots, which can anchor themselves in rock crevices, or those which grow in pockets of soil accumulated on ledges. The first group include thrift, familiar from its alternative seashore habitat, the succulent roseroot and pink-flowered moss campion. Those growing on ledges include the tall perennials such as globeflower, meadowsweet, wild angelica, greater woodrush, wood cranesbill, goldenrod, northern bedstraw, water avens and melancholy thistle. These plants are generally palatable to sheep and deer, and benefit from the protection offered by inaccessible ledges, where they grow and flower with a luxuriance unequalled in grazed situations. Higher up, real mountain specialists such as Alpine saw-wort and, in a few mainland localities on the richer rock types, small remnant populations of mountain willows, including downy willow and net-leaved willow, can be found in similar places.

The water of most hill lochs and lochans is acidic and nutrient-poor, supporting a limited but characteristic range of plants, including shoreweed, water lobelia, water horsetail, bottle sedge, white water-lily and, in the most acidic, awlwort. Some hill lochs have distinct populations of brown trout which have survived in isolation since the last ice age. Others have been augmented by stocking. The plaintive call of the common sandpiper characterises the hill lochans in spring, when it arrives to nest by the waterside.

Where acidic water seeps out of the ground spring-heads, highlighted by bright green fountain apple-moss and delicate starry saxifrage, dot the hillsides. Up in the corries, patches of scree may support populations of the appropriately-named parsley fern, whose crinkled leaves resemble the garden herb. Where snow lies late into the summer, a distinctive vegetation develops, with mat-grass, and on the mainland only, the clover-like Sibbaldia and dwarf cudweed. The high corries provide secure nesting sites for golden eagles and ravens and secluded pastures for calving red deer hinds. On the mainland the hill fox makes

Trailing azalea. © Iain Thow

its dens in the high rocks, and may occasionally be surprised foraging (or even sleeping) in broad daylight. Foxes are absent from the Western Isles and Rùm. The ring ouzel is another summer visitor, and its fluting song epitomises the high places.

High Tops

On completing your scramble you may emerge onto a windswept ridge or plateau. Here the vegetation will typically (on the mainland – some of these plants are absent from the Western Isles and/or Rùm) consist of low-growing woody shrubs such as dwarf willow, trailing azalea, and cushion plants including moss campion and cyphel. The spindly three-leaved rush, spiked wood-rush and stiff sedge stand vertical, defying the wind. On broader ridges and plateaux, the woolly fringe-moss forms extensive grey carpets, interspersed with plants of Alpine clubmoss and Iceland moss (which, perversely, is not a moss but a lichen). On the more fractured and angular rock types, for example the Torridonian sandstones and Cambrian quartzites, the summits and ridges may appear practically bare of vegetation. But a closer look reveals an intricate crazy paving of tiny lichens covering the rock surface.

Of the birds whose breeding is restricted to the high tops, ptarmigan are widespread in the north-west Highlands. They remain all year round, relying on their changeable plumage for camouflage (white in winter, mottled brown in summer). Snow bunting and dotterel have a more limited breeding distribution, using only the highest rocky summits and mossy plateaux respectively. All three species are absent as breeders from the Western Isles and Rùm, but snow buntings visit in winter to forage along the Hebridean coastline.

Weather

A Fisherfield temperature inversion seen from A' Mhaighdean. © Iain Thow

Weather

Although the weather in the Northern Highlands is in many ways less extreme than in the bigger hills further south, with lower rainfall and less snow, it is even more unpredictable. The cyclonic systems moving in off the Atlantic hit the rugged mountains of the indented west coast and often don't do what you (or the forecasters) expect. Year by year variation is huge but some general patterns can be picked out. Most obvious is that the west is wetter, mean annual rainfall being over 3000mm in Knoydart but only 750mm in Caithness. The east is usually colder, being less affected by the Gulf Stream, and this is particularly true in the north-east, with Altnaharra competing with Braemar to be the coldest place in Britain (-27.2°C has been recorded in both places). High roads such as that to Ullapool get around 140 days with ground frost a year, and up on the tops this total is higher. Conversely the west coast and the islands get only a few days of frost a year.

Snowfall in the area largely depends on altitude and distance from the sea, with the central ranges from Kintail to the Deargs getting the highest totals. Amounts are generally much smaller than in the Cairngorms or Lochaber though, with snow lying in northern glens for around 50 days a year (compared with twice that at Derry Lodge in the Cairngorms, for instance). On the bigger hills snow lies for much longer, of course, and in places such as the Affric hills there will be patches of old snow well into June. Snow falls usually start in November (sometimes October) and full winter conditions in May are not at all unusual. Conditions vary hugely across the area however, and in April or May areas such as Knoydart, Rùm or Harris may be virtually snow free when the Affric hills or the Fannichs are still in full winter garb.

Temperature changes drastically with height, 5°C in the glen will be below zero at Munro level even after the effects of wind chill and/or snow cover are discounted. The exception is during temperature inversions, common in autumn and winter, when cold air pools overnight in sheltered hollows (hence the Altnaharra figure). Both over the year and within the day the temperature varies less in places closer to the sea, especially on the west, and places such as Gairloch may be positively balmy when it is still winter on the big hills.

Winds tend to be stronger in the west, particularly in the Outer Hebrides, where most winters bring a few days with winds over 150km/hr. Even in other seasons it isn't unknown for big winds to stop the ferries and give you an unexpected extra day on the islands. Data for the Northern Highlands is much less plentiful than for the hills further south as there are no summit observatories comparable to those on Cairngorm, The Cairnwell or the Victorian one on Ben Nevis. Some things still apply however – the windspeed on the tops is usually at least double that in the valleys and often much more. 50km/hr on the tops is common. An 80km/hr wind will stop most people in their tracks and 120km/hr will pick you up. The current writer was once thrown 10m by an equinoctal gust on Beinn Choradail in South Uist. Even in less extreme conditions it pays to try and avoid walking into the wind on the more exposed parts of your route. On the positive side a good wind at least has the advantage of keeping the midges down!

The weather often varies hugely across the area of this guide at any

A Brocken spectre on Bivouac Rib, A' Mhaighdean. © Iain Thow

given time, and even within fairly small areas there can be a marked contrast. Gairloch often enjoys fine sunny days while it pours down only a few miles away in Torridon, for instance, and even on the same mountain good route choices can often make a big difference. Harris in particular often has very different weather on the two coasts, or in North and South Harris. Taking into account height and aspect will often get you an enjoyable scramble during a period of unsettled weather and reduce the chances of having an epic. Obviously north-facing routes will remain wet and unpleasant for longer than sunnier ones, and conversely they may provide welcome shade in a heat wave (they do happen in Scotland!). It's also worth bearing in mind the effects of weather on different rock

After a cloudburst, in the space of 10 minutes this small stream was turned into a raging torrent. © Iain Thow

types, with the rougher gneiss and sandstones keeping better friction when wet than do the schist and quartzite – see the section on "choosing a route" for more information.

Sometimes the weather can make even accessing the routes problematic. Streams can rise rapidly, especially in rocky areas such as Torridon or Knoydart. The Rough Bounds east of the latter contain several streams that can be uncrossable in wet weather, and people have been killed trying. It's always best to err on the side of caution when dealing with moving water, going the long way round and being late is obviously better than being swept away.

Of course the weather can produce positive effects too, with cloud seas not uncommon, especially in autumn, and scramblers on steep north-facing slopes are often in the right place to see Brocken spectres or fog bows. Showery weather can mean lots of rainbows and it is not uncommon on the windy west coast to see waterfalls being blown back vertically upwards. A sudden clearing when you are high on the hill can be absolutely magical. The rapidity of change can be impressive – the hills can change from cloud being above the summits to thick cloud covering all the ridges (or vice versa) in under a minute! The sheer variety and occasional ferocity of Scotland's weather means that it is worth paying close attention to both forecasts beforehand and changes during your day, but it is very rare that you can't find a worthwhile excursion to match the conditions.

Weather Forecasts
The one virtual certainty about the weather here is that it will vary over the area of this guide!

The Radio Scotland Outdoor Conditions forecast is a good source, at present at 6.25pm Mon-Fri and during the 7am and 7pm bulletins Saturday and Sunday.

On TV, Reporting Scotland includes a basic outdoor forecast in its early evening bulletins at weekends, and the BBC Countryfile Forecast on Sunday evenings gives a view for the week ahead targeted at those spending most of their time outdoors.

Online resources:
- www.mwis.org.uk includes useful details such as wind speeds and temperatures at 900m. They are often reachable in places with a poor mobile signal where bigger sites such as the BBC or Met Office fail to load.
- www.metoffice.gov.uk/mountain-forecast includes useful advice and excellent maps.
- www.bbc.co.uk/weather gives a good overview at 3 hour intervals.
- www.mountain-forecast.com shows the conditions on mountain summits at hourly intervals.
- www.yr.no and www.metcheck.com both show the weather in hourly intervals.

For the very short term the Met Office site has a rainfall radar map showing the current situation in great detail (every 100m!) so you can see what is just about to arrive.

Mountaineering History

The Triple Buttresses, Coire Mhic Fhearchair, Beinn Eighe.
© A.E. Robertson (May 1905), SMC Image Archive

For many years remoteness, poor roads and a moist climate combined to put off all but the most determined travellers from visiting north-west Scotland. The exploration of the mountains in the Northern Highlands and the Outer Hebrides has therefore been slower and more sporadic than elsewhere in Britain. Only a brief outline of events is given here. Fuller details of the early pioneers can be found in Ian Mitchell's book, *Scotland's Mountains before the Mountaineers*. For more recent ascents see three SMC climbing guides to the *Northern Highlands*.

Hunters, Cartographers and Soldiers

1250 — The naming of Coire Mhic Fhearchair (corrie of Farquar's son) suggests that Farquar MacIntaggart's son, William, visited the corries of Mullach Coire Mhic Fhearchair and Beinn Eighe around this time.

1580s — Fionnladh Dubh (Black Findlay), a famous archer and forester of Glen Cannich, shoots an intruder dead with a bow and arrow, and dumps the body in the loch below the summits of Càrn Eighe and Mam Sodhail. He is credited with the ascent of nearby Beinn Fhionnlaidh (Findlay's Hill) above Loch Mullardoch – the first recorded bagging of a Munro beyond the Great Glen.

1590s — Timothy Pont makes an extended cartographic study of Scotland. His sketches of the mountains suggest that he ascended some way up the hills. After his death his work was incorporated in the famous *Blaeu Atlas*.

1654 — Blaeu's *Atlas Novus* is published in Amsterdam. It makes Scotland one of the best mapped countries in the world.

1719 — The Battle of Glenshiel takes place on 10 June. 1,500 Jacobites including some 250 Spaniards are defeated by Hanoverian forces led by Major General Wightman. Contemporary paintings and drawings show Highlanders on the summit of Sgùrr na Ciste Duibhe and later their defeated Spanish allies being chased over Sgùrr nan Spainteach (Peak of the Spaniards). This was the last battle involving foreign troops to take place on Scottish soil.

1746 — On 16 April Charles Edward Stuart and the Jacobite cause are finally defeated at Culloden. The Prince criss-crossed all over the West Highlands, the Outer Isles and Skye that summer before eventually escaping to France from Loch nan Uamh on 20 September.

Naturalists, Geologists and the Ordnance Survey

1747 — William Roy joins a team led by Lieutenant Colonel David Watson, and spends eight years producing a map of the Highlands for the military at a scale of 1:21,560. Roy later becomes Major General and it is largely due to him that the Ordnance Survey is set up the year after his death in 1791.

1767 — James Robertson, in the course of carrying out a survey of Highland flora, ascends Ben Hope, Ben Klibreck, Ben Wyvis, Scaraben and Morven.

1770s — Rev John Stuart and John Lightfoot ascend many peaks, including Beinn Sgritheall, when botanising throughout the Highlands.

1800s — Legend has it that shepherds used to hear a wailing noise above a deep gash (Eag Dhubh na h-Eigheachd) just below the summit of Beinn Alligin, until one of them descends to investigate and falls to his death.

1811–21 — Dr. John Macculloch travels extensively while making the first geological map of Scotland single-handed. He writes 'four garrulous volumes on the Highlands and Western Isles'. In the North-West his climbs include Ben Lair, but his finest achievement is undoubtedly his ascent of An Teallach (Sgùrr Fiona) – the most significant ascent in the area to date.

1817 — William MacGillivray, aged 21, ascends An Cliseam '…in spite of hail and snow, and the furious whirlwinds or eddying blasts that swept the mountain'. He was a prodigious walker. (At the age of 11 he left Harris to study and travelled on foot from Poolewe to Aberdeen.) A keen but irascible naturalist, he later went on to become Professor of Natural History at Aberdeen University.

1819 — Captain Thomas Colby carries out an extraordinary season of 'station hunting' in the Highlands for the Ordnance Survey. (His career had nearly been brought to an abrupt halt in 1803, when he lost his left hand following an accident with an exploding pistol. A piece of metal remained lodged in his skull for the rest of his life.) While exploring Inverness-shire, Ross, Caithness and Orkney, with a party of artillery men, and afterwards the western parts of Ross and Skye with a fresh party, Colby traverses on foot an astonishing 1,099 miles in 45 days. During the course of this survey work – as part of the Principle Triangulation of Britain – several summits are visited, the most notable in the North-West being Slioch. Colby arranged mountain-top feasts for his men with huge plum puddings at the end of each surveying season. He went on to become the longest serving Director

	General of the Ordnance Survey (1820–1846), and was responsible for the first detailed mapping of Ireland.
1846	— The Inglis brothers – William, Charles and Robert – begin a life-long campaign of peak-bagging throughout the Highlands. Their numerous ascents include Ben More Assynt in 1863.
1850	— In the course of settling a boundary dispute a surveyor, George Campbell Smith, places cairns along the march between the estates of Gairloch and Torridon. His route takes him over the ridge of Beinn Eighe.
1851	— The first recorded ascent of Beinn Mhòr in South Uist is made by Corp. Jenkins of the OS, but trigonometers had been there a decade earlier.
1872	— Another boundary dispute sees an employee of Meyrick Bankes place a cairn on Beinn Tarsuinn – one of the most remote Munros.
1876	— The summit of the Great Stack of Handa is reached by Donald Macdonald (aged 26) in order to cull sea birds. He crosses hand-over-hand on a rope stretched across the enclosing geo by a team of men from Lewis.
1883	— Following a long running dispute over the geology of the North-West, Geikie appoints Peach and Horne to lead a team in mapping the Assynt area for the Geological Survey. One of the survey team, Lionel Hinxman, is a keen mountaineer.

The Climbers arrive

1888	— The Scottish Mountaineering Club is formed.
1890	— The second SMC Journal includes two articles on the North-West. Lionel Hinxman describes ascending Canisp with two friends, before climbing Suilven from its eastern end ('A Climb over Suilven'), and fellow geologist Henry Cadell describes 'The Mountain Scenery of the North-West Highlands'.
1891	— The fifth SMC Journal includes another article by Lionel Hinxman in which he gives an excellent description of Beinn Eighe and the Torridon Hills. The same year Hinxman makes an ascent of A' Chìoch of Beinn Bhàn in a thunderstorm.
1892	— Charles Pilkington and Horace Walker climb a prominent break on the right-hand side of the Grey Castle at the west end of Suilven. Prof Ramsay makes a repeat ascent in 1895.
1894	— Douglas, Hinxman, Rennie and Macdonald ascend Liathach by the *Northern Pinnacles*. They then walk through the hills to Strath Carron.

1898	— Norman Collie, probably with Cecil Slingsby, makes a part ascent and then full descent of the *Central Buttress* of Coire Mhic Fhearchair. He writes that he thinks he has discovered 'the finest rock climb in the British Isles'.
1899	— The first of two successive SMC Easter Meets is held at Kinlochewe. Lawson, Ling and Glover climb up the eastern end of Liathach and also a buttress on Sàil Mhòr, Beinn Eighe. Inglis Clark, Glover and Gall Inglis climb an impressive face just north-west of a large waterfall on Beinn a' Mhuinidh.
1900	— Ling, Mackay, Naismith, Raeburn and Gall Inglis (with an appearance by Munro) make the first winter traverse of Liathach's *Northern Pinnacles*.
1904	— Harold Raeburn and EB Robertson climb a buttress on Sgòrr Ruadh.

Raeburn (belaying) and Ling (seconding) on a route at the west end of Suilven, 29 March 1907. (SMC Easter Meet, Inchnadamph). © SMC Image Archive. Taken by Euan Robertson from Pilkington and Walker's route.

1906 — Dr, Mrs and Miss Inglis Clark and CW Walker ascend the steep western end of Stac Pollaidh (undergraded at Difficult in modern guides).

1907 — An audacious attempt on the Barrel Buttress of Quinag by Raeburn, Ling and Mackay only succeeds after an inspection on a rope from above. Ling and Sang attempt the Nose of Sgùrr an Fhidhleir. The fine *East Buttress* of Coire Mhic Fhearchair is climbed by Gibbs, Backhouse and Mounsey.

1908 — *A' Chioch* of Sgùrr a' Chaorachain is climbed by Glover and Ling.

1910 — Ling and Glover climb Beinn Airigh Charr (by a more direct line than their foray of the previous year). They also climb on Foinaven and Ben Hope.

1914 — Goggs, Arthur and Young climb the 'buttress left of Barrel Buttress', now known as *V Buttress*.

1930 — M Botterill does some of the first rock climbs in the Outer Hebrides.

1932 — Ling writes the *Northern Highlands* guide for the SMC.

1934 — Naismith edits the *Islands of Scotland* guide for the SMC.

1951 — A number of parties visit the north face of Beinn Lair and discover 22 new routes in a single summer. (They were so thorough in their exploration that there have only been a handful more summer routes added in the subsequent 70 years.) Frank Cunningham pens a review for the *SMC Journal* in which he describes climbing developments in the Northern Highlands since Ling's guide.

1952 — Scott and Molly Johnstone explore the climbing possibilities in the Outer Hebrides, and make new ascents, including the *Coire Dubh Slabs* on An Cliseam. (Notes appear in the 1954 SMC Journal.)

1954 — Donald Bennet & Donald Mill climb the spectacular *Red Slab* on A' Mhaighdean.

1955 — The Ling Hut is opened in Glen Torridon. MJ O'Hara begins the exploration of Maiden Buttress on Carnan Ban.

1957 — MJ O'Hara and WD Blackwood climb the superb *Fionn Buttress* at Carnmore. O'Hara then goes on to triumph on *Dragon* with GJ Fraser and among a number of other fine routes, also discovers the more amenable *Grey Ridge* with NC Peacock & RG Hargreaves.

Ling and Glover in old age – two former Presidents of the SMC and significant pioneers in the North-West Highlands. © Tom Weir

1967 — Two excellent routes are done the same day on Barkeval – *Broad Buttress* (J Matyssek) and *Narnia Arête* (Hamish Brown & AT Rollo).

1973 — A moratorium is proposed on the reporting of new routes west of the Great Glen (with the exception of Skye) by Ian Rowe and Graham Tiso.

1993 — The first comprehensive climbing guide to the Northern Highlands, (edited by Geoff Cohen) is published in two volumes. The flood gates open...

2004–07 — Three new comprehensive guides (edited by Andy Nisbet) are published to cover the explosion of new routes in the *Northern Highlands: North* (2004), *Central* (2006) and *South* (2007).

The area north of the Mallaig railway is dominated by east-west chains of rugged peaks, with the Rough Bounds of Knoydart in particular being amongst the craggiest areas of the Highlands. Despite this continuous rock lines are few, with most of the scrambles here made up of a succession of outcrops, but some are fine scrambles nonetheless.

Some of the routes are accessible in a day from the Fort William to Mallaig road or the minor roads up Loch Arkaig and Glen Garry, but many require a longer trip. There is a regular boat service from Mallaig to the village of Inverie and this provides a good base for those in Knoydart proper.

Also included here is the compact group of hills overlooking Loch Lochy, where two very accessible Munros have long but rather vegetated scrambles on their south-east flanks.

The Great Glen to Knoydart

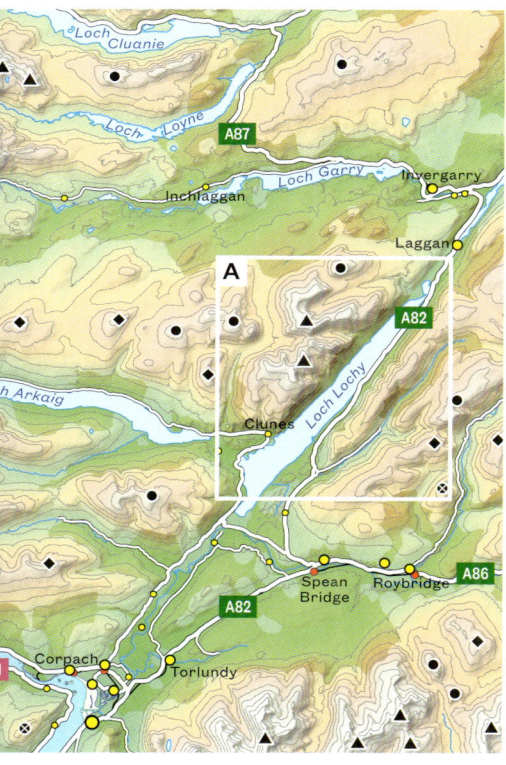

A. Loch Lochy Hills	Routes 1–3	P.72
B. Glenfinnan Area	Routes 4–7	P.78
C. Morar, the Rough Bounds & Knoydart	Routes 8–17	P.86

Loch Lochy Hills

Sròn a' Choire Ghairbh and Meall na Teanga are a popular round from either Kilfinnan at the north end of Loch Lochy or Clunes to the south. They give easy though quite steep walking on good paths with extensive views over the Great Glen and west to Knoydart and Kintail.

1. **Meall na Teanga**   Routes 1 & 2   P.73
2. **Sròn a' Choire Ghairbh**   Route 3   P.76

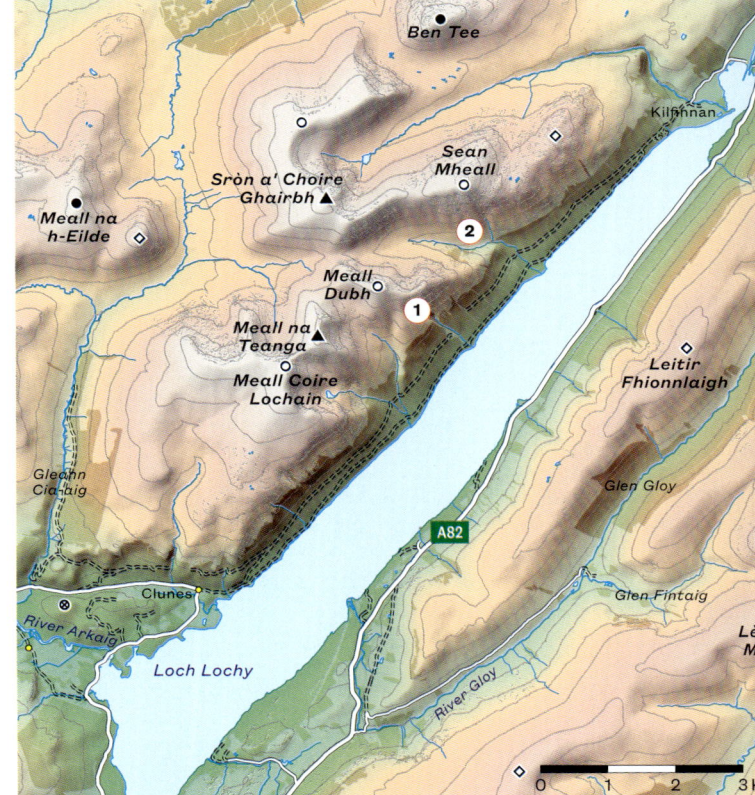

Meall na Teanga 918m

This steep-sided hill has three tops linked by pleasant grassy ridges, with the highest summit just scraping into Munro status. The described scrambles are on the north-east top, Meall Dubh, which has a rocky face overlooking Loch Lochy. The hill is usually combined with its neighbour Sròn a' Choire Ghairbh, and scrambles on both can be included with a little cunning. Both routes are quite vegetated in places but the rock is generally sound psammite.

- PAGES 71 & 72
- OS LR 34
- SOUTH
- PSAMMITE

1 Central Buttress, Meall Dubh — Grade 2 or 3

| ⌖ NN 236 927 | 🚶 2HRS 20 | ◿ OUTCROPS | ⊤ +200M |

A very steep and indirect approach, but the scrambling is quite good once it gets going.

Approach
From the bend in the road at Clunes (NN 201 886) follow the forest road towards Loch Lochy, taking the upper fork after a few hundred metres. After about 6km this ends at a stream (Dearg Allt, not named on the Landranger map). Go steeply up its south bank (brief detour into the trees necessary) and once above the forest carry on up the spur, with excellent views of the scrambles, to reach a small col at 530m. Take a deer track slanting down right onto the main face. This passes 10m below a prominent small pine and crosses a deep gully with a stream. Central Buttress is beyond, starting as two lower bluffs, the right-hand one bigger and cleaner, with a larger pine tree on the right-hand side.

The Route
Gain the top of the right-hand bluff either from the heathery groove between the bluffs or by climbing a short slab 3 metres right of the larger pine tree, pulling up on heather then moving back left to the top of the bluff. Carry on up the crest, with more rock gradually appearing and things getting much more pleasant. At a steep slabby buttress go left and climb a heathery recess before rejoining the crest. At twin buttresses above this either climb the right-hand slabby one on small sharp holds (Grade 3) or more broken rock on the left side of the left-hand buttress. Easier rock leads to the top.

2 Right-Hand Buttress, Meall Dubh — Grade 3

| ⌖ NN 237 927 | 🚶 2HRS 25 | ◿ OUTCROPS | ⊤ +200M |

More broken than the previous route but the scrambling parts are better.

Approach
As for the previous route to the gully beyond the small pine, then continue on the deer path below the two bluffs and across another wet gully onto the buttress beyond.

The Route
Grovel up steep heather on the left-hand angle of the buttress, with traces of path and occasional rock. Arrive at much steeper rock, split into two buttresses by a chimney groove. Climb steeply up the right edge of this on good holds (a little extra rock can be found rather artificially by starting a little further right, going up to a steep slab and traversing left across the lower part of this to reach the right edge of the groove). The groove itself is less exposed but not much easier. Either way reaches a heathery area with steep rock above. From the top left of the heather pull awkwardly up left to reach another heather slope and go right across the bottom of this to the rib beyond it. Climb the rib on positive holds (some loose), first left then right to finish up the skyline.

A little higher are twin buttresses. Climb the left arête of the left one airily on excellent holds. The right arête is only slightly harder if you use the heather on the right just below the top. Now walk up a nice narrow arête with occasional rock to climb an enjoyable final buttress by the left-hand of two spurs on good small holds.

The right-hand slabby buttress, Central Buttress, Meall Dubh (Route 1, Grade 3). Scrambler: Jamie Hageman. © Iain Thow

Sròn a' Choire Ghairbh   935m

Steep sided and flat topped, this Munro is easily combined with its neighbour on good paths. The scramble is on the south face of Sean Mheall (887m), a subsidiary top 2km east of the main summit. This has plenty of rock, but it is well guarded by purgatorial grass and heather.

 PAGES 71 & 72
 OS LR 34
SOUTH
PSAMMITE

③ South Face, Sean Mheall — Grade 2 or 3

○ NN 244 937　　　🏃 1HR　　　⟋ OUTCROPS　　　⊤ +500M

A good finish spoiled by a scrappy middle. Starts up a stream gully then, when this forks, follows the buttress between the gullies.

Approach
This route is most easily approached from Kilfinnan to the north but it can be done after one of the previous routes by dropping down the east ridge of Meall Dubh to the forest edge.

From the road end at Kilfinnan follow the forest road south-west, keeping on the higher track when the Great Glen Way drops down left. After about 3km take a well-used but smaller path up right into the forest (cairn). Cross the stream at the forest edge, then in 300 metres reach another stream which is the start of the route.

The Route
Go up boulders and short falls, quite lichenous in places. Eventually you are forced out of the gully bed by a slimy slabby fall. Go up the right bank and up steep grass and heather until the stream forks. Descend into the right fork above its first pitch, then go out left onto the heathery buttress between the two branches of the stream. From two small birches zigzag up heather, with traces of path. Where the path starts to peter out mossy cascades in the stream bed on the right are a better option. Follow these until better rock starts to appear on both banks. Go left back onto the buttress and things improve.

After an easy start climb slabs left of centre (Grade 3, easier to the right), then a central rib. Go left into a mossy niche and pull out steeply leftwards on big flakes. After an easier ridge go up between two big boulders to easy ground. The next step can be climbed by a steep juggy pillar on its right or avoided further right. Then you have the options of an easy finish or harder slabs both left and right.

Loch Lochy Hills

Sròn a' Choire Ghairbh

Glenfinnan Area

The two Munros of Sgùrr Thuilm and Sgùrr nan Coireachan are a well-known round from Glenfinnan, but few engage with the rocky faces below the ridges west and south of the latter peak. These provide long slabby scrambles on mostly excellent psammite with a remote feel. A mountain bike is useful for Riabhaich Slabs but the approach to the Beinn Gharbh routes is steep, rough and pathless. At the other extreme the hidden slabs on Sgùrr Mhuidhe have one of the shortest approaches in this guide.

1.	Sgùrr nan Coireachan	Route 4	P.79
2.	Sgùrr Mhuidhe	Route 5	P.83
3.	Beinn Gharbh	Routes 6 & 7	P.83

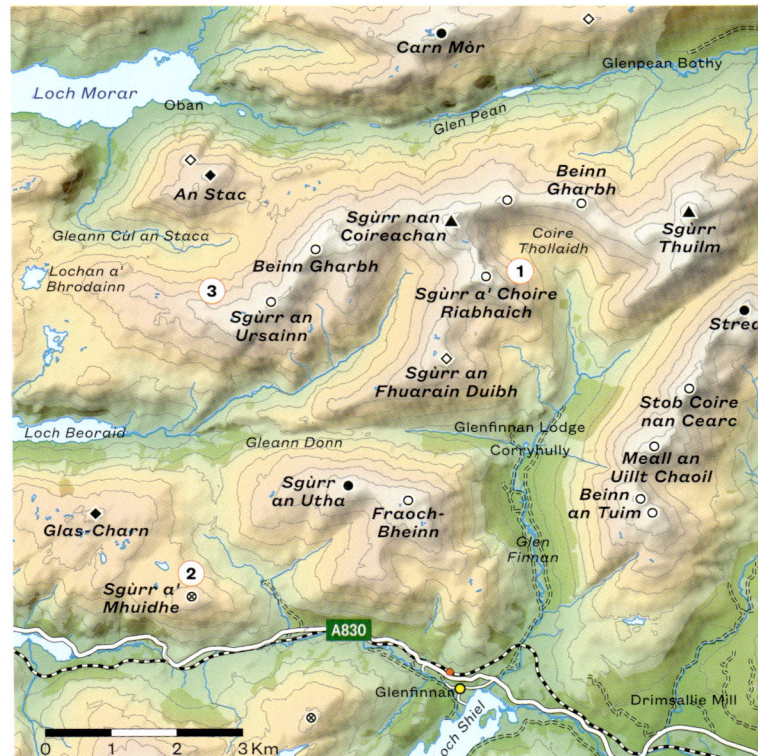

Sgùrr nan Coireachan 956m

Almost always climbed as a pair with Sgùrr Thuilm, and usually by the path up the south-east ridge, but this rocky Munro deserves further exploration. As well as the described scramble, Coire Carnaig on the south side has lots of slabs to play on, which are very scenic but don't make as good a line.

- PAGES 70 & 78
- OS LR 40
- NORTH-EAST
- PSAMMITE

4. Riabhaich Slabs — Grade 2 or Moderate *

○ NM 914 873   🏃 2HRS 45   ◿ SLABS   ⊤ +350M

The north-east flank of Sgùrr nan Coireachan's subsidiary top of Sgùrr a' Choire Riabhaich has a long slabby scramble on excellent psammite. Two short sharp Moderate sections are avoidable, making the route Grade 2.

Approach
Park at the visitor centre car park at Glenfinnan (NM 907 807, pay and display, often very busy with Harry Potter fans). Follow the tarmac estate road up Glen Finnan for 2.5km, then turn right to Corryhully bothy. A mountain bike is useful to here and useable a little further but with rapidly diminishing returns. About 1km beyond the bothy the track crosses the stream at a bridge. Turn left up the far bank on a smaller path, which carries on up into Coire Thollaidh, petering out at around 350m. Continue up to cross the stream at the lip of the upper corrie (400m), with the crag up to your left. The left-hand edge is a blunt spur with minor scrambling, then right of this is a mass of clean slabs, then broken ground leading to a minor ridge high up. The route follows the left edge of the main slabby mass, starting about 100m above the stream.

The Route
Start at the bottom left of the slabs and go up steeply on positive holds, then up a big sweep of easy patterned slabs. At the top bear right up grass to a steeper tier. This can be climbed centrally at Moderate or avoided on the right. To climb it walk a few metres left and go steeply up a broad rib, left then right, to reach a grass ledge. An awkward grassy traverse then leads left to enable a pull up onto a big grass terrace. The avoiding route comes in here.

Above the middle of the terrace is a clean steep slab with lots of small spiky holds. This is Moderate if tackled centrally or Grade 2 by its left edge. Carry on up short slabs and one big easy one. Walking-angle slabs then lead to another steepening, which has two vertical walls. Go up just right of the smaller left-hand one, passing right of a large boulder. Carry on up easy steps until past the steep walls on your right, then walk right to the skyline and go up a big slab.

More easy slabs carry on in the same line (a steeper sidewall on the left is nice, on sharp fingerholds). The angle eases off briefly, then steepens again into a long angular rib with a steeper left side. The start of this is excellent and it continues pleasantly until it eventually runs out to grass. Climb a short steeper prow on its left side, then more slabs and short steps, gradually easing and becoming grassy. After a short walk there is a final upthrust of steeper rock, but this is quite vegetated and harder than it looks so is best avoided on its right. Arrive just left of the rocky peak of Sgùrr a' Choire Riabhaich, an excellent viewpoint.

Riabhaich Slabs, Sgùrr a' Choire Riabhaich (Route 4, Grade 2 or Moderate). Scrambler: Noel Williams. © Iain Thow

Sgùrr Mhuidhe 526m

A shy and retiring peaklet which from most angles merges into the bigger hillside behind it. It is very rocky however, and has a pointed summit with an excellent view. Most of the outcrops are small, but the hidden north-east flank has more substantial slabs.

- 🌐 PAGES 70 & 78
- OS LR 40
- NORTH-EAST
- PSAMMITE

⑤ North-East Flank — Grade 2/3 ✱

| ○ NM 864 826 | 45MINS | SLABS | +200M |

An accessible set of psammite slabs useful for an evening trip or short day.

Approach
About 2km beyond the bridge over the railway west of Glenfinnan a hydro road goes up northwards into woods (NM 876 818, parking across the road just west). Follow this up to the new dam then cross the stream and head north-westwards across boggy ground. Keep low until past the spur on the left then head up towards the obvious crag, which is not marked on the OS Landranger map. It has a vertical foot and a slabby left flank, up which the scramble starts.

The Route
Come in from the left and go up slabs into the centre of the buttress. This could be made quite hard if desired as parts of it are quite slick, but there are always easier options available. The main slabs peter out after 100m but a big walking-angle slab up left leads to a small steeper bluff, then easy rock continues almost to the top of the hill. There is also an irresistible pinnacle at NM 868 819.

Beinn Gharbh 896m

Considered a subsidiary top of Sgùrr nan Coireachan, but actually quite an independent hill (with another three metres of drop it would be a Corbett). It has a fine summit and a rocky north-west face of steep slabs. The minor tops along its south-west ridge have plenty of rock too, with the north flank of the top west of Sgùrr an Ursainn providing the best scramble.

- 🌐 PAGES 70 & 78
- OS LR 40
- NORTH-WEST
- PSAMMITE

North-East Flank, Sgùrr Mhuidhe (Route 5, Grade 2/3).
Scrambler: Jamie Hageman. © Iain Thow

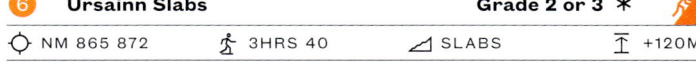

6 Ursainn Slabs — Grade 2 or 3 ✱

| ◯ NM 865 872 | 🚶 3HRS 40 | ◿ SLABS | ⊤ +120M |

An excellent main slab of rough psammite with easy slabs below and outcrops above. A long walk in by any route.

Approach
The quickest way in is from the road 2.5km west of Glenfinnan (NM 876 818). Take the new hydro road for a kilometre until it forks. Take the left track until it bends left, then take an indistinct boggy path ahead to cross a broad col and descend to the stream junction just east of Kinlochbeoraid. Cross both streams, the second of which can be tricky. In this case there is a large boulder jammed in the gorge 100 metres upstream which provides an exposed crossing.

Go up steeply to the saddle west of Sgùrr an Ursainn (NM 866 867). Descend a grassy stream/ramp northwards until lower than the slabs on the left. Traverse left (west) to reach a rock terrace below a two-tiered steep wall. There are easy slabs below this to provide a longer start.

For the adventurous, an interesting approach is to kayak up Loch Morar to Oban, though the bothy (NM 863 900) is now closed.

The Route
At the right end of the steep wall a tongue of slab descends from the upper tier to reach the terrace. Climb this (the only bit of Grade 3 on the route, avoidable by grass on the right) to reach a huge slab. Go leftwards up this then rightwards to its apex, almost walking for the confident. Smaller but steeper outcrops lead up to the summit, finishing with another delicate slab. There is a beautifully perched paddling pool just east of the summit.

To reach the North-West Face of Beinn Gharbh go back down the approach rake then traverse north-east to the col with An Stac. There are several short slabs of superb rock just below and west of the col, all around Moderate. Also nearby, the upper parts of An Stac (NM 866 889) have lots of fun short outcrops but no lines and the north-east ridge of Meith Bheinn (NM 822 872) has many short easy slabs of rough psammite.

7 North-West Face  Grade 2/3

| ○ NM 883 883 | 🚶 4HRS | ◿ INTRICATE | ⊤ +250M |

Acres of slabby psammite, much of it excellent, but there are no strong lines, and sadly most of the slabs are too steep to be called scrambling so the end result is disappointing. Anyone happy soloing at around 4c would have a field day here. The ramps between the slabs make a good winter Grade II.

Approach
The route fits in well after Ursainn Slab as described above, but an alternative is to come up Glen Pean from the head of Loch Arkaig. Go through a huge landslip (an amazing place) and turn left up a stalkers path at NM 889 895. At the 350m contour slant right up a grass shelf to reach the col below the cliff. Using Glen Pean bothy markedly shortens this approach.

The Route
The nature of the face produces lots of route choice, so the following is just a suggestion. At the bottom left of the face is a steep buttress with a prominent boulder on its top. Reach this from the right, then find a way through the steep slabs above, probably using the grassy grooves between them. A grassy ramp now runs up right, follow its rocky outside edge. Near the top of this cross the ramp to the right edge of a steep slab which provides a continuation (exposed but easy). Above this are lots more slabs at a more amenable angle which lead to the ridge about 300 metres north-east of the summit.

Morar

This range of small but very rocky peaklets between Loch Nevis and Loch Morar is home to two unfrequented scrambles perched above the sea, with scope for several more. The views are superb, out to the isles of Rùm and Eigg, across to Knoydart and east to the bigger peaks of the Rough Bounds.

The map below shows Morar, the Rough Bounds and Knoydart.

1. Cnoc a' Bhac Fhalaichte	Route 8	P.88
2. Sgùrr an Eilein Ghiubhais	Route 9	P.89
3. Garbh Chìoch Mhòr	Route 10	P.92
4. Beinn an Aodainn (Ben Aden)	Routes 11 & 12	P.93
5. Beinn na Caillich	Route 13	P.97
6. Ladhar Bheinn	Route 14	P.99
7. Stob a' Chearcaill	Route 15	P.100
8. An Caisteal	Route 16	P.102
9. Meall nan Eun	Route 17	P.104

Morar

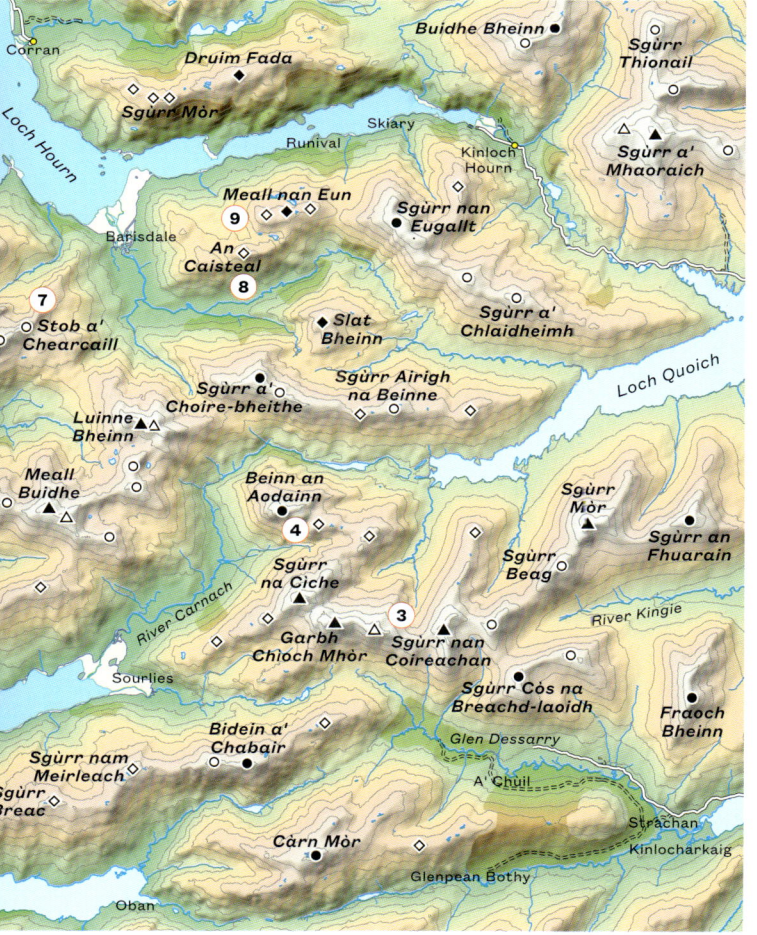

Cnoc a' Bhac Fhalaichte   388m

Only a minor summit, but a splendid viewpoint, with a steep slabby west face which dominates the tiny settlement at Tarbet. The energetic could use it as an approach to the remote peaks of Sgùrr Mòr and Bidean a' Chabhair.

- PAGES 70 & 86
- OS LR 40
- SOUTH-WEST
- SCHIST

8 Tarbet Slabs   Grade 3 or Moderate

| NM 797 919 | 2HRS | INTRICATE | +250M |

Not as impressive as it looks from a distance but well worthwhile, with good flaky schist slabs after a scrappy start. Sadly some of the best slabs are too hard to be called scrambling, forcing detours onto grass ledges and cracks.

Approach
Tarbet can be reached by boat from Mallaig (Western Isles Cruises, arriving at around 3.30pm, pick up also available, same time, Mondays to Fridays from April to October). Alternatively take the beautiful path along the north shore of Loch Morar, one of the best easy walks in the country. Looking east from the cairn which marks the top of the pass south of Tarbet you can see a big vertical crag off left and a smaller vertical crag well right, with broken rocky ground between (lots of bracken later in the season).

The Route
Start up the left-hand edge of the broken area, left of birch scrub. Short steep outcrops lead to bracken and grass. Go up past a split boulder to more juggy shattered craglets, then steep broken ground becomes slabs leading to the top of the first tier. The deer fence above has no stile and is best crossed using an old straining post a little left of the obvious arrival point. Above this a short juggy wall leads to a big grass shelf.

Walk right along the shelf, almost to a minor summit, to where a pyramidal boulder lies below the cliff ahead. The slab behind the boulder followed by a grassy groove is the best of several options. Climb a steep crack with a small holly, then rough slabs to another shelf below a steep rock band. Traverse left below this until past an easy square-cut gully. Climb the left edge of the rib left of this (the rib direct is Moderate), then continue up to a minor top.

Across the saddle ahead are three slabby ribs. Climb the right-hand one, starting steeply on big sharp holds and finishing up a flaky groove. Cross another minor summit and a boggy col. Now climb a slab behind two boulders, going up left to a right-slanting rib and finishing up a groove. The next slab is easy, then a final tier has either twin cracks on sharp holds or easier slabs to the right.

If carrying on to Sgùrr Mòr then many more outcrops can be found in the rough backlands.

Sgùrr an Eilein Ghiubhais 522m

A very rocky hill with a steep north face and a tremendous view out over Loch Nevis. There is scope for a lot more scrambling than the described route, but much of it is steeper than it looks and often quite hard.

- PAGES 70 & 86
- OS LR 40
- NORTH
- PSAMMITE

⑨ Right-Hand Rib Grade 3

○ NM 726 977   🏃 1HR 45   ⟋ OUTCROPS   ⊤ +300M

The central rib on the face looks terrific from a boat but is too hard for scrambling, but the easier-angled right-hand rib has some excellent scrambling on rough psammite, despite the copious heather.

Approach
From the end of the minor road running east from Mallaig (very limited parking) take the track round to Mallaigmore. Before reaching the cottages traverse right across the stream to a ruin. The coast from here can be followed but is extremely rough, so it is easier (and probably quicker) to go up eastwards to the top of the steep slope at around 350m, traverse along to the top of Coire Liath at NM 719 972 then descend its west side. This does mean dropping back down to about 50m to pass below the lowest cliffs on the north-west shoulder of the peak.

If coming in via the coast go up slightly from the ruin to pass over the first hump, then slant down to sea level. Go up steeply to pass over the top of Sròn Raineach at around 70m ('Bracken Nose' – a good reason to go high later in the season). Descend a steep narrow gully to sea level again and go along for about 1km before gaining about 60m to pick up a rough deer path through the heather round into the foot of Coire Liath, where the two approaches join.

Below the main face a wide heathery ramp slants up left and some short steep slabs can be found on this, providing quite tricky scrambling on superb rough rock. Looking up, the face has a steep blunt central spur rising from a heathery bay, with less defined but quite steep rock to the left and an easier-angled spur to the right. The latter is the described route, curving up right from the foot of the heather bay, with very steep heathery ground to its right.

The Route
From the left edge of the lowest rock on the spur go up a clean slabby rib to heather (harder than it looks). Continue up right on rock steps and more heather, awkward in places but with the steps generally climbable fairly directly. The rib soon opens out to more heather with some easy slabs. When the ground steepens again go right to the skyline and climb this, crossing a distinctive oblique trench. Climb a short steep wall, either by its reachy left edge or more easily right to left, then gentler slabs lead up to the top of the main steep section. The ground soon eases to walking, where you can either slant up left and string together minor outcrops all the way to the summit or walk up and right for some distance to gain shorter but more sustained slabs.

From the higher approach, if you can't face losing all the height then nice slabs on the east flank of Coire Liath (NM 724 973) are also good fun.

A fun slab on the high-level route back to Mallaig from Sgùrr an Eilein Ghiubhais.
Scrambler: Keith Hoole. © Noel Williams

The Rough Bounds

The peninsula of Knoydart proper is fringed by some of the roughest ground in Scotland, jaggy peaks with many rock outcrops (although few natural lines). The scrambles here will mainly be done as part of a backpacking trip, but can be reached in a long day using either of the winding roads up Loch Arkaig or Glen Garry. Allow nearly an hour for the drive from the main road in either case.

Garbh Chìoch Mhòr   1013m

The twin Munro to the more famous Sgùrr na Cìche is just as rocky as its neighbour but not as distinctive a shape. It is notable for the example of extreme wall building that follows the ridge crest. There is a short steep buttress below the main summit on its north side, but by far the best scrambling is on the huge triangle of slabs below Garbh Chìoch Bheag.

 PAGES 70 & 87
 OS LR 33
 NORTH-EAST
 PSAMMITE

10 Coire nan Gall Slabs — Grade 2 *

◇ NM 926 963   🏃 3HRS 15   ◿ SLABS   ⊤ +400M

A vast acreage of psammite slabs, mostly easy-angled but with some overlaps and steeper sections. It is unlikely that any two people would follow the same route so only the general line is described.

Approach
From the head of Loch Arkaig (parking at NM 987 915) follow the track up the north side of Glen Dessarry past the lodge, then the rougher path up to and along the top side of the forest. Cross the Allt Coire nan Uth and turn right up the next stream to go up steeply to the col between Sgurr nan Coireachan and Garbh Chioch Bheag. Descend the other side into the east branch of Coire nan Gall. You can either drop down to the 500m contour and start up a narrow slab just right of a stream or traverse in higher up below a line of steeper outcrops.

The Route
From the narrow slab more slabs lead up to a large grass terrace where the traverse comes in. Above this steeper slabs or easier ground on the right lead to broad slabs with overlaps, which gradually ease in angle to walking. These take you to the main ridge a little east of the summit of Garbh Chioch Bheag. A slightly steeper finish can be found by moving left to arrive on the ridge at a subsidiary top.

If continuing over Garbh Chioch Mhor to Sgurr na Ciche there are outcrops on the east shoulder of the latter that are easily gained by going up right from the col between the two. These are rather discontinuous but can be made fairly hard if required.

Beinn an Aodainn (Ben Aden)   887m

Hidden away in the wild heart of the Rough Bounds, this rather squat-shaped but tremendously rocky peak is one of the most remote hills in this guide. All approaches involve river crossings which can be difficult and occasionally impossible (Abhainn Chosaidh on the Loch Quoich approach is notorious). Fatalities are not unknown and the golden rule is 'if in doubt, don't do it'. Apart from the two scrambles mentioned the North Face looks promising, but steeper slabs mostly push you out onto grassy ramps.

⊕ PAGES 70 & 87
⋈ OS LR 33
⇔ SOUTH & EAST
⌂ SCHIST & PSAMMITE

![South Face photo]

11 South Face   Grade 2

| ⌖ NM 899 980 | 🚶 2HRS (SOURLIES) | ⌁ OUTCROPS | ⯯ +350M |

A long run of slabby outcrops of good but often lichenous schist and psammite following the right-hand side of the face. Not particularly good scrambling but in an impressive setting.

Approach
By far the best base for this route is Sourlies Bothy (NM 869 950) or a wild camp nearby (the quite small bothy can get very busy). From the bothy go round west into the Carnoch valley and follow the south-east bank of the river up to the Allt Achadh a' Ghlinne. Go up the south bank of this (sketchy path) until above a small gorge and beyond the spur projecting from the South Face of Beinn an Aodainn which forms the start of the route. Cross the stream at around NM 900 978 to reach the right-hand side of the spur, just left of a steep stream.

The Route
Go up steep grass to gain the spur at a flattening above its steep initial

section. Mossy ribs and more steep grass then lead up for 100m or so to a small col. Climb a pinkish rib to another small col, then walk up to a third one. A large grey slab off right is unfortunately too hard so climb the mossier rib and pink slab directly ahead, left of the stream. Above is a spill of gigantic boulders with a vertical 'Cenotaph Corner' rock face to their left. Go right up easy slabs past the boulders, then up grass to a clean rock band right of a black wet wall. Zigzag up ledges about 30 metres right of the black wall, then climb a harder slab by a left-to-right line of small flakes, delicate to start. Go left up a grass runnel, then easy rough slabs lead up to a big terrace, with the skyline of the East-North-East Ridge up left. This is easily gained up steep grass, then followed to the summit, but the bouldery landslip on the left is worth investigating on the way – it has some quite impressive holes in it!

12 East-North-East Ridge   Grade 1 or 2 ✶✶

| ◯ NM 921 994 | 🏃 3HRS | ◿ OUTCROPS | ⫟ +600M |

A long slabby ridge of excellent schist and psammite, mainly walking but with some good steeper bits.

Approach
The only feasible day trip version of this route from a road is to come in via the head of Loch Quoich, a 30km outing, while a more reasonable day involves using Barrisdale as a base, around 22km but involving two crossings of the 500m Mam Unndalain. For the former, start at the two-bar 'bridge' at NG 985 036 and head south-east across either pathless bog or mudflats depending on the height of the reservoir. The remains of an old road help you round to the shore of the main loch, then a rougher path takes you to the mouth of Gleann Cosaidh. The river here can be difficult or even impossible to cross after wet weather. Continue along the rough lochshore for 1km until the remains of a construction road appear a little above the shoreline. Follow this to the head of the loch, cross both dams and stay on the track for another 200 metres or so. A smaller path now heads off right over a minor col and descends to the head of Lochan nam Breac. At the stony saddle 300 metres before the loch the Allt Coire na Cruaiche comes in from the left. The two approaches join here.

For the Barrisdale route cross the bridge by the bothy and take the path up over Mam Unndalain. On the other side a good path slants down to the head of Lochan nam Breac, and another stream that can be hard to cross after heavy rain (not an uncommon event in Knoydart). Cross the beach and take the path up eastwards for 300 metres to the foot of the Allt Coire na Cruaiche.

The Route
Ascend the west bank of the Allt Coire na Cruaiche until it opens out, then go right up slabs (mostly walking angle) to reach the crest overlooking Lochan nam Breac. Continue south-west up more easy slabs with optional steeper bits (usually mossy) to reach the main east-north-east crest at around 450m. Follow this up on delightfully rough rock, mostly

Looking up the East-North-East Ridge of Beinn an Aodainn (Route 12, Grade 1 or 2). © Iain Thow

easy but with the odd harder section. A steep quartzy slab on the right side of the ridge is a highlight (Grade 2). Above a prominent step the ridge bends left and narrows, before reaching a large rock platform. The cracked prow above is Grade 2 by the left hand crack, or avoid it on the left. A narrow but easy ridge now leads over a minor top to a grassy col with a big pointed flake. The flake is Moderate, but beware the wobbly jug, and of course it must be reversed. More sensibly, go up slabs right of the flake and over another minor top, then an easy broad ridge leads to the summit.

Knoydart

Although Knoydart is on the Scottish mainland it is only reachable either by ferry or a long walk, and many of these routes are best enjoyed as part of a multi day expedition, using either bothies or a tent. Routes 13 and 14 are usually climbed from Inverie, reached by ferry from Mallaig, while routes 15, 16 and 17 are usually done from Barrisdale, gained by a delightful coastal walk from the end of the remote minor road at Kinloch Hourn. Allow nearly an hour for the drive from the main road and plenty of time for the coastal walk, which is hillier than many expect.

Much of Knoydart is very rocky and several areas not described here are worth exploring. The tiers of short slabs on the south flank of Sgùrr Sgeithe (NM 857 980) give some technical fun, although with no real line. The central north corrie of Meall Buidhe (NM 854 992) has loads of easy-angled rock to play on, and there are two short lived but nicely positioned towers on the East Ridge of Sgùrr a' Choire Bheithe (NG 904 010). Creag Mhòr of Meall Bhasiter (NM 845 973) has a prominent sharp rib, but this is harder than it looks and forces you off onto steep vegetation. Lower down and a good option when the higher hills are clagged in is the South-East Rib of Druim na Cluain-airighe (NG 758 032), short but on excellent rock.

Beinn na Caillich　　　　　　　　　　785m

A remote and rugged hill with a sense of being poised above the ocean, this is quite a complex sprawl of broad ridges and hidden corries.

 PAGES 70 & 86
 OS LR 33
 SOUTH-EAST
 PSAMMITE

 South-East Slabs　　　　　　　　Grade 3 ✶✶

 NG 801 061　　 2HRS 10 (INVERIE)　　 OUTCROPS　　 +250M

A long route up tiers of psammite slabs with lots of possibilities, both hard and easy. Open and sunny in aspect and quick to dry, but not a good choice in the wet.

Approach

From Inverie take the track north-west over Mam Uidhe to the forestry just beyond the saddle. A few hundred metres after reaching this turn right and go through the wood for 1.5km to join the Abhainn Inbhir Ghuis-erein. About 1km beyond the forest cross the river and take a smaller path alongside the Abhainn Bheag. In a little under 3km the slabs are obvious, up to the left. They slant up leftwards, bounded by a stony gully

to their left, and are quite steep in the middle. At the lower right-hand end there are prominent twin cracks with a birch tree up right and a mossy tier below.

The Route
The mossy tier is feasible if dry, then climb the slab left of the twin cracks and a smaller slab above by a knobbly crack. Walk left up a rock ramp until more slabs lead up to easy ground. Climb a small clean slab, then broken ground to two more slabs, the second climbed with relish using the left-hand of two diverging cracks. More easy craglets run up to a thin boulder field angling up left.

The outcrops above are steeper, so move 50 metres left and go up a pink rib above a small pointed pinnacle (the spike on the right is loose). Up left is a larger crag, where several possibilities converge past a big rock crevasse to finish up a steep wide crack (avoidable on the right). Two small outcrops lead up to another large crag, climbed on big blocks near its right edge, weaving about a bit. The general angle now starts to lean back at a heathery section, but there are still several fun outcrops above, starting with a steep crack on jammed flakes. The craglets finally peter out about 100m below the summit.

Beinn na Caillich has lots of other scrambly outcrops to play on, the slabs on the west side of the north top (666m) being particularly good, although short.

Ladhar Bheinn   1020m

Knoydart's reigning peak is some people's candidate for the finest hill in Scotland. Certainly the tremendous Coire Dhorrcail on the north-east of the summit is a dramatic sight, especially in winter. The scrambles on this side are very vegetated though and win no prizes despite their situation. The North-East Ridge of Stob Dhorrcail, though prominent, is mainly steep grass. By far the best scramble on the hill is on the much less impressive western spur, An Dìollaid.

⊕ PAGES 70 & 86
◁ OS LR 33
✥ WEST
⌂ PSAMMITE

14	**An Dìollaid**		Grade 3 ✶✶
◯ NG 801 047	🚶 1HR 40 (INVERIE)	◿ SLABS	⫯ +350M

Another long route, linking together steep slabs of excellent psammite, where inward-dipping holds allow quite steep rock to be climbed in comfort. Many of the outcrops are quite sustained (although not hard) and slightly taller than you would prefer, making this very much a route for those not worried by exposure.

Approach
As for route 13 as far as the Abhainn Bheag. About 1.5km after crossing the river you reach a large cairn-like shattered boulder just above the path. From here the crag is obvious up right. The centre of the face is

steeper and quite mossy, so the route follows the cleaner right-hand side, before moving left as the angle eases (slightly!).

The Route
Start up purplish clean slabs on the right-hand side of the face, fairly continuous but little more than walking. Follow small outcrops above until they run out, with bigger steeper cliffs off left. Walk over to these. The toe is steep and easily avoided, but small sharp holds make it much easier than it looks. Above this much easier slabs lead up to a large clean slab with more good holds. After a broad slab the ground becomes grassier, but still with small scrambly craglets which run up to a wide shelf below the upper face.

Climb the first outcrop above the shelf, then traverse horizontally left to the first crag on the far side of a small stream/gully. Starting this direct is Moderate, but by coming in from the left big holds allow you to climb the rest of the rib direct. Continue up left on excellent rock to boulder slopes. Just left is an irresistible steep pink slab above a small pool, climbed direct on superb holds. These continue on easier rock, although getting mossier, to the top of the main face. Off left is a steep square outcrop – reach over the biggest bit of the overhang to get a nice surprise! Easy pink rock continues past perched boulders to the top of the tier. Several more short walls provide more fun with fantastic sharp holds before the 650m shoulder arrives all too soon.

If carrying on up the ridge in mist note that the trig point is not the summit of Ladhar Bheinn, the cairn 300 metres further on being 10m higher.

Stob a' Chearcaill 840m

This is the jutting rock peak that forms the southern flank of Ladhar Bheinn's Coire Dhorrcail, included in the classic horseshoe from Barrisdale. The huge north-west face carries several classic winter climbs but the schist is too vegetated for good summer climbing.

 PAGES 70 & 87
 OS LR 33
NORTH-EAST
SCHIST

15. North-East Ridge — Grade 1

NG 847 031 | 2HRS (BARRISDALE) | INTRICATE | +100M

The rearing prow is impressive from below but turns out to be fairly grassy, giving a rather wandering scramble.

Approach
This will almost always be climbed from Barrisdale, taking the path into Coire Dhorrcail and leaving it as it contours round the foot of the ridge to follow the crest up over Creag Bheithe.

Approaching the North-East Ridge of Stob a' Chearcaill (Route 15, Grade 1).
© Chris Eilbeck

The Route
The nose of Stob a' Chearcaill looms up intimidatingly, and direct routes are as unpleasant as they look. Better and much easier is to go round left and up well-trodden steps in a steep gully. On regaining the crest go up a left-slanting ramplet and zigzag up grass until the ground gets steeper and rockier. Go up the first step, then traverse horizontally right to a jammed flake. Squeeze up behind this, exit right and go up a steeper groove on good holds. Zigzag up more grass steps, then climb an awkward left-slanting weakness. Everything above is much easier. The route is sometimes descended, but this is considerably more awkward, both technically and in terms of route finding.

An Caisteal 522m

A very rocky hill with steep slabs on its north face giving climbing at around VS and a steep but broken South Face which makes an excellent scramble. The west summit is higher and has the best view. Many more scrambling lines are feasible, notably a left-hand finish to the described route, more direct but less good in detail.

 PAGES 70 & 87
 OS LR 33
SOUTH
PSAMMITE

16 South Face — Grade 3 ★★

◇ NG 898 035   🚶 50MINS (BARRISDALE)   ⊿ OUTCROPS   ⊤ +400M

A long scramble of linked psammite outcrops, mainly on steepish slabs with sharp holds and good friction. Quite tricky in places but not sustained. This route will mainly be of interest to those staying at Barrisdale, either camping or in the bothy, but it can be done as a long day trip from Kinlochhourn by following the coast path to Barrisdale and returning by slanting down from Meall nan Eun to meet the track at the col west of Skiary.

Approach
From Barrisdale follow the track up Glen Barrisdale for 3km to the foot of a knoll just beyond a small stream running down south-east from the col between Meall Bhuidhe and An Caisteal. At the foot of the knoll there is a small steep slab just beside the path, which returns to the main river about 100 metres further on.

The Route
Climb the small slab then easier slabs to pass left of a steep wall with an obvious quartz vein and continue to the top of the knoll. From the col beyond dodge a steep wall on the left, then another on the right. Go up to a pointed boulder and climb the rock behind just right of a small birch tree. Easy slabs then lead up to a group of trees below a long steep wall.

Walk left up a wide bouldery ramp, occasionally using slabs on its outside edge. Just before the ramp ends, about 10 metres right of small trees, go right onto a ledge with small boulders, then bear left up delicate slabs (easier on the right) to the top of the tier. Stepped slabs then lead to a larger slabby wall. Walk right below this and climb its delicate right edge bearing left (easier the further right you go). Go up to reach the next rock band just right of a wet area. Climb a stepped weakness up right to the broad crest and go up a left-slanting ramp. This leads easily to the crest, but a more exciting finish quits the ramp after 10m and goes right up flakes, finishing up exposed slabs on positive holds.

Walk up to a bigger buttress with a long steep wall at its foot. Climb a juggy staircase on the extreme left end of the wall, then traverse horizontally right onto the buttress proper and take either of two lines slanting up right onto the front (the lower one is easier). Climb a right-slanting groove to heather, go up left to a niche and traverse right onto a slab above its smooth start. Climb this to easy ground. Small outcrops now lead up to a large terrace below the upper face.

Head up right to more clean slabs and trend up right past a perched block, delicate at first. Either carry on in the same line or take a harder direct finish up slabs with sharp rippled holds. Walk up right below one outcrop to reach a larger face with a left-slanting vein of pink pegmatite. Climb the easy first part of the vein to a grass ledge, then a more sustained section to a niche. Pull steeply out of this, then step left to a ledge and finish up a thinner quartz vein. An easier version moves right from the grass ledge then up directly. Climb easy slabs past quartz, then a couple of steeper outcrops, after which more short walls and slabs lead up to the summit ridge. The actual summit is a few hundred metres up left, the western top being the highest.

Meall nan Eun 623m

The twin hill to An Caisteal, a broad knobbly ridge with great views out over Loch Hourn. The west face has four buttresses with clean rock climbs in the lower grades. The right-hand, biggest and steepest is Severe; the middle two are slabby, set back a little and around V Diff, while the left-hand and longest gives two easy-angled Diffs, of which the following is the better.

 PAGES 70 & 87
 OS LR 33
 WEST
PSAMMITE

Immaculate rock on Cannonade, Meall nan Eun (Route 17, Difficult).
Climber: Nicky Gear. © Iain Thow

Cannonade, Meall nan Eun (Route 17, Difficult).
Climber: Nicky Gear. © Iain Thow

17 Cannonade — Difficult, Moderate or Grade 3 **

NG 895 051   1HR 30 (BARRISDALE)   SLABS   +200M

A clean slabby rib of superb psammite, mostly Grade 3, with harder variations on the top slab. It makes a good follow on from Route 16.

Approach
From the top of the scramble on An Caisteal (i.e. well right of the two summits) descend northwards fairly steeply, cross a sluggish stream then slant left up a ramp below a steep wall (nice bouldering). Drop down the other side of the spur to the outlet of the lochan, then bear left before slanting down rightwards below the middle two buttresses to reach the foot of the left-hand one. The foot of the buttress breaks into two ribs and Cannonade starts up the right-hand one.

The Route
Climb the groove up the front of the rib to easier rock. At the top of this climb the clean slabby left side of the rib (or the easier crest). Climb a slightly steeper section by a left-slanting groove, then go right to the arête and up to easy rock. Swing up left steeply onto the crest of the next rib and go up it to grass. Up left is a larger clean slab, the crux. Climbing the right edge of this direct is Difficult, whilst meandering around a bit following the lines of weakness brings the grade down to Moderate. The groove on the right avoids it altogether at Grade 3.

Less sustained slabs above lead to easier ground, then more scattered outcrops continue almost to the west summit, often with surprising holds just where you need them. The central summit is a metre higher but the west summit has by far the finer view.

The two ridges either side of the massive through-valley of Glenshiel/ Cluanie are a paradise for ridge wanderers. Although the main ridges themselves are easy, several side ridges provide good scrambles, with the Forcan Ridge of The Saddle being a classic. These are mainly schist hills, so some of these routes are a bit vegetated and/or discontinuous, but they are still worthwhile, especially as a prelude to a leisurely wander along the Cluanie Ridge or the Five Sisters. Closer to the coast more isolated hills such as A' Ghlas Bheinn or Beinn a' Chapuill can also provide entertainment, with the stream scramble on the former being the longest (and probably wettest) route in this guide.

Not described here but worth including if passing are the scattered outcrops on the west face of Beinn Clachach (NG 869 106); the steep slabs low on the Glen Arnisdale flank of Druim Fada (NG 885 092); a long but broken slabby line on Creag a' Mhaim (starting at NH 095 078); and the short Mod to Diff rock climbs on Boc Beag (NG 909 245).

Kintail

1.	Beinn a' Chapuill	Route 18	P.110
2.	The Saddle	Route 19	P.111
3.	Sgùrr na Sgine	Route 20	P.113
4.	Aonach air Chrith	Route 21	P.114
5.	Sgùrr nan Conbhairean	Route 22	P.115
6.	A' Chràileag	Route 23	P.116
7.	Mullach Fraoch-choire	Route 24	P.117
8.	Sgùrr nan Spainteach	Route 25	P.117
9.	Sgùrr na Ciste Duibhe	Route 26	P.118
10.	Sgùrr an t-Searraich	Route 27	P.119
11.	Beinn Fhada	Route 28	P.121
12.	A' Ghlas-Bheinn	Route 29	P.122
13.	Càrnan Cruithneachd	Route 30	P.123
14.	Biod an Fhithich	Route 31	P.126

Beinn a' Chapuill   759m

This knobbly plateau north-west of Beinn Sgritheall has a lot of rock on its steep sides, as well as being an excellent viewpoint. There is scope for far more scrambling than just the route described, while the north-east ridge is a delightful walk up from Gleann Beag.

 PAGE 108
 OS LR 33
 SOUTH-EAST
 PSAMMITE

18 East Slabs   Grade 2 *

○ NG 837 146	🚶 2HRS	⊿ OUTCROPS	⊤ +300M

A steep hillside scattered with psammite slabs, giving lots of route choice. Harder variations can easily be found.

Approach
Start from the forest track leaving the road at NG 780 136 (parking 50 metres up the track). Follow the track through the recently felled wood, then keep ahead up the Allt Gorm and cross over to Loch Bealach na h-Oidhche. From the saddle north-east of this traverse northwards,

descending slightly. Pass under the first slabs, which are steep and often wet, to reach cleaner lower slabs slanting up left.

The Route
Climb the right-hand side of the lowest rib (the flaky crack just left of the foot is Difficult). Carry on up slabs until they run out into the hillside. Traverse right below boulders and up more slabs. Follow these onto the next open buttress, with a wide choice of route. Link together slabs and boulder problems until the rock starts to peter out. Bear up left to reach more clean slabs which provide a nice finish, arriving at the plateau just south-east of the summit lochan. A slightly lower top marked Beinn a' Chapuill (742m) on OS maps lies a further 750 metres north-west.

The Saddle   1010m

A superb hill with three craggy ridges, the best of which is the famous Forcan Ridge. The circuit of the whole hill from Shiel Bridge is a great long day, while a shorter but still excellent route takes in just the Forcan Ridge before moving across to the neighbouring Munro, Sgùrr na Sgine, and climbing its north-east ridge (Route 20).

- PAGE 108
- OS LR 33
- EAST
- SCHIST

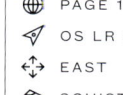

19 Forcan Ridge   Grade 2 or Moderate ✶✶✶

◯ NG 947 131   🏃 1HR 30   ◁ ARÊTE   ⊤ +350M

One of the best scrambles in Scotland, a knife-edged ridge, quite exposed but not difficult. All the awkward bits can be avoided at Grade 1, but this misses out the best part of the route. The direct descent from Sgùrr na Forcan is much harder than anything else on the route and most scramblers avoid it.

Approach
A good stalkers' path leaves the A87 at NG 968 143 (parking just north). Follow this up to pass right of Meallan Odhar to the foot of the ridge.

The Route
A short well-used slab starts the scrambling (harder options exist to the right). An obvious route zigzags up through outcrops until the ridge bends right then left at around 800m. The ridge now narrows, with easier options on the right. A short tower at around 850m is passed by an exposed step up left, then just before the summit of Sgùrr na Forcan itself another tower is climbed direct on steep flakes. Both these can be avoided on the right.

The descent from Sgùrr na Forcan is steep and intimidating but on good holds (Moderate). There are easier options down gullies on both left and right, most go left. From the col a sharp ridge with an optional slabby knife edge (avoidable on the left) leads to a minor top, then more broken scrambling leads to the main top of The Saddle, with the slightly lower trig point just beyond.

The Forcan Ridge (Route 19, Grade 2).
Scrambler: Jacqueline Jeffrey. © Jason Hoffman

Sgùrr na Sgine   946m

A steep hill with a pleasant curving ridge, although rather overshadowed by The Saddle. The scramble described makes a good follow-on to the Forcan Ridge.

- PAGE 108
- OS LR 33
- EAST
- SCHIST

Kintail

Sgùrr na Sgine

20 **North-East Ridge**			Grade 2
NG 949 115	2HRS	BUTTRESS	+200M

A short steep ridge on rough quartzy schist, quite exposed but easy.

Approach
The route can be approached directly up Coire Toiteil, but it is better to include it after the Forcan Ridge. Descend to the Bealach Coire Mhalagain, then go up steeply to the col between Sgurr na Sgine and Faochag. Turn right, then head left along an obvious shelf crossing the north face. Where this ends slant down to reach a very steep outcrop at the foot

of the north-east ridge, the lowest rock on the face, with large boulders below it. Start just beyond this at quartzy rock, the right-hand of two ribs. This point can also be easily reached from the saddle between Sgùrr na Sgine and Sgùrr a' Bhac Chaolais.

The Route
Climb steeply onto the quartzy rib and follow it up, quite exposed at times. Where it ends go up steep vegetation and minor craglets until a sharp ridge develops. Follow this up on big flakes and boulders to arrive directly at the summit cairn.

Aonach air Chrith 1021m

The popular Cluanie Ridge has several enjoyably narrow subsidiary ridges, the best being on Aonach air Chrith.

⊕ PAGE 109
◁ OS LR 33
✥ NORTH
⌂ SCHIST

21 North Ridge Grade 1 or 2 ✱

◯ NH 058 101   🚶 45MINS   ⟋ OUTCROPS & ARÊTE   ⟂ +550M

A route in two parts, a series of rather gloomy outcrops (Grade 2) then an airy narrow ridge (Grade 1). The first part can easily be bypassed by traversing in to the saddle beyond A' Chioch from the north-west.

Approach
From the layby at NH 044 114 follow the good path towards Druim Coire nan Eirecheanach. At around the 300m contour head south-east across the Allt Coire an Eirecheanach to the outcrops starting at around 450m on the north end of A' Chioch, the broad rounded top north of Aonach air Chrith (unnamed on the 1:50k map). Start at the lowest slab, on its right.

The Route
Climb the furthest right-hand edge of the slab, then minor craglets lead up to a larger outcrop with an overhanging prow and a big groove on its left. Climb the left edge of the groove, steep at the top, then traverse right along a shelf below a vertical wall. Clamber onto the right-hand end of this to reach open ground. A short wall on the left is worth including before a grassy walk up to another larger outcrop. Go right of this and up its right-hand edge, finishing through a slot, then more grass leads to the top of A' Chioch.

Cross the saddle ahead and go up right to join the north ridge proper, which is narrow and rocky. Keep on the crest for the most fun, passing over a minor top, from where two flaky towers and a narrow arête lead to the main summit.

Sgùrr nan Conbhairean 1109m

A graceful peak with pleasant grassy ridges and a prominent spur falling north-east into the wild upper reaches of Glen Doe. It is a superb viewpoint.

 PAGE 109
 OS LR 34
 EAST
 PSAMMITE

Kintail

Sgùrr nan Conbhairean

 North-East Spur Grade 2 *

| ⌖ NH 135 138 | 🚶 2HRS 40 | ⊿ OUTCROPS | ⊤ +350M |

A good line linking psammite outcrops up an airily-positioned spur. Much better than it looks from a distance and easily added on to a round of the Cluanie Munros. There is some exposure, but with positive holds, and there are lots of possible variations, with almost everything avoidable if desired.

Approach
The easiest approach is to climb Càrn Ghluasaid using the good path starting from the parking at Lundie (NH 145 104). Follow the ridge west-

wards over Creag a' Chaorainn and descend northwards from the Glas Bhealach beyond it. Descend the upper corrie until it drops away steeply at around the 750m contour, then start at a jagged buttress on the left (west) just above the drop.

The Route
The central rib is a loose Difficult but there is an easier rib to the right. Above this boulders lead to a flattening, then go right under steep cliflets. Climb a long rib up the right-hand side of these on jugs, finishing with a patterned slab. Go up another easy rib, then go right to climb a series of ribs on the skyline. At a steeper section go up left from the lowest point by a juggy rib and a vegetated weakness. Follow the skyline easily, then move right to a slab poised above the drop on the right. Carry on up the nose on positive holds to an easing. Above climb a steeper buttress direct on good holds. Steep walking leads to the summit. In spring the top of this ridge usually has an impressive snow crest, giving the route an almost alpine feel.

A' Chràileag   1120m

A big grassy mountain with nice ridges and a real feeling of height. The stream described provides an alternative approach to the usual slog up from Cluanie.

- PAGE 109
- OS LR 33 & 34
- SOUTH
- PSAMMITE

23   Allt Choire a' Chait   Grade 2

◯ NH 107 113   🚶 5MINS   ◿ STREAM   ⊤ +250M

A long and scenic series of falls, not sustained and all avoidable. The schist slabs are beautifully patterned, but wickedly slippery when wet.

Approach
There are parking places on the A87 a few hundred metres either side of the stream.

The Route
100m above the bridge the first gorge is climbed by pocketed slabs on the left. Just after large boulders in midstream go up patterned slabs on the left. At a narrowing stay on the left, close to the water at first, then up a gnarled slab. Keep on the left until an impassable pool forces you out. A few metres higher a horizontal ledge leads back in, followed by an awkward move up onto slabs on the left. At the top cross back right by a boulder. Avoid two pools, then drop back into the stream bed and climb two sets of lovely slabs. Keep right, avoiding one pool, until the bed opens out.

Go up the left bank to a larger fall, climbed by a quartzy wall well left of the water. Cross back right and go up a few steps to easy ground. At an upper fall take the right-hand branch, keeping right when it forks. Higher up another fall is climbed on the left by a delicate traverse and slabs, then another by more slabs. A couple of higher falls need to be avoided.

Mullach Fraoch-choire   1102m

A well-defined top with three ridges, the southern one of which has some easy scrambling over pinnacles, nicely positioned on a sharp ridge. Routes 23 and 24 can easily be combined, giving a full and very varied day out. The summit itself is a splendid viewpoint.

- PAGE 109
- OS LR 33
- SOUTH
- SCHIST

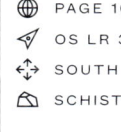

24 South Ridge (Na Geurdain)   Grade 1 or 2 ✶

| NH 095 165 | 3HRS | ARÊTE | +100M |

A series of pleasant pinnacles add interest to a narrow ridge. Difficulties can be sought or avoided by a clear path.

Approach
Almost invariably reached over A' Chràileag. Follow the ridge north over a subsidiary top to the saddle. The ridge ahead is narrow but easy at first, then there are a few optional easy scrambles before the pinnacles are reached.

The Route
Follow the crest over the sharp first pinnacle. A path now avoids all difficulties on the left, but the crest is better. Climb the next steep tower either direct on steep jugs (Grade 2) or by squeezing through a gap on the left, then up right to the arête. Crossing the top of the tower is airy, then descend on the right. The rest is easy.

Sgùrr nan Spainteach   990m

This is the forgotten sixth Sister hidden away from the popular viewpoints, but with a nice summit poised above Coire Dhomdain. The buttress below the summit provides some rather vegetated scrambling.

- PAGE 109
- OS LR 33
- NORTH
- SCHIST

25. North Buttress — Grade 2

- NG 994 153
- 2HRS
- BUTTRESS
- +200M

A blunt schist buttress with a wide choice of route and little exposure. Some technical moves, easily avoided. Slow to dry and slippery when wet.

Approach
Either descend grass slopes east of the summit to the foot of the buttress, or more scenically traverse in from the Bealach an Lapain at the east end of the Five Sisters ridge. There is a small path at first, rounding the initial spur, then traverse to and across a small shelf before slanting down to the foot of the buttress, about 1.5km from the Bealach. Start at an ill-defined bouldery ridge down left from two triangular faces.

The Route
Follow the ridge until above the triangular faces, then traverse right to another triangular face above the others. Climb the right-hand edge of this. Follow a broken ridge until a traverse right leads to another triangular face, climbed from left to right (hard but avoidable). Go up blocks, then climb a short wall crossing the buttress, starting just left of a spike. Go up left to the skyline and follow it to boulders. A short steep section above a niche leads to more boulders and the top.

Sgùrr na Ciste Duibhe — 1027m

The rightmost of the Five Sisters in the popular view, with long rough slopes falling to Glenshiel and a hidden craggy north side.

- PAGE 109
- OS LR 33
- NORTH
- SCHIST

26. North Buttress — Grade 1

- NG 985 153
- 2HRS 40
- BUTTRESS
- +120M

A rocky ridge with only limited scrambling but good positions. Easily included in a traverse of the Five Sisters.

Approach
Either traverse from the Ciste Duibhe/Carnach col (easy), or use a steeper traverse from the strange offset saddle east of Sgùrr na Ciste Duibhe. In the latter case slant down northwards from the west end of the saddle, keeping below slabs until it is easy to slant up to the ridge.

The Route
An easy ridge leads to boulders, then a narrowing leads to a notch. A short steeper section on good holds and more boulders lead to a minor top, then a short loose descent and walking takes you to the summit.

Sgùrr an t-Searraich — 576m

This subsidiary summit of the Five Sisters is a superb viewpoint and has a series of slabby ribs running south from the summit, well seen from the Glen Shiel road. These make a good short excursion ideal for an evening.

- PAGE 108
- OS LR 33
- SOUTH
- PSAMMITE

Kintail

Sgùrr an t-Searraich

Grade 3 start

27

The initial slab on South Ribs, Sgùrr an t-Searraich (Route 27, Grade 3).
Scrambler: Noel Williams. © Iain Thow

27 South Ribs — Grade 3 *

○ NG 946 184   🏃 15MINS   ◁ OUTCROPS   ⊤ +500M

A long string of schist and psammite outcrops, some steep with juggy flakes, some slabby and delicate. There are some hard moves but little exposure, and with lots of options available it is easy to make it only Grade 2. The psammite is quick drying but slippery when wet, and the route is best in spring or autumn as bracken low down makes for hard going in summer.

Approach
From the Shiel Bridge shop cross the bridge and turn right soon afterwards to follow a path along the river. At the first fence head up left through bracken to reach a gate. Follow a small path along to the reedy Loch Shiel. At a stone wall just before the far end of the loch go up right past small clifflets to the bottom right of the main slabs.

The Route
Go up the slabs (Grade 2) or climb the centre of the buttress via a niche, a ramp and a juggy wall (Grade 3). Climb a steeper wall on good flakes, then slabs and heather lead to an easing. Walk up the spur via a couple of minor outcrops. At the top walk up left to reach the next outcrop above its main steeper cliff. Go up this via a left-slanting groove, then climb the right edge of slabs. Cross the next hump and go up to climb the left-hand end of the crag above. Go right to a grassy ramp and either climb the rib above its foot (Grade 2) or a clean slab further right (Grade 3). Next come a juggy rib and a steep slab on sharp edges, then more little outcrops can be included as you go up the spur.

At a minor summit go horizontally right to the next spur. Climb the front of this on jugs, then several more short steep outcrops. Where the spur runs out climb the obvious clean slab ahead, then outcrops working up left, aiming for a larger crag on the skyline. Climb the groove in the centre of this, then either make a long and scary step right onto a nose (Difficult) or escape left.

More outcrops follow, still heading up left, notably a left-sloping groove with a hard start (or the much easier dogleg groove just left) and the left-hand side of a steep juggy wall. Finish up easy left-sloping slabs with a short walk to the summit.

Beinn Fhada   1032m

A long ridge running from Strath Croe to the head of Glen Affric with some easy scrambling on the north-west end. The slabby schist buttresses below this on the north-east impress from a distance but are horribly loose. In low water there is also some nice scrambling in the Allt Coire an Sgairne (NH 003 211).

⊕ PAGE 109
 OS LR 33
 SOUTH
 SCHIST

28. Bealach an t-Sealgaire (Hunters' Pass) — Grade 1

◯ NG 993 204   🚶 2HRS 20   ◿ ARÊTE   ⊤ -50M

A broken ridge with one short harder descent. Not exposed but quite awkward and not avoidable.

Approach
From the foot of Gleann Lichd (limited parking at NG 966 210, more space 500 metres further back) take the road crossing the river to Innis a' Chrotha and fork left. Turn right onto a signed path and use this to get beyond the buildings. Leave the path and go up the grassy slopes ahead to a stile, then continue up Beinn Bhuidhe. The ridge curves rightwards as you gain height and becomes rockier over Sgùrr a' Choire Ghairbh.

The Route
The first minor summits provide a few small outcrops to play on, but the best scrambling is on the descent to the notch of Hunters' Pass. Go down into a slabby groove, avoiding the steeper bottom section by a ramp on the left. A pleasant ridge leads over Ceum na h-Aon-choise and Meall an Fhuarain Mhoir before a stroll across the plateau to the main summit.

A' Ghlas-Bheinn   918m

This knobbly Munro blocks the end of Strath Croe, with several prominent gullies running down its south-west slopes. These have some scrappy scrambling low down, but the hidden stream running down further east into Gleann Choinneachain is much better.

⊕ PAGE 109
◁ OS LR 33
✣ SOUTH-WEST
⛰ SCHIST

29. Allt Loch a' Chleirich — Moderate ★★

◯ NG 997 220   🚶 1HR   ◿ STREAM   ⊤ +550M

A very long and sustained stream scramble, with most falls climbable in low water, albeit in the stream at times. Save it for a dry spell and still be prepared to get very wet! Serious and committing in places and much harder (or impossible) in higher water.

Approach
From the foot of Gleann Lichd (limited parking at NG 966 210, more space 500 metres further back) take the road crossing the river to Innis a' Chrotha. Fork left then turn right on the signed path into open country. In just over 1km fork left to slant down and cross the footbridge over the Abhainn Chonaig. Go up to turn right onto a forestry road, which soon swings right over a bridge. Follow the road up the far bank and round right to slant into Gleann Choinneachain. Where the road

turns sharply back left go straight on, still on a good track, to emerge from the (recently felled) forest at a bridge, with the stream just beyond.

The Route
Climb the first fall by traversing in from the right above the pool. Three more falls follow, taken on the right, left and right respectively to reach the end of the first gorge. A large fall now comes in on the left. Start this on the right, cross at the initial pool, then start up a clean rib on the left. This gets harder and forces you off right into a grassy groove (serious). Gain a grass ramp further right awkwardly and follow it to the top of the rib.

Regain the stream above the big fall and cross its top (easy but exposed). Go up a central rib, then cross the stream leftwards again to climb a short steep wall on sharp holds. Cross slabs rightwards and go up a runnel left of the main flow. Cross again twice in quick succession and go up easily to a gorge. Although initially looking promising, this has a horrendously slimy exit, so is better avoided on the right. Descend into the stream above the next falls, climb a clean rib on the far bank, then follow the left edge. The next gorge starts easily, then at the first fall pull up onto a shelf on the left, traverse along it and climb a niche left of the fall. The next fall is passed by a technical traverse low on the right wall, and the next by going up right of the fall. Exit the gorge on the right and rejoin the stream above.

Climb a fall in the flow and avoid the next by starting up a small side stream on the right, then traversing back in across steep grass. Climb another fall on the left on small holds, then the stream forks. Take the right branch. After one fall and an easy section a more serious obstacle is passed by a traverse across the wall on the right on loose spikes. Easy little falls follow, then the last big fall is avoided by a grassy gully on the left. Another easy section leads to a succession of small falls, one climbed in the stream on sharp red holds. None are hard (in low water) and most are avoidable as the gorge opens out before arriving at the lochan. The summit of A' Ghlas Bheinn is 200m higher, best reached by going right then left.

Càrnan Cruithneachd   729m

An unfairly neglected hill, probably as it isn't easily seen from Kintail. From Glen Elchaig, however, it is a prominent spiky peak with a large broken north face. An ascent using the rib above the pass between the two glens makes an enjoyable longish half day, or it can be combined with A' Ghlas Bheinn to the south.

 PAGE 109
 OS LR 33
 SOUTH-WEST
 PSAMMITE

30   South-West Shoulder   Grade 2 *

| ○ NG 987 256 | 2HRS | SLABS | +200M |

A slabby rib of clean psammite with little exposure and lots of possible variations. High so open to bad weather and slippery when wet but with lots of good holds. If the steep nose low down and the quartz band high up are avoided it is only Grade 1.

Approach
As for the previous route, but instead of swinging right over the second bridge go up ahead to reach another forestry road. Turn right on this, then soon after fork left on a less used track. About 500 metres later this starts to zigzag up the slope to the left. Follow it left, right and left, then take a smaller steep path up right to emerge above the forestry. Carry on up to the saddle and the route starts up to the right just before the col.

The Route
Start at the lowest rocks and go up left to a slab (or an easier staircase to its right). Continue easily up left to climb a steep nose. Traverse right onto the next buttress, which consists of slabs followed by a knobbly wall and then easy outcrops. Climb a more sustained section, best near the right edge, to a levelling off.

    Easy rocks and grass lead to a steepening, climbed by any of three ribs (the left-hand one the best, the middle one easiest). A shattered quartz band leads to easy ground, then once over a minor summit a small outcrop leads to an excellent steep slab, climbed by another shattered quartz band. Gradually diminishing craglets lead to the first of two summits. The second and highest summit is a superb viewpoint perched high above Glen Elchaig.

South-West Shoulder, Càrnan Cruithneachd (Route 30, Grade 2).
Scrambler: Jamie Hageman. © Iain Thow

Biod an Fhithich   330m

A rather vegetated north-facing crag with a clean slabby right-hand side overlooking the River Glennan in the wild land north of Dornie.

 PAGE 108
 OS LR 33
 NORTH-WEST
 PSAMMITE

31 Ankle Ridge — Difficult ✶

◯ NG 914 275   🚶 35MINS   ◢ BUTTRESS   ⊤ +150M

Slabby psammite ribs scattered with incut holds. Easy for the grade with lots of possible variations, although the buttress itself is not escapable. North-west facing and accessible so a good summer evening route.

Approach
From Bundalloch on the east side of Loch Long (NG 896 278) take the track up the River Glennan for 1.5km. Cross the river and slog up heather to the right-hand edge of the lowest buttress.

The Route
Climb the right-hand edge of the buttress on positive holds to a heather terrace below the main crag. From the highest point of the terrace climb orange rock moving right. Make an awkward step right onto a rib and go up its right-hand edge to the edge of the crag. Go up the arête (easy-angled but quite delicate). Where this is split by a heathery groove the left-hand rib is better. An overhanging nose can be climbed on its right or avoided on its left to reach a large niche. Go left to the obvious rib and follow it to the top.

There is good bouldering just beyond the top. Descend well to the left (looking out), as the gullies either side are unpleasant.

1. **Toll Creagach** — Route 32 — P.130
2. **Càrn Eighe** — Route 33 — P.130
3. **Sgùrr na Lapaich** — Route 34 — P.131
4. **Beinn na Muice** — Route 35 — P.132
5. **Càrn Eiteige** — Route 36 — P.133
6. **Creag Ghlas** — Route 38 — P.135
7. **Bidein a' Choire Sheasgaich** — Route 38 — P.136
8. **Lurg Mhòr** — Route 39 — P.138
9. **Bidean an Eòin Deirg** — Route 40 — P.139

Glen Affric to Strath Carron

This area is a peak-baggers' paradise, with summits spread out along sweeping ridges running west to east, separated by broad deep glens. The north-western hills are usually accessed from Glen Carron and form a more compact knot. Distances are long here, but the good estate track up the Allt a' Chonais makes the approach easy (a mountain bike is useful). The other hills rise above Strath Conon, Glen Strathfarrar, Glen Cannich and Glen Affric and are easily reached from the east.

Although this area is not one of the rockier parts of the North-West, there are still good scrambles to be had. Most of them are on the ridges linking the major peaks of the area and fall into the category of incidents in a mountain day spent traversing a number of hills rather than being objectives in themselves. A pleasant contrast with most of the North-West is that the glens carry a fair amount of woodland, including sizeable areas of ancient forest. The Scots pines of Glens Affric and Strathfarrar in particular are outstanding, and add greatly to the pleasures of a day here.

Toll Creagach   1053m

This large rounded Munro has broad ridges and a rough north-east corrie with a prominent psammite slab on its west side.

 PAGE 128
 OS LR 25
EAST
PSAMMITE

---

32 Toll Creagach Slab   Grade 3 ✳︎

◇ NH 204 287   🚶 1HR 50   ◿ SLABS   ⬍ +100M

The tall narrow slab is quite smooth in places but also has plenty of good square holds. It is sustained but mostly quite escapable. It would be a poor choice in the wet.

Approach
From the south side of Mullardoch Dam (NH 223 310) follow the lochshore for a short distance then head up into Fraoch-choire, all very rough going. Carry on up the corrie to the 600m level then go up right to the slab. It is also possible to climb Creag a' Bhaca first, go up the ridge to the 750m level (where it starts to steepen again), then traverse in to the slab along a horizontal grassy shelf. This is easier going but tricky to identify and gives no advance view of the route.

The Route
Start at the tapering lowest point of the slab and climb it, bearing slightly left. The rock is clean, with intermittent cracks and grooves to help, although there are also some delicate sections. Occasional small ledges and islands of heather provide refuges and these can also be used to avoid harder sections or escape altogether. The top half broadens out but easy ground is still not far away if required. Near the top the angle eases off a little, then the slab finishes just below the ridge.

Càrn Eighe   1183m

The highest summits north of the Great Glen, Càrn Eighe and its twin summit Mam Sodhail, are the focal points of a sprawl of ridges between Glen Affric and Loch Mullardoch. Most of these are grassy, but the east ridge breaks into a row of shattered pinnacles about 1.5km from the summit, forming the climax of the classic horseshoe around Gleann nam Fiadh.

 PAGE 128
 OS LR 25
EAST
SCHIST

33. Càrn Eighe Pinnacles — Grade 1

◯ NH 137 263   🏃 3HRS 40   ⊿ ARÊTE   ⊤ NEGLIGIBLE

A sharp spiky ridge, avoidable on its south flank. Snowy well into spring.

Approach
The pinnacles are usually traversed from east to west while en route from Tom a' Chòinnich to Càrn Eighe. After the steep rise to Sròn Garbh (NH 145 264, unnamed on the OS 1:50,000 map), pass over the minor top of Stob Coire Dhomhnuill (NH 139 262) to reach the sharp ridge.

The Route
A narrow ridge and an easy blocky pinnacle lead to a broad saddle, then go up steep spikes to cross the first pinnacle. Climb a bigger pinnacle easily, descending leftwards just before the top. Go up the second large pinnacle, dodging its summit on the right to reach a steep juggy descent. Blocks lead up to Stob a' Choire Dhomhain and the end of the difficulties.

Nearby, the waterfall and stream below Loch Lapaich are worth including if passing (hardish Grade 1). Start up lovely square steps left of the stream at NH 163 245. The start is the best bit but it continues further than you expect, finishing with a baby gorge. Sadly the interesting looking ridge on the left side of the main face is very mossy and quite loose (Moderate).

Sgùrr na Lapaich — 1150m

One of the dominant peaks of the area, this has a pointed summit and several good ridges, although only one of these runs to scrambling.

🌐 PAGE 128
📐 OS LR 25
↔ EAST
⛰ SCHIST

34. East Ridge — Grade 1

◯ NH 167 351   🏃 3HRS   ⊿ ARÊTE   ⊤ +250M

A bouldery schist ridge, narrow in places and quite mossy but not particularly exposed. There is plenty of choice of route but generally the crest is best.

Approach
Although it can be approached directly from the power station in Gleann Innis an Loichel (NH 183 381, short but steep and rough) the ridge is most often climbed during a traverse of the Mullardoch Munros. From the saddle between Càrn nan Gobhar and Sgùrr na Lapaich start up a gentle ridge, then go right to join the rocky crest at a large square-cut boulder.

The Route
Climb onto the boulder from the left, step right across a gap, then go left and through a flaky gap in a steep face. Boulders and moss lead up to a grassy ridge, then move right onto a slabby crest. Avoid a steeper slab, or climb it by a grassy crack and quartz nodules at Grade 3. As the ridge narrows keep to the crest for the most fun and cross a minor summit. A clamber up large boulders leads to the main summit.

Beinn na Muice 693m

This isolated hill rises steeply above the Monar Dam, giving superb views. The south flank is very rocky, especially at its western end, running up to the nicely perched summit ridge.

 PAGE 128
 OS LR 25
 SOUTH
 SCHIST

35. South-West Slabs — Grade 2 or 3

◇ NH 209 399   🏃 15MINS   ◿ SLABS   ⊤ +300M

The hillside is scattered with slabs of excellent knobbly schistose grit, varying from walking-angle to 50 degrees, becoming more sustained and steeper towards the top. There is a huge choice of route.

Approach
The road up Strathfarrar is private, with a gatekeeper, but in summer vehicle access is allowed from 9am until 6–8pm (depending which month), up to a maximum of 25 vehicles. It is closed all day on Tuesdays and until 1.30pm on Wednesdays.

Park 0.5km before the Monar Dam, where a rough vehicle track goes off northwards. Where this swings left and starts to gain height leave it and cross the streamlet just right. Head north-west up the hillside to the first slabs. At the top are two larger masses of rock, and the best route links together slabs up leftwards aiming for clean rock on the skyline below and left of the left-hand one.

The Route
Choose any slab that looks appealing and work up left, taking in the cleanest slabs. These can be quite smooth, but are scattered with knobbly holds. As with most slabs, small changes in angle make a big difference. They become more sustained, then you arrive on the ridge at a big easy-angled slab just below and left of the left-hand steeper buttress.

The buttress can be tackled direct (harder than it looks, Moderate), or zigzagged up at a serious Grade 3, while a spiky groove near the left edge provides a good line at Grade 2. There are minor outcrops on the ridge above this, or a steep traverse right (slightly down) takes you below the right-hand buttress to its far edge, which consists of enjoyable Grade 3 slabs. A pleasant ridge then leads to the summit. The highest summit is near the eastern end, but the western top has a better view.

Càrn Eiteige   882m

This pleasantly narrow ridge runs out south-westwards from the west end of the Strathfarrar Munros. It descends to a couple of rocky knobbles just above the foot of Loch Monar, the higher of which, Creag a' Chaobh, has steep slabs on its south face.

🌐 PAGE 128
✈ OS LR 25
⇕ SOUTH
⌂ PSAMMITE

36. Creag a' Chaobh — Grade 3 ✶

◇ NH 197 406   🏃 30MINS   ◿ SLABS   ⊤ +200M

These steepish psammite slabs are quite vegetated but have plenty of clean sections too. Quite serious at the start but easing after 50m, with lots of choice of route. It is feasible to start further left at around Diff.

Approach
The road up Strathfarrar is private, with a gatekeeper, but in summer vehicle access is allowed from 9am until 6–8pm (depending which month), up to a maximum of 25 vehicles. It is closed all day on Tuesdays and until 1.30pm on Wednesdays.

Park on the left just before Loch Monar dam (NH 204 395) and follow the private access road along above the north shore. Pass above the first building and turn left almost immediately (through the welcoming barbed wire gate) then slant up to join a small path passing well above Monar Lodge. This contours along between the new planting higher up and the two small older woods on the lochshore before descending slightly to a gate. Creag a' Chaobh is obvious just ahead and you leave the path about 200 metres beyond the gate, at the top of a slight rise. At the right-hand foot of the crag is a mossy slab topped by a long vertical wall. Start 10 metres left of this at a cleaner slab.

The Route
Go up the stepped slab to heather, then up the left edge of a steeper slab to grass (crux, avoidable on the left). Bear left up more broken rock towards a pinker quartzy area, then climb this to easy ground at the top of the first section. Slant left up easier-angled rock (still exposed) then climb the left edge of a vertical wall (beware the large loose flake just below the top). Grass and walking-angle slabs then lead to the half-height easing (possible escape right).

Walk up ahead to climb a short stepped buttress, then go up left on pink quartzy rock to the skyline. Climb an excellent long pink rib to a steeper finish. Grass and a couple of minor outcrops then lead to the top of Creag a' Chaobh, a good viewpoint. It is easy to carry on up the blunt spur to Carn Eiteige, but if just doing the scramble then head north-east first to get beyond the crag before descending southwards between the new planting and the east flank of the hill.

Creag Ghlas 686m

This subsidiary top of the Strathconon Corbett, Sgùrr a' Mhuilinn, has a large south-west face consisting of two buttresses of steep schistose grit. The West Buttress has the best climbs but the larger East Buttress is broken into a series of slabby tiers which can provide a devious scramble, a good way to start a loop around the two Corbetts.

 PAGE 128
 OS LR 25
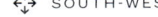 SOUTH-WEST
 SCHIST

37 East Buttress — Grade 3 ★★

| ⌖ NH 246 544 | 🚶 1HR 10 | ◿ SLABS | ⌶ +300M |

The left-hand edge is taken by the broken rock climb *Oh Dear* – given the strange (but accurate!) grade of Difficult to VS. This makes an excellent scramble if the harder parts are avoided. Climbers may prefer to take rock boots and tackle these more directly, giving an extended series of short routelets. The crag gets plenty of sun and dries fast despite some vegetation, but would be nasty in the wet. Avoid February–July due to nesting raptors. (See Mountaineering Scotland website.)

Approach
From Glenmeanie in Strathconon (NH 284 528) take the forestry track up Gleann Meinich to NH 244 541, then turn right up a break in the forest. Once above the trees slant up right to the base of the cliff. Start at the left-hand end of the main slab, just right of a narrow gully.

The Route
There are various cracks on the slab at Severe to VS, but scramblers should start by a vegetated groove on the left, stepping right onto the slab as the angle eases. Go up a right-slanting groove until a step left leads to a ledge and the top of the tier. Follow easy slabs (best on the left) to a steeper tier. Go down right to climb steps leading back up left (awkward), then go left to the edge and up. Avoid the next slab by a grassy groove on the right (delicate Very Difficult direct). A broken groove leads up the next tier (or thin cracks near the left edge, Difficult). The slabs now ease until a short vertical wall is bypassed to reach a larger wall. A broken groove on the left leads to a cleaner finish (the steep square-cut corner on the right leads to a juggy finish at Very Difficult). Numerous slabby boulder problems now lead to the east summit. From the saddle on the left clean easy-angled ribs lead to the higher west summit.

Bidein a' Choire Sheasgaich — 945m

A remote Munro with a lot of rather vegetated crags, including the 150m high North Face which falls in two steep tiers to the Bealach an Sgoltaidh. It is almost always combined with Lurg Mhòr on the basis that once you've done the enormous walk in for one you might as well climb both.

- 🌐 PAGE 128
- ⟁ OS LR 25
- ⇵ NORTH
- ⌂ PSAMMITE & SCHIST

38 North Face — Grade 3

| ⌖ NH 048 422 | 🚶 4HRS 20 | ◿ SLAB & BUTTRESS | ⌶ +150M |

A scramble in two disjointed halves, a lower tier of steep but positive psammite slabs, and a more serious upper tier of juggier but looser schist. Basically a way of adding interest to a steep path.

Approach
The usual approach is from Craig (NH 040 493), crossing the railway and taking the vehicle track (take the higher forks in the forest) to NH 074 468. Fork right (small cairn) and cross the river (usually a two-wire bridge at 076 466), then take the path up to the Bealach Bhearnais. Either climb Beinn Tharsuinn or traverse across its south-east shoulder (not quicker), then descend to the Bealach an Sgoltaidh. On the crest of the pass is a wall. From the south end of this follow a steep path zigzagging up left. Pass right of a steep slab, then above it walk 100 metres left to a larger clean slab, just left of a wide grassy gully. Start at the bottom right-hand corner of this.

The Route

Delicate moves lead up the edge to a ledge at 5m. Follow this left across the slab until just before the left-hand edge. This point can easily be reached direct, but with less fun. Go up on good holds, moving right near the top to avoid a dirtier section. Go up minor outcrops and grass to another slab and climb it just right of the left-hand edge on good holds. Follow a large terrace up right to meet the path below a steep grassy gully.

The path exits up the gully, but if in search of more excitement walk a long way right below the upper tier until the steep cliffs above begin to break up into shattered ribs. Take the first rib right of the overhangs, quite broken and mossy at first, but cleaner and juggy above (some loose holds). The rib ends on steep grass with a mossy slab above and overhangs to the left. Go up left and cross the top of a minor gully to get onto the next rib above the overhangs. Climb this airily on big holds. Another exposed rib then leads to the top of the crag. A few boulder problems can be found further up the ridge, notably two superb rippled slabs just before and after the largest lochan.

Lurg Mhòr   986m

One of the most remote Munros, with a nice summit ridge perched above the head of Loch Monar. The section between the two tops has a short section of unavoidable scrambling, which has to be crossed by anyone collecting Munro Tops.

- PAGE 128
- OS LR 25
- EAST
- SCHIST

39   Meall Mor Ridge   Grade 1

| ⬡ NH 067 404 | 🏃 6HRS | ⟋ ARÊTE | ⊤ NEGLIGIBLE |

A couple of awkward steps on a narrow ridge, brief but quite exposed.

Approach
Lurg Mhòr is a very long way from anywhere. It is most commonly approached by climbing Bidean a' Choire Sheasgaich first (as for Route 38). Descend south-east to a saddle and climb broad slopes to Lurg Mhòr.

The Route
From the summit follow the ridge eastwards and descend a sharp slabby crest (path to the right). Make an exposed step down, then descend another sharp crest to a saddle. Go up steeply to a minor summit, then pass airily left of a small tower to a notch. Go up the far side on big flakes, then an easy narrow ridge leads to the rounded top of Meall Mòr.

Bidean an Eòin Deirg 1046m

This subsidiary top of the sprawling Sgùrr a' Chaorachain has a nice pointed summit and a steep, sharp north-east ridge.

- PAGE 128
- OS LR 25
- NORTH-EAST
- SCHIST

40 North-East Ridge — Grade 1 or 2

| ○ NH 105 445 | 3HRS 40 | OUTCROPS | +250M |

A bouldery spur, but with a few short outcrops. If the first two slabs are avoided the route is only Grade 1.

Approach
From Craig (NH 040 493) cross the railway and take the forestry road up the Allt a' Chonais for 8km (take the upper track at forks) until just short of Glenuaig Lodge. Head south-east up grassy slopes into the valley of An Crom Allt and follow this up to the saddle below the west ridge of Càrn nam Fiaclan. Traverse south-east below some steep slabs, then head up to a prominent pink slab at the foot of the main spur.

The Route
Climb the pink slab, then traverse left past a smaller ridge to another slab. Go up the left arête of this. Easier slabs then lead to a broad spur, mainly grassy. As the ridge narrows more easy slabs can be included, then short outcrops alternate with boulders. The spur narrows and steepens, still mainly boulders, but with a few small outcrops. At the top a steeper rib and mossy boulders lead directly to the cairn.

Bounded by the deep trenches of Glen Torridon and Strath Carron, this area has a clutch of individual peaks, all quite distinctive in character. All of them have large amounts of rock too broken for good rock climbing but which can provide excellent scrambling. Some are quartzite but the majority are largely of Torridonian sandstone, which provides the best routes. On the western edge of the area the latter forms the huge tiered cliffs of Beinn Bhàn and Sgùrr a' Chaorachain – famous for their winter climbs and the classic rock climbs of *Cioch Nose* (Severe) and *Sword of Gideon* (VS). Further east are the Ben Damph and Coulin Forests, whose rocky peaks rise steeply from wild lochans. These are threaded by a good network of stalkers' paths, making it easy to link several scrambles on different hills into a lengthy scrambling day.

Applecross & Coulin

1.	Meall Gorm	Route 41	P.142
2.	Sgùrr a' Chaorachain	Route 42	P.143
3.	Beinn Bhàn	Route 43	P.144
4.	Beinn Damh	Route 44	P.147
5.	An Ruadh-Stac	Routes 45–47	P.149
6.	Maol Chean-dearg	Routes 48–50	P.151
7.	Fuar Tholl	Routes 51–54	P.156
8.	Sgorr Ruadh	Routes 55–56	P.161
9.	Beinn Liath Mhòr	Routes 57–59	P.163
10.	Sgùrr Dubh	Routes 60–61	P.166

Meall Gorm   710m

The terraced sandstone cliffs rimming the southern flank of Bealach na Ba feature in many a photograph. Most of the buttresses are too steep for scrambling, but there are exceptions. The broken buttress left of the narrow *Blue Pillar* (Very Difficult) near the right-hand end of the cliff has a nice finish, but the route described below is better.

 PAGE 140
 OS LR 24
 NORTH
SANDSTONE

 41 Long Buttress   **Grade 2**

 NG 788 408    10 MINS    OUTCROPS   +160M

This is the long stepped buttress running down to the step in the corrie floor. Generally follow the right-hand edge, up short steep walls with a wide choice of route. Parts are hard for the grade but everything is avoidable.

Approach
Halfway up the Bealach na Ba road there is a small parking place on the right just above the step in the corrie floor (NG 787 412). Cross the corrie to a small outcrop with a large perched block at half height.

The Route
Climb the right-hand edges of the first two outcrops. The next outcrop is steep, so climb a rib right of a grassy rake. More short buttresses follow, with many possible lines, a small detached pinnacle and a flaky prow being worthwhile. Bear left up short walls to finish up an excellent slabby wall. Harder variations are possible taking the larger buttresses direct.

Sgùrr a' Chaorachain 792m

Very impressive from a distance, this sandstone dome dominates Loch Kishorn, and some good rock climbs are found along its sides, including the classics *Cioch Nose* (Severe) and *Sword of Gideon* (VS).

 PAGE 140
 OS LR 24
 SOUTH-EAST
 SANDSTONE

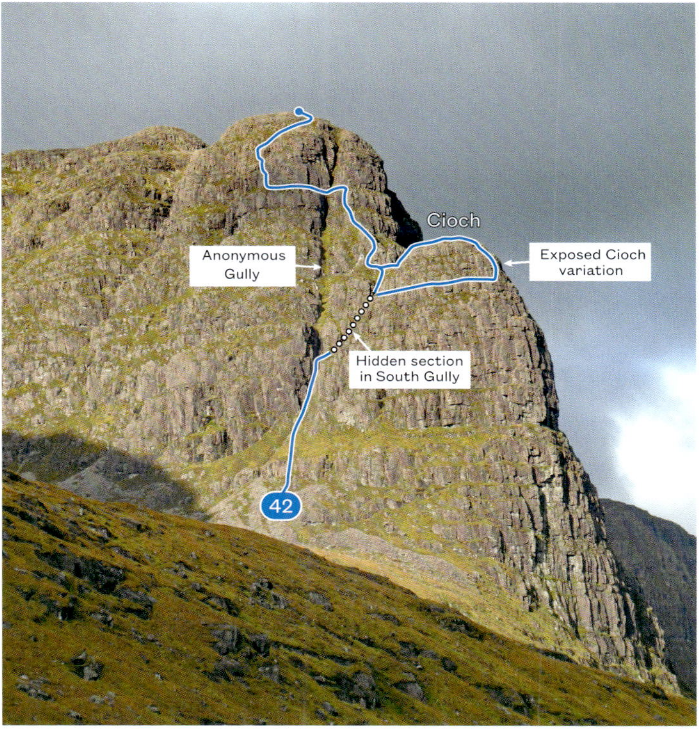

42 Cioch Indirect — Difficult *

◯ NG 796 426　　🏃 50 MINS　　⟋ INTRICATE　　⊤ +350M

Basically a way of doing the eye-catching ridge above the Cioch without climbing the Nose. Still an intimidating outing though, exposed in places and technical in others. The line is not always obvious and, although big ledges often mitigate the exposure, the situations are impressive and the positions serious. Only two short sections are Difficult.

Approach
Park at the bridge over the Russel Burn (NG 815 413) and from the next bend take the track to Loch Coire nan Arr. From the far end of this slant up north-west into the mouth of Coire a' Chaorachain, with the Cioch looming ahead. Start below South Gully, the major gully left of the Cioch, just left of a scree patch.

The Route
Climb two short outcrops to the mouth of South Gully. Go up easy rocks just right of the gully, then either traverse into it and climb it damply to a steep wall, or climb the left-hand edge of a chimney just to the right (steep), then traverse into the gully below the steep wall.

Go left into a subsidiary gully (Anonymous Gully), up this for 10m, then right again to rejoin South Gully above the steep wall. Climb the gully, with a short hard pitch (usually wet). The col behind the Cioch is now easy to reach, but more fun is to walk right along a terrace to the arête and climb this on wildly exposed flakes and blocks to the top of the Cioch.

Beyond the col dodge the first step on the left (path) and continue up the ridge. This steepens, with an airy step right near the top, before reaching a good ledge below a large vertical wall. Follow the ledge left across Anonymous Gully and out to the arête. Just beyond this climb a steep open groove slanting left, just left of a pile of blocks (exposed). At its top step left and go up a short wet gully, then right along a ledge to the skyline. Climb this airily on big rough flakes. Now follow the ridge over a series of towers, with some easy scrambling up them. The first, third and fifth towers have steep awkward descents.

A good continuation is to carry on round to the main top of Sgùrr a' Chaorachain and descend the south-east shoulder, which is steep, with occasional short bits of scrambling and great views.

Beinn Bhàn　　896m

The highest of the Applecross hills, with a magnificent line of corries on its north-east flank. The three finest are (left to right) Coire na Feola, Coire na Poite and Coire nan Fhamhair, and these are separated by the prominent ridges of A' Chioch (Moderate) on the left and A' Phoit (Severe) on the right.

 PAGE 140
 OS LR 24
 EAST
 SANDSTONE

43 A' Chìoch — Moderate ✶✶

○ NG 819 446   🏃 1HR 20   ◿ BUTTRESS   ⊺ +450M

A major expedition up a steep-sided ridge with awesome situations. Even the easiest sections are exposed, and although individual scrambling sections are short there are lots of them. There are numerous possible variations and most tricky bits can be avoided, the only unavoidable Moderate section being the narrow gully near the top. This doesn't feel exposed psychologically but an unroped fall would go a long way. Although there is some vegetation (and the occasional loose block) the route is still reasonable in the wet as holds are large and the sandstone is clean and rough.

Approach

From the bridge over the River Kishorn at Tornapress (parking just east at NG 835 423) take the path running up northwards. Leave it after about 2km (small path) to follow the stream up into Coire na Feola. A' Chìoch is the right-hand arête.

The Route

The ridge starts as a broad buttress, where a steep bouldery start leads to broken rocks. Cleaner slabs to the left give a good harder variation. Once over the first crest more bouldery walking leads to a row of stepped ribs on the right. The left-hand one is excellent, finishing up a flake-crack. The ridge now narrows before another steepening. Vertical rocks on the right can be climbed on their left edge on good holds or avoided on the left. Broken tiers lead to the top of A' Chioch.

Go down a narrow ridge to grass, then either descend awkwardly on the crest or more easily use a gully on the left and an exposed grassy

ramp. From the notch beyond either climb the steep rib of blocks ahead (some loose) or use the gully on the left to reach the next top. Descend on the right, then take a narrow ledge left to a notch. More direct descents are steep and loose. Pass left of the small pinnacles to reach the very steep headwall. A well-used route climbs this just right of the arête, quite vegetated, until the ground opens out below a steeper tier. Climb the awkward narrow gully in the centre using a handy jammed block, then go up and left to more open slabs and a final easy ridge. The summit is a few hundred metres to the right.

Beinn Damh 903m

A steep-sided broad ridge with tiered sandstone cliffs on its east flank. The main section is very vegetated but there is cleaner rock at the southern end. The prominent ridge leading up over Stuc Toll nam Biast looks impressive but contains very little scrambling.

- PAGE 141
- OS LR 24
- NORTH-EAST
- SANDSTONE

44. North-East Spur — Grade 3 *

| ⌀ NG 897 507 | 🏃 1HR 45 | ⊿ OUTCROPS | ⊤ +350M |

A long scramble up a blunt shoulder with lots of short tiers, quite hard in places but rarely exposed.

Approach
From the Torridon Inn (NG 889 541) go behind the pub to cross the stream and turn left up to the road. A good path leads up through the woods west of the stream into Coire Roill. Fork left once outside the woods (just after the fork a detour left to the waterfall is usually well worthwhile). Cross the stream and follow the path, which cuts back left initially (easy to miss) before slanting up along the east side of the corrie. At the lochan on the col go right to pass beneath cliffs below a higher saddle. Start at the lowest clean buttress of the North-East Spur, with a deer track at its foot.

The Route
Climb the lowest buttress, quite tricky and with some loose blocks, then smaller outcrops lead to another deer track. Climb a slab and groove right

of the steepest nose (technical but not exposed), then an open scoop to heather. A short step leads to a steep slab, too hard for scrambling. The groove just right is harder than it looks (V Diff) so go up steps right again to an arête. Small outcrops follow, gaining an overhanging prow from the left, then work left easily to a large shelf below a steep cliff. All this can be avoided by slanting in from the upper saddle on the left.

From the highest point of the shelf climb a rib between two grassy grooves to a grassy alcove, then small ledges lead out right to the skyline. The ground now opens out to numerous small craglets. When things steepen again climb a detached block and step off it onto a nose and up. Take the next steep slab direct to a square-cut groove, then climb a slabby nose to easy ground. One easy tier remains before a pleasant walk up the ridge, which becomes quartzite. Just before the summit a final steepening is an easy clamber.

An Ruadh-Stac 892m

An excellent peak that just fails to reach Munro height. The quartzite slabs on the east flank provide good scrambling, and the Allt Loch Mòine a' Chriathair makes an entertaining approach.

- PAGE 141
- OS LR 25
- SOUTH-EAST
- SANDSTONE & QUARTZITE

45 Allt Loch Mòine a' Chriathair — Grade 2 or 3 *

○ NG 951 465   🏃 25MINS   ⟋ STREAM   ⊤ +200M

First a bouldery gorge, then better and more open scrambling up steep sandstone steps beside scenic falls. The route is escapable in numerous places, while the better upper part can easily be done on its own.

Approach
Start from Coulags in Strath Carron (parking just west of the bridge, NG 956 451). Start up the access track to the house just east of the bridge, then go left (signed) alongside the river to rejoin the track beyond the house. Usually it is easy to cross the main Fionn-abhainn at the mouth of the Allt Loch Mòine a' Chriathair (and if it isn't then you shouldn't be doing this route!). There is a bridge 600 metres upstream.

The Route
An easy gorge leads to the first fall, climbed on the right with a hard pull-up to start. Follow a central rib to more boulders. Climb the next fall on the right, followed by a very slippery shelf. A large boulder (avoidable on the left) leads to an easy section. Leaning walls then force you out of the gorge. Return briefly for an easy bit, then two more falls need avoiding. Return as the gorge opens out, where pretty slabs and a couple of small falls lead to a long level open section.

Enter the next gorge by a delicate move to a slippery shelf on the left, then cross and go along a ledge past a holly. Climb the next fall either by a jump on the left (slippery landing) or a precarious shelf on the right. Pass the next fall by a chimney on the right to reach an easy section, terminated by a big fall coming in on the left.

The character now changes to steeper and more open falls, and the route can easily be started here to take in just the best scrambling (Grade 2). Climb juggy walls right of the stream to a long shelf. Halfway along this cross and climb the wall on the left on good holds to another shelf. At the far end of this climb cracked boulders and a short wall to more slabs and the finish. A short walk leads up past a lochan to the next route.

46 Eastern Slabs — Grade 2 or Moderate

○ NG 928 481   🏃 2HRS   ⟋ SLABS   ⊤ +350M

Open slabs of excellent quartzite, delicate in places and quite serious, then a bouldery walk leads to an easier but looser finish. The slabs would be a bad idea when wet.

Approach
If not coming from the previous route you can traverse in from the lowest point of the saddle east of An Ruadh-Stac. Traverse south-west below easy slabs to the second smooth slab, directly above the largest lochan.

The Route

Climb the easy slab, then walk up broken ground to go up another smooth slab with a vertical right-hand wall. Where this reaches steeper steps go left along a ledge below steeper rock into the central bay. Direct routes from here are delicate and around Moderate, but the best line is to carry on along the ledge until below a slabby corner with a vertical left-hand wall. Tiptoe delicately up the corner in a superb position. At the top climb the first overlap by stepping in from the right, then climb the second overlap direct to easy ground. Walk up boulders for 150m or so, then near the top of the ridge a short detour right leads to small buttresses which give a pleasant Grade 2 finish.

---

47 **North-West Shoulder** — **Grade 2**

◯ NG 920 483   🚶 3HRS   ⊿ OUTCROPS   ⊤ +100M

A couple of steep quartzite steps and some smaller outcrops are a convenient way of adding some interest to an ascent of An Ruadh-stac from the north. They are easily avoided on the right if you have non-scramblers in your party.

Approach

The route can be approached from the south via the track from Coulags (as for the previous routes) by crossing the triple col between An Ruadh-Stac and Maol Chean-dearg, but this involves losing 150m of height, so it fits in much better with an ascent from Annat on Loch Torridon. The track leaves the road at NG 894 544 and slants up south-eastwards to Loch an Eoin below Maol Chean-dearg. Fork right at the loch and go round to Loch Coire an Ruadh-staic. At the loch head southwards across the stream and go up the north-west shoulder of An Ruadh-Stac (head right at first for easier ground). The shoulder steepens into cliffs at the top, with the scramble directly ahead.

The Route

Start on the right, at the lowest rock, and string outcrops together (including a nice slab) to reach a steeper buttress. Climb a groove right of the nose (the nose direct is Moderate). On the next tier start at the bottom right and work left up stepped grooves. Finish up shattered craglets just below the summit area. This consists of numerous stony mounds, confusing in mist, the true summit being at the southern corner.

Maol Chean-dearg — 933m

A fairly easy Munro when approached from the south-east, while the north side of the hill is steep, wild and little frequented.

🌐 PAGE 141
⟵ OS LR 25
⇕ NORTH-EAST
⌂ SANDSTONE & QUARTZITE

48 Ketchil Buttress — Grade 3 or Difficult ✱

| ⌖ NG 931 492 | 🚶 2HRS 20 | ◿ BUTTRESS | ⊤ +120M |

Steep quartzite steps on good square-cut holds. An enjoyable alternative to the steep scree-ridden section on the usual path.

Approach
Start from Coulags in Strath Carron (parking just west of the bridge, NG 956 451). Start up the access track to the house just east of the bridge, then go left (signed) alongside the river to rejoin the track beyond the house. Follow the path northwards up the Fionn Abhainn and 1km beyond the bothy fork left and follow the zigzag path as far as the 500m contour. Now head up right to a quartzite face. The left-hand side of this is a long line of cliffs low down, while the right-hand side has two bigger buttresses at a higher level. Ketchil Buttress is the left-hand one. Start at twin ribs separated by an alcove. The right-hand buttress is a similar grade, but looser and a poorer line.

The Route
Climb the left-hand rib (the right-hand one is a loose and awkward

Difficult). Climb another step above, then a steeper step using flakes just right of the nose. Easier rock then leads up to a final steep wall, which can either be tackled direct (Difficult) or dodged by a ramp on the right.

Ketchil Buttress (Route 48, Grade 3 or Difficult).
Scrambler: Iain Thow. © Noel Williams

49 East Shoulder — Grade 3

◇ NG 932 501   🏃 2HRS 30   ⟋ INTRICATE   ⊤ +150M

A series of steep tiers separated by easy ramps gives a rather winding line but good situations. Some tiers are quite hard but all are short, mostly with lots of possible variants. The bedrock is excellent rough sandstone but there are quite a lot of unattached blocks sitting about and the moss on the ledges is nasty when wet.

Approach
As for the previous route to 1km beyond the bothy then continue on the glen path past Loch Coire Fionnaraich and up to the Bealach na Lice (NG 933 509). This point is also easily reached from Annat as for Route 50. Leave the path and go southwards up broken ground, passing a small lochan, until the spur flattens out below the north face of Maol Chean-dearg. Ahead is a shallow corrie with a steep left wall and the left rim of this is a blunt shoulder with ramps running up rightwards. Go up left to the shoulder and start just right of the left-hand edge of the initial line of cliffs.

The Route
The basic idea is to slant rightwards up the ramps, breaking through the steep tiers where seems appropriate/feasible, until you reach the prow of the cliff, then zigzag back left to easier ground and up.

Start leftwards up slabby rock to grass then move right up a narrow ramp for a short distance to find a way through the rock above. Keep working up right, breaking through small tiers to reach a big right-slanting bouldery ramp with a deer track. Go right on this and up the right-hand side of a slabby arête above boulders (easier further right). Go up the left edge of a small tier, then a stepped-groove a bit further right to reach another ramp. Follow this right until the small tier above eases, then go up to the next ramp, arriving by a big pile of cracked boulders.

Follow the ramp rightwards below vertical rock to the prow of the cliff and the most committing section of the route. Go up left (usually wet) to climb a steep V-groove. Traverse well left to more open ground and go up to a wider grassy rake. From here there are lots of options. Basically work up and right, taking in any outcrops you fancy until the angle eases off at the top of the shoulder.

East Shoulder, Maol Chean-dearg (Route 49, Grade 3).
Scrambler: Nicky Gear. © Iain Thow

50 North Flank Grade 1/2

◇ NG 929 501　　🏃 2HRS 40　　◿ OUTCROPS　　⊤ +350M

Mainly steep walking, but the final ridge is good and the setting wild and impressive. Slow to dry and much harder in the wet. The higher parts can be avoided by steep grass to the left but this still feels precarious.

Approach
From Annat on Loch Torridon (NG 894 544) take the signed footpath running up south-east from the shore road about 100 metres west of the phone box, starting in a small wood. Follow this to Loch an Eoin, then fork left to the Bealach na Lice (NG 933 509). Go up southwards past boulder problems and follow the shoulder up until it runs into the main hill. Ahead is a shallow corrie with a steep cliff on its left and a ramp leading up right. The ramp becomes a gully higher up (Hidden Gully) and the route follows the right edge of this.

The Route
Start up a broken buttress on the right of the main bay. This is steep to start, then gradually eases to walking. Walk rightwards up the ramp, with a few outcrops, then when the gully becomes more defined cross to the right bank. A series of short steps are tackled direct, then a fun knife edge. The next vertical step is climbed by a groove on the right, then a few more steps lead to easy ground just below the summit.

Fuar Tholl 907m

A fine peak, whose complex flanks provide a host of possibilities for scrambles. On the south and south-east sides are clean slabs of excellent sandstone which can be interlinked in a variety of different ways, the one giving the best scrambling being to start up An Leth Chreag, traverse left to include the 'fine slab' then use the Link Rib to gain the top part of the South Flank. The north and north-east sides are steeper and looser but worthwhile scrambles can still be found.

⊕ PAGE 141　
◁ OS LR 25　
⇔ VARIOUS　
⌂ SANDSTONE

51 · South Flank — Grade 1 or 3 ✱

◇ NG 984 484 🚶 1HR 15 ◿ SLABS ⊺ +400M

The face above Sgùrr a' Mhuilinn is a huge sweep of sandstone slabs. The rock is excellent, although much of it is fairly easy-angled.

Approach

From parking at Achnashellach (NH 005 484, often busy, please park sensibly – i.e. at right-angles to the road) go up to the station, cross the line and follow the forestry road up right. Take the first turning left, then after 0.5km a smaller path is signed off left. Follow this up until above the forestry then at a battered signboard go left to the River Lair. The easiest crossing is one waterfall higher than the place where the path meets the river, but even this can be difficult or impossible in spate, necessitating either a descending traverse in from much higher up or a different choice of route. From the usual crossing a rough deer track leads up steep bog and a heathery spur just right of a small stream, then slants left below boulders to go up to the plateau of Sgùrr a' Mhuilinn at around 400m. From here the most direct line follows the left-hand rim of Fuar Tholl's south-eastern corrie (the Fuar Tholl itself, 'cold hollow' in Gaelic), but other possibilities include the fine slab mentioned in Route 52, which is directly above, and 500 metres left a prominent clean slab gives easy scrambling with a steep wall at the top, climbed by a left-to-right ramp (Grade 1).

The Route
Go up easy slabs by their right-hand edge, then smoother slabs offset to the right until these curve over to walking. A little higher two steeper ribs off right are worthwhile, then more slabby walking follows. A steeper band crosses the ridge above – easy direct, or Grade 3 by a vertical wall of spikes to the right. Boulders lead to another steep wall, climbed by a groove at its highest point. An easy slab and two short walls lead to easy ground, with the summit not far away.

The fine slab on Leth Chreag, Fuar Tholl (Route 52, Grade 3).
Scrambler: Lucy Williams. © Noel Williams

52 Leth Chreag — Grade 2 or 3 *

◇ NG 986 487   🚶 1HR   ◿ SLABS   ⊤ +500M

The slabs below the right-hand edge of the main corrie give a good scramble, which leads on to an easy but nicely narrow ridge. It is also possible to move left after the first section to climb a fine slab, the best single bit of scrambling on the hill, then use the Link Rib to join Route 51.

Approach
As for the previous route but just after passing below the boulders head up rightwards to a narrow line of stepped slabs.

The Route
Go up the slabs, mostly Grade 1 but with occasional harder steps, until they peter out after 60m or so. Here the logical line is to move right and follow more broken slabs up the edge of the face to pass left of an overlap and reach a minor top at 650m. Alternatively, better (but harder) scrambling can be found by traversing left across rough heather to cross below the prominent steep band slanting up right and reach the fine slab behind it. Climb directly to a prominent circular depression, then carry on up delightful slabs until they ease to walking. They are quite blank in places but with excellent friction (Grade 3). Several cracklines offer welcome rests. From the top of the slab bear right up easier slabs to reach the 650m top.

Beyond the 650m top walk up the rocky shoulder until it steepens, then zigzag up broken ground and cross a short shattered arête to reach the summit.

From the top of the 'fine slab' you can extend the scrambling by heading left via minor slabs to reach a small lochan, with a clean rib up and left (Link Rib, Grade 3, NG 983 487). Climb the rib just right of a roofed groove, avoiding the steepest section on its right to reach a huge block. Slabby outcrops above take you up to join Route 51 just above the two steeper ribs.

53 Spare Rib — Moderate

◇ NG 976 494   🚶 1HR 45   ◿ BUTTRESS   ⊤ +200M

Steep in places and the sandstone is sometimes quite loose, with a precarious crux, but a good line with an excellent ridge to finish.

Approach
From Achnashellach start as for Route 51 but stay on the path once out of the forestry and follow it up into Coire Lair. Turn left at the crossroads at NG 990 502, cross the stream and follow the path up to the 550m contour, then traverse left to the cliff. This is split by three deep gullies, dividing it into four buttresses. The left-hand one is The Pile (Difficult, with a steep tower at half-height). Spare Rib is the next right.

The Route
Start up small outcrops on the right-hand side of the buttress, just left of the gully. These get more sustained, then steepen considerably. Take

![Photo showing route 53 with The Pile and crux labelled]

grass ledges leading left, then go back up right to make a precarious mantelshelf into a niche left of the nose. Climb steeply out of this, hard and exposed. The worst is now over.

Go up vegetated steps left of the gully, then up the easy crest on loose blocks. Climb the next steepening by a tricky groove in the centre, then move right and climb a cleaner groove on the crest, finishing up big spikes. Start the next step on the right, then climb a crampon-scratched groove left of the crest. Finish up the spiky crest, to reach easier loose blocks. Traversing up and right leads into the north-west corrie below the next route.

54 Summit Rib — Grade 3 *

| ◯ NG 975 490 | 🏃 2HRS 30 | ◢ BUTTRESS | ⊤ +100M |

Short but excellent scrambling in good positions. Only a minor detour if you are coming from Sgorr Ruadh.

Approach
This is the middle of the three buttresses just under the summit on its north-west side. It can be reached easily up the north-west corrie, or by traversing northwards from the col between the impressively steep Mainreachan Buttress (NG 972 489) and the main summit. The rib has

an open easy gully to its right and a deep cut narrower one to its left. Start at the lowest point.

The Route
Go up a juggy rib, then a steep quartz slab on small sharp edges. Swing right-to-left up a vertical wall, then follow more juggy steps on the left edge (quite loose). The angle eases off, with a steep flake-crack off to the right giving a hard variation. Higher up a juggy prow leads to a narrow arête, then easy ground goes up to the summit.

Sgorr Ruadh 962m

The highest peak of the Coulin Forest throws down two huge sandstone buttresses into Coire Lair to the north-east. Most of this is very steep, but variants of the two best known rock climbs make good scrambles.

- PAGE 141
- OS LR 25
- NORTH-EAST
- SANDSTONE

55 Academy Ridge, Lower Slabs — Grade 3

| ⌖ NG 970 507 | 🏃 1HR 45 | ⊿ SLABS | ⊤ +100M |

The lower part of this Very Difficult climb is mostly easy slabs, with a couple of short awkward sections. It makes a good prelude to Raeburn's Buttress.

Approach
From Achnashellach start as for Route 51 but stay on the path once out of the forestry and follow it up into Coire Lair. At the crossroads of paths at NG 990 502 continue ahead until beyond the loch. The two buttresses up on the left are Academy Ridge on the left and Raeburn's Buttress on the right. Start at the bottom right-hand corner of the former, right of a vertical wall with slabs above.

The Route
Climb the right-hand arête until forced right below blanker rock. Go back up left as soon as possible to a nose. Keep moving up left until a flake-crack allows access to the arête. Follow the skyline, with plenty of scope for variation, until it eases to walking. The top part of Academy Ridge is a serious Very Difficult, so traverse off right into a shallow corrie (escapes both upwards and downwards). Continuing further right below steep cliffs reaches the next route.

56 Raeburn's Buttress — Grade 3 ✱✱

◇ NG 966 509　　🏃 2HRS　　◿ BUTTRESS　　⊤ +250M

This is the right-hand of Sgorr Ruadh's two buttresses as seen from Coire Lair. Avoiding the hard start to the original summer route provides nicely positioned juggy scrambling, steep and exposed in places, but with good holds and friction. Intimidating and high in the grade.

Approach
From Achnashellach as for the previous route then either approach direct from Coire Lair up the shallow corrie between the two buttresses or traverse right after completing Route 55. On the right-hand side of the shallow corrie is a narrow gully just left of the skyline. Start here.

The Route
The original summer route starts up steep rock right of the gully and is Difficult, so climb the gully until above the chockstone. Bear up right to a stony shelf and follow this right to the skyline. Climb the steep central nose (some loose holds) to a pinnacle. Climb the right-hand of two ribs to a ledge, then make an awkward step up left into a mossy groove. Carry on up this and its right-hand arête. Where this fades go up left to the skyline and continue up this, with the odd problem.

   A short walk then takes you to the sting in the tail. The ridge narrows and bears right. Climb the first tower starting on the left and bearing up right to take the nose direct. Climb a second nose direct, then a third larger nose direct too. This last looks highly unlikely, but good holds make the exposure bearable. Walking leads to the north-east summit.

Beinn Liath Mhòr　　926m

This is a steep-sided east–west ridge with three summits. Most of the rocky flanks are very broken, the only continuous rock being on the south flank of the easternmost summit. Most of these sandstone buttresses have hard sections but a couple are feasible for adventurous scramblers.

⊕ PAGE 141
◁ OS LR 25
✥ SOUTH
⌂ SANDSTONE

57 Lochview Slabs — Grade 2/3 ✱

◇ NG 979 511　　🏃 1HR 40　　◿ SLABS　　⊤ +120M

Unimpressive from a distance but the clean slabby steps of rough sandstone have good holds and lots of choice of route. Makes an enjoyable approach to Apex Buttress.

Approach
From Achnashellach start as for Route 51 but stay on the path once out of the forestry and follow it up into Coire Lair. At the crossroads at NG 990 502 go straight ahead for a little over 1km to the closest point

to Loch Coire Lair. Up right are a succession of left-curving outcrops. Go steeply up right to their bottom right corner.

The Route

Work up leftwards on excellent rock to reach a big easy slab slanting up left along the top of the tier. On the next tier two narrow ramps slant up left. Climb one of two grooves just right of the upper one (right-hand easier), then a steeper wall with a convenient spike. Easier rock leads to another gentle left-slanting slab topping the tier. The third tier can be tackled anywhere to reach another wide ramp below the bigger fourth tier, which has an apron of short slabs below its centre. Start just left of the apron up steeper rock, zigzagging a little to finish just left of a nose. There are minor outcrops above leading towards the col between the central and eastern tops of Beinn Liath Mhòr, or alternatively you can take a deer path rightwards to the foot of the next route.

58 Apex Buttress — Grade 3 or Moderate

◯ NG 982 513   🏃 1HR 55   ◿ BUTTRESS   ⊤ +180M

A longer but more broken route, quite steep in places. The underlying rock is sound and juggy but there are lots of loose rocks lying around on the ledges and the rock isn't as clean as the Lochview Slabs. The last main buttress is excellent, but the rest is nowhere near as good.

Approach

As for the previous route but leave the path 200 metres earlier and go steeply up grass, or (much better) do the previous route and traverse rightwards along the deer path. Either way the buttress is the one just left of a broad grassy ramp running steeply rightwards up the face. It has a vertical wall at its foot with a horizontal pale band at its start.

The Route

Avoid the vertical start by coming in from the right up vegetated steps to a big ledge. Either climb a leaning wall on awkwardly-placed but smile-inducing jugs (Moderate) or avoid it on the left. Easier rock leads to grass. Go up left to a bigger face and work leftwards up this, avoiding the steep top wall on its left by a slabby weakness left then right. Climb a more sustained steep clean wall on big rough holds, with a bit of zigzagging around, then easier rock leads to the top of the main section. Outcrops carry on up ahead, mostly on the left (avoiding the sharp ridge with the huge detached flake seems like a sensible plan). Sadly the outcrops don't continue all the way to the ridge, leaving you with 60m of steep heather and scree to finish.

59 South-East Rib — Grade 3 ✳

◯ NG 987 509   🏃 1HR 25   ◿ BUTTRESS   ⊤ +200M

This rib on the far right-hand edge of the main cliff is short, but has excellent clean rock, providing an enjoyable alternative to the steepest part of the path. The first nose is intimidating, but hidden holds round the left-hand arête make it easier than it looks.

Approach

As for the previous routes but about 400 metres beyond the crossroads head up right to the lowest buttress at the far right-hand end of the cliff. Start on the left-hand side of this at a steep clean nose.

The Route

Climb the left-hand edge of the nose, which is very steep, but with good holds (some hidden round the left arête). Another steepening is climbed right of the arête, then rocky slopes lead up to a scree patch. Climb a steep wall by a square-cut groove right of centre, quite awkward at the top. Easy rock now leads up to grassy slopes, then a few more outcrops can be incorporated before the angle eases. The path at this point is well off to the right.

Sgùrr Dubh 782m

This predominantly quartzite hill dominates the south side of Glen Torridon. Although it is extremely rocky most of the crags are very short, the best being the prominent slabs above the Ling Hut and the gorge that runs through them.

- PAGE 141
- OS LR 25
- NORTH-WEST
- QUARTZITE

60 North-West Slabs — Grade 3

◇ NG 964 553   ⚲ 1HR   ◿ SLABS   ⊤ +200M

These are quite technical in places, but escapable virtually anywhere. The strata slope inwards, giving positive holds, but the fine-grained quartzite is very slippery in the wet.

Approach
Follow the path starting just east of the Coire Dubh car park (NG 958 569) past the Ling Hut up to around 200m, then slant up left to the prominent slabs. The lower left-hand tier has two slabby areas separated by a zone of small overhangs. Start below the right-hand slabby area at a separate slab about 30m lower, right of a scree patch. This is the lowest slab on the face.

The Route
Climb the slab, then a higher slab guarded by a small overlap. Go up left and climb a larger but more broken tier, then two more small slabs to reach the main cliff. Climb shattered slabs below and left of a large cracked pillar. Continue up smoother slabs by the delicate central crack to reach easy ground.

Ahead is a gorge, with cleaner steeper slabs up to the right. Cross the stream and go up to the left end of these, just left of the first vertical section. Gain a niche and exit up steep flakes on the right wall, then bear left up a slabby rib. More slabs lead past a sandstone boulder to the top.

Higher up there are sandstone slabs at NG 971 550, above two small lochans, then several more outcrops of both sandstone and quartzite can be found between here and the summit.

61 Sgùrr Dubh Gorge Grade 3

◯ NG 964 551   🏃 1HR   ⊿ STREAM   ⊤ +200M

A deep gorge with a definite crux, only escapable at mid-height. Contains a stream but this is mostly avoided.

Approach
As for North-West Slabs but start at the gorge right of the lower slabs.

The Route
The lower gorge is boulder hopping at first, then when it turns left things improve. Pass a small fall on the left to reach a longer cascade. Start on the left and work up leftwards to climb the crest of a rib. Straddle the next small gorge then go left of a pool to another fall. A metre or so up this escape left up a steep rib (or avoid the fall altogether by a narrow loose arête on the right). Pass the next fall on the right, delicate at first, to a levelling, then several small falls lead to the top of the lower tier.

Enter the large gorge ahead, often dry at first, then clamber up blocks, finishing with a steep groove on the left to arrive at the main fall. Cross the pool below this and climb a steep juggy wall on the right (crux) to reach a grassy rake leading steeply up rightwards. Go up the rake until it is possible to traverse left on exposed heather to easy ground (an easier alternative is to go higher up and slant back in above). Above are three small falls climbed strenuously on the left, then the gorge eases. A steep tower on the left makes a fine optional finish, vertical but on big holds.

Other scrambling possibilities on Sgùrr Dubh are the sandstone ribs below the minor summit at NG 976 559 (quite hard), the pleasant south-east facing sandstone slabs above Coire an Leth-uillt and the more serious quartzite slabs on the north-west face around NG 972 564.

The crux of Sgùrr Dubh Gorge,
(Route 61, Grade 3).
Scramblers: Paul Mather (above),
and Steve McCallum (below).
© Scott Muir

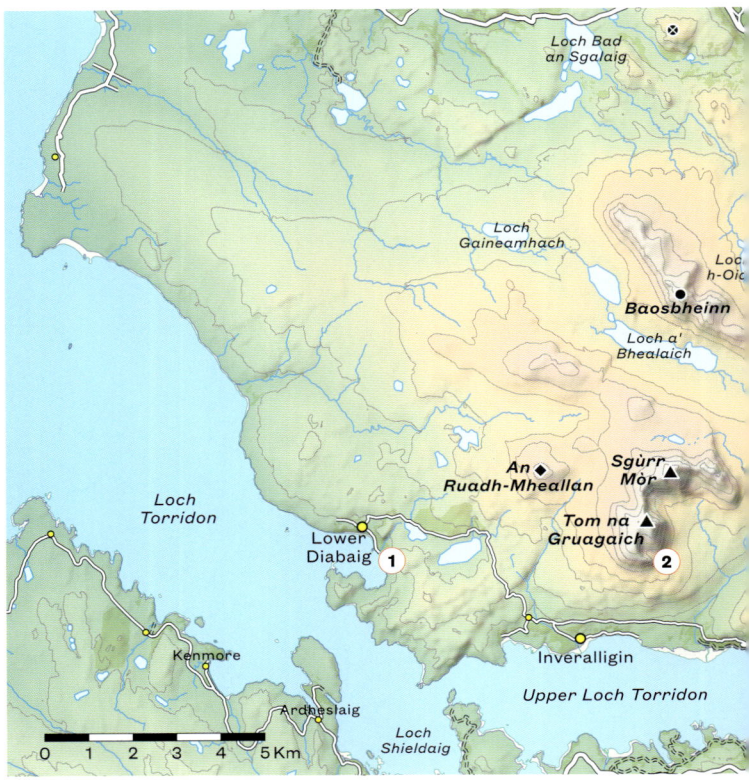

A superlative area, with huge amounts of scrambling in a stunning setting. The ridges of Beinn Alligin, Liathach and Beinn Eighe are popular classics, but there are also routes on the more obscure peaks and many good alternative ways up onto the main ridges.

The peaks are largely of Torridonian sandstone capped by quartzite, with the boundary between the two descending eastwards so that the east end of Beinn Eighe is purely quartzite and Beinn Alligin purely sandstone. The sandstone tends to produce steep tiers and blocky pinnacled ridges, while the quartzite often comes in huge sweeps of slabs. At lower levels Meall Ceann na Creige at Diabaig has a lot of excellent scrambling suitable for an evening's exploration, as well as being a well-known climbing ground.

Torridon

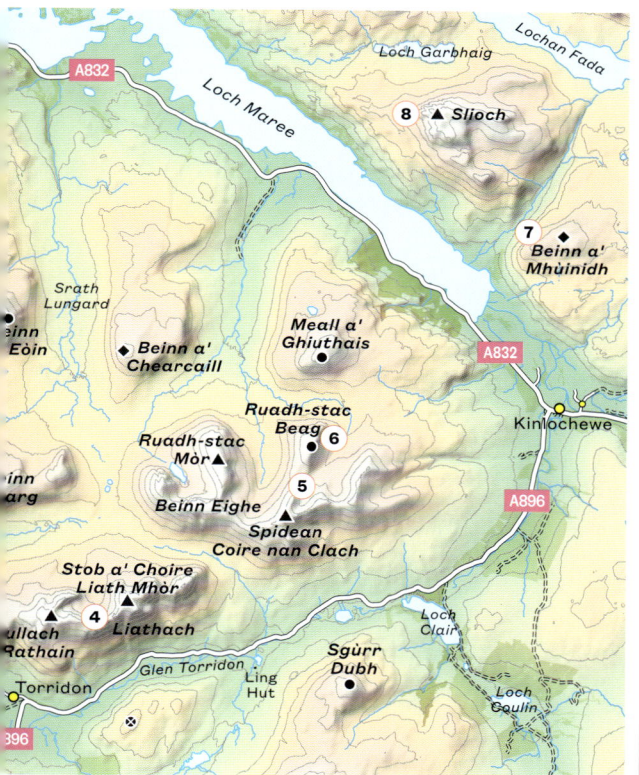

1.	Meall Ceann na Creige	Route 62 P.172
2.	Beinn Alligin	Routes 63–65 P.175
3.	Beinn Dearg	Routes 66–67 P.178
4.	Liathach	Routes 68–74 P.180
5.	Beinn Eighe	Routes 75–81 P.190
6.	Ruadh-stac Beag	Routes 82–83 P.197
7.	Beinn a' Mhùinidh	Route 84 P.199
8.	Slioch	Route 85 P.201

Meall Ceann na Creige — 270m

The hills behind Diabaig may be small, but they are very rocky, with a superb outlook. Better known for its rock climbs, this area also offers excellent scrambling, with the described route just one among many possibilities. Diabaig is often sheltered from the worst weather and much sunnier than the nearby hills.

- PAGE 170
- OS LR 24
- WEST
- GNEISS

---

62 West Spur — Grade 3 ✶✶

| ○ NG 799 596 | 🏃 5MINS | ◿ BUTTRESS | ⊤ +270M |

Sea to summit on slabby gneiss outcrops with very little walking in between. Intimidating in places, but with lots of possible escapes.

Approach
From the road end at Diabaig pier follow the shoreline along until stopped by a steep spur with slabs to its left. At high tide you need to cross the bridge at the road end and follow the path up into the wood. Keep on this up and right until just after it flattens out, at which point

you cross the route. This misses out some good scrambling so it might be preferable to wait at the beach until the tide goes out and savour the superb setting, after all this is the land where mañana is much too frantic a concept!

The Route
Go up the easy-angled but delicate slabs, then right up steps to a small rowan. Climb the blocky rib above this to a wide terrace. Up left is a steep rib, gained by a right-to-left weakness, steep but on good holds. Climb blocks above, then go left through trees and up a small slab to a heathery niche on the next rib. Go up steeply to more heather, then easy slabs lead up left to a terrace and the path (high tide access).

A steep wall lies ahead, avoided by a vegetated right-slanting groove a few metres left. Continue up right, then climb a short steep crack and easy slabs to another large terrace. The spur above is too steep, so avoid it by a greasy rib in the gully on the right. Go up left onto the slabs above the steep section. Climb these, breaking through the intimidating bulge above by a weakness on its right (crux, but much easier than it looks). More slabs lead to another bulge. This is Difficult, so avoid it by climbing slabs about 10 metres right. Follow a ledge round onto the front of the buttress and go up this to an easing. Slabs lead to the top of the cliff, with more slabs and problems on the short distance to the summit.

Approaching the crux of West Spur, Meall Ceann na Creige (Route 62, Grade 3).
Scrambler: Nicky Gear. © Iain Thow

Beinn Alligin 986m

This distinctive mountain gives a classic traverse, with easy but exposed scrambling over the Horns, easier and much less sustained than the traverses of Liathach or An Teallach. The circuit is much better going anticlockwise, as you are then taking most of the scrambling in ascent rather than descent. The flanks contain a lot of rock, but the tiered nature of the sandstone produces few scrambles.

- PAGE 170
- OS LR 24
- VARIOUS
- SANDSTONE

63 Na Fasreidhnean, Tom na Gruagaich — Grade 1

| NG 862 591 | 1HR 10 | BUTTRESS | +300M |

The south rim of Coire nan Laogh makes an enjoyable alternative to the path. Much easier than it looks. Frequently descended but this usually involves missing the best bits.

Approach
From the car park at the foot of Coire MhicNobaill (NG 869 577) take the path on the west side of the stream leading directly up towards Beinn Alligin. Follow this to the foot of Coire nan Laogh.

The Route
Go up left to the skyline, where a minor path leads up short bouldery steps. At a steeper prow climb a slab to its right, then a steep groove and a short wall. The path avoids the first two on the right and the third on the left. Easy scrambling along the line of the path now leads to a grassy ridge.

64 Horns of Alligin — Grade 1/2 **

| NG 876 612 | 2HRS | ARÊTE | +200M |

The climax of the traverse, a jagged ridge with some easy scrambling over its three summits, mostly on an obvious path. A couple of brief sections border on Grade 2.

Approach
From the car park at the foot of Coire MhicNobaill (NG 869 577) follow the path up the east bank of the stream. Fork left just after crossing the stream to head up towards the Bealach a' Chomhla. Soon after crossing the Allt a' Bhealaich a steep path (with some easy scrambling) branches up leftwards onto a shoulder, then up to the Horns.

The Route
Go up a few short rock steps to the first Horn, then zigzag down grooves left of the crest (briefly exposed). The second Horn can be taken either direct or via an easier zigzag on the left (awkward move to get onto a

boulder). The third Horn is tackled direct by a steep chimney. At the cairn bear left and descend steeply on a well-used path. The mossier lower part of the ridge is usually avoided on the left, but can be easily included at the price of a few awkward steps at the far end. A few minor bits of scrambling can also be found on the ascents to Sgùrr Mhòr and Tom na Gruagaich.

65 Backfire Ridge  Grade 2

| ⌖ NG 875 617 | 🚶 2HRS 20 | ◿ OUTCROPS | ⬍ +250M |

A good line with a wild and remote feel. Sustained at Grade 1 with the odd harder move and some airy positions. Greasy in the wet, with some loose rock.

Approach
As for Route 64 to the Allt a' Bhealaich, then carry on along the lower path to reach the Bealach a' Chomhla. At the lochans just beyond the pass head up left to reach a rocky shelf just east of Loch Toll nam Biast. From here the ridge leading up to the highest of the Horns is obvious, but the way onto it isn't.

The Route

Pass the first low rock tier to reach flat slabs and go up to a larger vertical tier. Follow a shelf left below this until above the Bealach a' Chomhla, where the angle of the face above eases. Climb the first section by steep steps, the next by slabs, and a third hidden section by a right-to-left ramp at its left-hand end. The angle now eases below the ridge proper.

Scramble up steep piles of blocks right of the grassy runnel running up the centre of the ridge. As the ridge narrows the runnel itself is used in a couple of places. The ridge levels out and small easy towers and one steeper one lead to a grassy shelf below a long tier. This can be climbed on the right on steep jugs, but the finish is very loose and better avoided. The next tier is taken direct, then a jutting nose gained from the right provides a good finish, arriving by the summit cairn on the third Horn.

The slabs below Backfire Ridge (Route 65, Grade 2). Scrambler: Nicky Gear.
© Iain Thow

Beinn Dearg 914m

Often neglected in favour of its larger neighbours, Beinn Dearg overlooks some tremendous wild country. As well as the two routes described, the north-west ridge of Stùc Loch na Cabhaig has a few easy steps on a nice airy ridge, while the obvious step in the main ridge consists of two steep blocks passed by central cracks, then a narrow bouldery arête (Grade 1).

- PAGES 170-171
- HARV. TORRIDON, OS LR 19 & 24
- VARIOUS
- SANDSTONE

66 **South-West Face**			Grade 3
◯ NG 889 607	🚶 1HR 30	⟋ OUTCROPS	⊺ +250M

A succession of boulder problems adding interest to a steep ascent, all avoidable. The main frontal face is similar, but with steeper and often wetter faces.

Approach
As for Route 64 to the Allt a' Bhealaich, then stay on the east side of the stream and slant up to the foot of the face. Start on the left-hand edge of the third gully left of the main frontal face.

The Route
Work up left, including outcrops as desired until the buttress gets more defined. Here a steep band crosses it, with a choice of cracks and arêtes on perfect rock. Another steep step then leads to a third with a pinnacle. Climb this and step off the top. There are several more steps before the buttress peters out into grassy slopes leading up to the summit ridge. The main summit is up right, but Stùc Loch na Cabhaig to the left is worth the detour on a clear day for the tremendous view.

---

67 North Ridge, Càrn na Feola — Difficult ✶

◯ NG 917 617   🚶 2HRS 30   ⟋ BUTTRESS   ⊤ +350M

Steep tiers of sandstone in a remote setting with a sting in the tail. A serious route, although the hard bits are short.

Approach
From the Coire Dubh car park (NG 958 569) follow the path up between Liathach and Beinn Eighe, forking right onto the path to Coire Mhic Fhearchair. Where this turns east go down north-westwards and cross rough ground past Loch nan Cabar to the vertical foot of the North Ridge. The route can be reached up broken ground to the left of this, but better is to follow the foot of the cliff up rightwards until above the first two tiers. A narrow grass ledge then leads left below another vertical tier.

The Route
Keep going left until the tier above shrinks to only 5m or so, then climb any of several weaknesses. Work back rightwards up grass and short steps to a band of steep clean slabs directly above the nearest point of Lochan Càrn na Feola. Zigzag up these near the right-hand end. More small outcrops lead to a larger greasy tier. Start below an overhang (hard) and move up left (or avoid the tier further right). Above is a smooth curving scoop, climbed by a right-slanting weakness. Carry on up, passing right of a greasy tower, then moving left up blocks.

The ridge narrows below a steeper tier, climbed on the arête by steep blocks. The top move is scary, but there is a useful hidden jug round to the right (this tier can be avoided by going a long way left). The next tier is climbed by a niche with a hard start and a wide bridge to finish. Blocks left of a prow then lead to a large terrace. The vertical cliff beyond this is climbed on its left arête by a wide crack. This is quite strenuous, but with good sharp holds in the crack. It can be avoided by going a long way left. Easier rocks now lead to the top of Càrn na Feola.

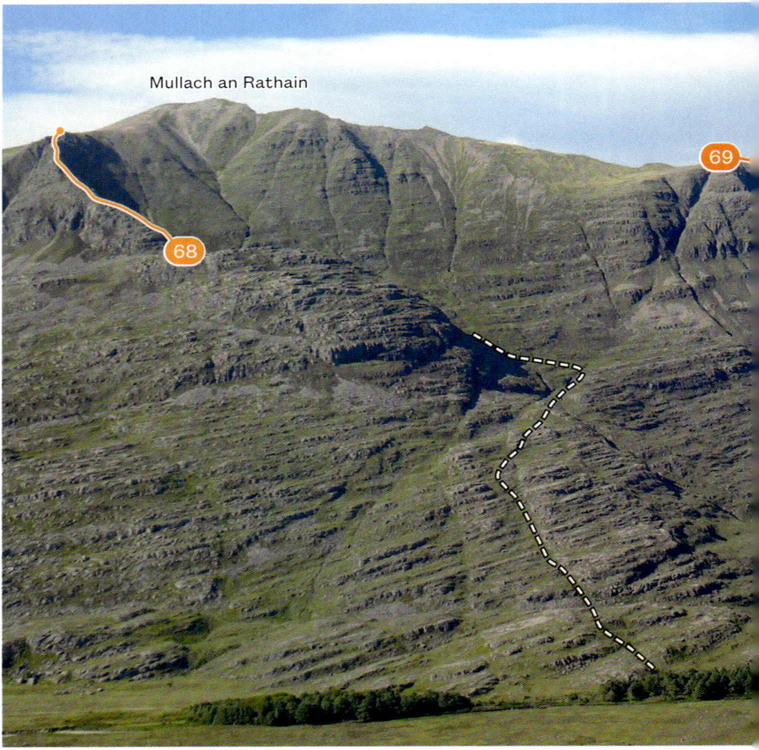

Liathach 1027m

A contender for the grandest hill in Scotland, the summit ridge is a classic scramble, exposed but not hard, while its steep sandstone flanks contain numerous other possibilities.

- 🌐 PAGE 171
- ⊲ OS LR 25
- ⇔ VARIOUS
- ⌂ SANDSTONE

South Ridge, Mullach an Rathain		Grade 2 **
○ NG 911 569	🚶 1HR 30	⊿ ARÊTE ⊤ +200M

A well-positioned scramble leading to Liathach's western summit, making a good prelude to the main traverse.

Approach
From the road at NG 914 554 (limited parking) follow the path up the west side of the Allt an Tuill Bhain (past brilliant bouldering) into the hollow of Toll Ban, then bear left to a shoulder. The rock tier below the shoulder offers some scrappy Grade 2 scrambling following vegetated ribs, steep at first, then easy.

The Route
At the first rock band go up a gully a few metres left of a detached block (several harder alternatives). Easy steps lead to a grassy groove in the middle of the ridge. The rocks on either side are more fun, first right, then left. Go up right to climb steeper rocks, with the path giving easy options, then zigzag up to cross an exposed narrow arête (path on the right). Pass an overhanging pinnacle by a groove on the left to reach a level ridge, then go up boulders to a leaning tower. Climb the steep slab immediately left of this (crux, reachy) to arrive at easy ground with surprising suddenness. This last section is easily avoided on the right.

South Ridge, Mullach an Rathain (Route 68, Grade 2).
Scrambler : Noel Williams. © Iain Thow

69 Am Fasarinen Traverse — Grade 2 ✶✶✶

○ NG 925 575   🏃 2HRS 40   ⟋ ARÊTE   ⊤ +200M & -200M

This lovely pinnacled ridge links Liathach's two Munros, giving airy positions without too much difficulty. The sandstone is clean and not too badly affected when wet, but strong winds make the traverse a bad idea. Most of the rock is solid but the shattered gully just west of the lowest col on the main ridge is notorious for people knocking bits of it onto those below – take care and if you can avoid climbing above or below others then do so. A path along ledges on the south side misses all the fun (but is still very exposed). The ridge is usually done east to west, but west to east gives better scrambling. Both ways are described.

West to East
From Mullach an Rathain go down to where the ridge narrows, then over a minor bump. From the col beyond (the traversing path goes off right here) go up easy steps, then climb two towers direct (or dodge them on the right). Cross the Munro Top summit of Am Fasarinen, descend steeply and pass right of a flat-topped tower. A steep ascent leads to two level sections, then the ridge bends left and right. Descend a steep shattered gully on the right, then go left and rejoin the ridge. Drop to a col, the lowest, and traverse to another col. Climb the next large tower on the left at first, then direct, steep at the top but easily avoided by a path on the right. Keep on the ridge across another notch and summit, then over blocks to drop to a col. The final two towers can be climbed direct or avoided on the right. An exposed knife-edged descent from

Am Fasarinen Traverse (Route 69, Grade 2).
Scrambler: Kaeryn McDowell. © Al Halewood

them leads to easy ground. A path slants up right of the ridge (or follow the spine) to reach the steep bouldery ascent to Spidean a' Choire Leith.

East to West

From the start of the sandstone after the descent from the main summit a good path slants down to the first pinnacle. Either dodge the first two pinnacles by a path on the left, or go over them direct (exposed start and steep descents). From the notch beyond go over a blocky top, pass left of the next summit, then descend to another notch. Follow the ridge over the next top, descending to join a good path on the left. Carry on down to a col and traverse to another col, the lowest. Go up broken ground on the ridge before traversing left to climb a shattered gully. Stay on the crest over two level sections, down to a notch, then over a flat-topped tower and up steeply to reach the Munro Top summit of Am Fasarinen. The final section has two steep descents on the crest, both easily avoided on the left. The traversing path comes in here. Cross a minor bump to reach easy ground, where a good path leads up to Mullach an Rathain.

70 East Buttress, Am Fasarinen — Difficult ✱

○ NG 926 574   🏃 2HRS 20   ⊿ BUTTRESS   ⊤ +150M

A serious and quite technical route with a spectacular finish. The top 50m (by far the best bit) is easily added to a traverse of the main ridge.

Approach
Either traverse westwards from the usual ascent path up Liathach, or descend steeply from the main ridge. For the former route follow the well-used path up the Allt an Doire Ghairbh from the layby at NG 936 566 into Toll a' Meitheach. Where the path goes up right below the top tier of cliffs leave it and traverse left below the upper cliffs. Go up a short groove about 10 metres left of the waterfall coming out of Coire Liath Mor (cairn at the top). Slant up left to the skyline then traverse left below the steeper rock of Pyramid Buttress to the open corrie south-west of the summit.

Descend slightly to a stream junction, then continue left on a broad sloping terrace to reach the top one of two prominent scree patches (smaller patch just beyond). If the ledge you are on becomes narrow, go back and take a lower one – the correct ledge is wide, with a well-used deer path, other ledges are dead ends. Start 45 degrees up right from the highest point of the upper scree patch, at the foot of the first rock band that completely crosses the buttress.

This same point can be reached by descending steeply from the col at the east end of the Fasarinen Pinnacles to reach the stream junction referred to above at about 750m.

To do just the top part of the route descend 30m from the lowest col on the Fasarinen ridge, then take a wide but steeply sloping grass ledge eastwards. Slant up on the upper branch of this to arrive at the skyline below the steep final tier of the route.

The Route
Climb a corner with an overhanging right wall until forced left to a grassy groove. Exit right to grass, then climb serious vegetated ground to the top of the tier. On the next tier climb a steep groove with a prominent crack in its left wall, swing right onto a nose and go up to the top. More small tiers follow, one with a neat little face climbed by a thin Y-crack (Very Difficult but easily avoided). Climb the next big tier by a groove on the left, a hard start leading to good open scrambling up a ridge. On the next tier climb a square-cut groove on the left, exiting right to a shelf, then go up to the large top tier.

The top tier is serious and committing but can be avoided by the large open gully on the left. Go up left on scrappy ground to a narrow grass ledge at one-third height. Step right to climb the right-hand of two mossy grooves to blocks and a small ledge. Finish up a prominent steep corner on big holds, a strenuous grand finale. Equally good is to move further right to a platform on the arête and finish airily up this.

The final tier of East Buttress, Am Fasarinen (Route 70, Difficult).
Climber: Iain Thow. © Noel Williams

71   East Ridge, Stùc a' Choire Dhuibh Bhig   Grade 1 or 2

◯ NG 945 585   🏃 2HRS   ◿ OUTCROPS   ⊤ +50M

Only minor scrambling, but a good line up the hill.

Approach
From the Coire Dubh car park (NG 958 569) follow the path northwards up to about 330m. Go left up walking-angle slabs, then steeper boulders to heather. Traverse right to reach the ridge above the first tier of steep dank rock. Carry on up the ridge to a short scramble near the top.

The Route
Climb the first tier by a steep chimney left of the arête then the second by a tower of blocks, both Grade 2. Easier options exist nearby. Quartzite boulders lead to the summit of Stùc a' Choire Dhuibh Bhig.

72   North Ridge, Spidean a' Choire Leith   Grade 1/2

◯ NG 927 583   🏃 2HRS 15   ◿ OUTCROPS   ⊤ +300M

A slog to reach, but a nice airy upper ridge.

Approach
From the Coire Dubh car park (NG 958 569) follow the path up between Liathach and Beinn Eighe, forking left at NG 934 594. Just beyond the first loch head south-west, slanting rightwards up very rough ground to reach the broad foot of the ridge between Coire na Caime and Coire Dubh Mòr.

The Route
There are a few problems near the bottom, then a long steep grass slope (traces of path) leads to two steeper tiers. Climb a central blocky rib on the first, with a similar rib above. Climb the second by steep blocks just left of a flying buttress. The ridge now eases, with all difficulties avoidable on the right. Following the true arête gives three steep prows and some enjoyable easy ridge, all with huge drops on the left.

73   PC Buttress   Difficult *

◯ NG 921 577   🏃 2HRS 40   ◿ BUTTRESS   ⊤ +250M

A good line and good rock, although with the odd loose block. Steep and serious, with a hard crux and some exposure. Probably the hardest route in this guide.

Approach
From the lochan in Coire na Caime, usually approached as for Route 72, PC Buttress is directly above, dividing the upper corrie in two. Go up right to a rock terrace below the preliminary tiers in front of the buttress.

Access from upper corrie

The Route
Climb a slabby rib in the centre of the lowest tier, then a groove in the nose above. Climb the next tier by steep steps right of the central weakness. The angle now eases and broken rock leads to the start of the main buttress.

Climb a weakness just left of the tallest section of the tier, then walk left up steps and grooves to a grassy terrace. The next section is the crux, and is hard for the grade, but can be avoided by unpleasant vegetated ground further left. Climb a delicate slab right of overhangs to the next terrace. You are now committed! Follow grooves up left then take a ledge horizontally right to a prominent huge block. Bridge up behind the block then work up left to the skyline, where the route eases.

Continue up the crest to a terrace, then go up a slabby nose right of a mossy groove and up to a level section of ridge. A large flake blocks the way, climbed airily on its crest. Another slabby tier now leads to easy ground and a subsidiary top. Easy steps link this with the main ridge.

 Northern Pinnacles Moderate ✶✶

◯ NG 918 581   🚶 2HRS 40   ⟋ ARÊTE   ⊤ +350M

A serious and exposed route, especially by the direct version. The hardest part of the pinnacles themselves can be avoided, making a Grade 3 version if the approach from upper Coire na Caime is used.

On the ridge below Meall Dearg, Northern Pinnacles (Route 74, Moderate).
Climber: Iain Thow. © Noel Williams

Approach

The usual way in is to take the good path up Coire Dubh from the car park at NG 958 569, forking left at NG 934 594. Just beyond the first loch head south-west, slanting rightwards up rough ground into the mouth of Coire na Caime. Right-slanting ramps help but try to avoid going too high. Once in the corrie go in to reach the lochan, with the route up right.

If just doing the pinnacles on their own they can be reached by descending a rough gully two cols east of Mullach an Rathain into the top of Coire na Caime at around 800m, then ascending broken ground to the col between Meall Dearg and the Pinnacles themselves. The Munro Top of Meall Dearg is easily reached from here, useful for non-scrambling baggers. This approach is marginally quicker than the Coire Dubh one even if doing the whole route but in that case it adds over 300m of ascent onto an already sizeable total.

Another alternative start uses a ramp system on the north flank of Meall Dearg, which is good in winter but in summer is steep grass (usually wet) in a serious situation.

The Route

For the longer start from the lochan in Coire na Caime avoid the first cliff on the left to reach the second steep tier. Climb a small preliminary tier, then take a left-slanting weakness close under the steep face. This is harder than it looks and quite exposed at the top (detours left help in places). Reach a large grass shelf, go up right and climb a short steep groove. Big but greasy steps now lead up left. At the top of these go up right to the ridge. Follow this up better rock with short problems until it eases. Cross a minor summit and at the col beyond dodge the pinnacles on the right. Go up to an easing then follow the arête over the summit of Meall Dearg.

At the next col the easy approach from upper Coire na Caime comes in from the left. Take the first easy pinnacle direct, then the second by a slab and steps on the right, finishing up a gully. The third and longest pinnacle is taken direct, sometimes using a groove to the left, finishing up a greasy chimney on the right. The fourth pinnacle is started direct, then for the Grade 3 version go right along ledges to finish up a short chimney. For the direct finish go up left to an exposed move onto a slab (hard if damp). Above this there is another airy pull up before the ridge eases. The summit of Mullach an Rathain is just beyond.

Beinn Eighe   1010m

A complete range in itself rather than a single peak, Beinn Eighe has three wild northern corries which provide climbs and scrambles with a 'big mountain' feel. The complete traverse of the mountain is a classic day out which includes a couple of sections of easy scrambling, while side spurs provide possible harder starts.

 PAGE 171

 HARV. TORRIDON

 VARIOUS

 SANDSTONE & QUARTZITE

75. Lawson, Ling & Glover's Route — Grade 2 *

NG 938 609 | 2HRS 45 | BUTTRESS | +250M

A slog to start, but an enjoyable clamber up a blocky ridge higher up. Technically easy for the grade but sustained and committing (there are no easy escapes at any point). The pinnacle looks ridiculously intimidating from the lower part of the route but turns out to be much easier than it appears. The crux is on clean sandstone and doesn't get much harder if wet, but the mossier rock lower down does.

Approach
From Coire Dubh car park (NG 958 569) take the path up between Liathach and Beinn Eighe. Fork right to go round into Coire Mhic Fhearchair. At the loch go steeply right up scree to the mouth of a large gully.

The Route
Go up easy rock steps just right of the gully, then slog up steep grass, heading for a blocky rib centrally placed on the slope to the right. Go up this, then continue in the same line to reach the ridge just above a small blunt pinnacle. Follow the bouldery ridge until it narrows, then climb a stepped-groove in the arête (the only unavoidable Grade 2 section on the route). This brings you out onto the pinnacle, really more of a shelf. From the col behind climb either a series of problems on the left or easier broken ground to the right. Climb a steeper tower to a flattening,

then more rounded towers before the ridge slackens off into boulders leading up to Sail Mhor. Nearly everyone will continue along the ridge to the next route, although escapes are possible (unpleasantly) from the col between them.

76 Ceum Grannda — Grade 2 *

◇ NG 941 601   🯅 3HRS 30   ◿ BUTTRESS   ⊤ +50M

Short and sweet – an airily positioned ridge scramble. The hardest part is avoidable.

Approach
On the ridge between Coinneach Mhòr and Sail Mhòr, often descended from the former as part of a traverse of the main ridge, but easily reached over Sail Mhòr by the scramble described above.

The Route
A preliminary clamber over quartzite blocks and through a cleft pinnacle leads to a small col. Climb any of three steep corners, then continue up an open slab (gained more easily from the right). Finish up a bouldery ridge. In descent the lower corners can be awkward so it is arguably better to cut left from the foot of the bouldery ridge and descend the open gully (loose but easy). Obviously this can also be ascended but it isn't much fun.

77 East Buttress, Coire Mhic Fhearchair   Difficult ✶✶✶

◯ NG 946 603   ⚲ 3HRS 10   ◿ BUTTRESS   ⊤ +200M

A superb line in a magnificent situation. Steep, exposed, intimidating and serious, but covered in positive holds. Perhaps the best route of its grade in Scotland.

Approach
As for Route 75 to Coire Mhic Fhearchair. The route is the left-hand of the Triple Buttresses that dominate the corrie. The lower sandstone section is steep, wet and best avoided. Traverse in from the left along Broad Terrace, at the base of the quartzite tier. Some easy scrambling can be found on the way up to the left end of the terrace and there is one scary step halfway along. Start 10 metres left of where Broad Terrace reaches East Central Gully.

The Route
Climb a steep open groove on big square-cut holds, then move right and go up a crack in the gully wall. Return to the crest and go up easily to a terrace. Climb the crest to another shelf, then go up left into a steep shattered area and out onto the front of the buttress. Climb this (easiest right of centre). It is steep and exposed, but still on good holds. Alternatively there is a less airy but very steep corner round to the right. The angle now eases off and short steps lead up to the plateau.

Pitch 2, East Buttress, Coire Mhic Fhearchair (Route 77, Difficult).
Climber: Andrew Thorley. © Vicky Hunter

There are a couple of minor scrambles nearby, neither anything special but both in dramatic situations. The sandstone rib just right of the start of Fuselage Gully (the gully just right of the West Buttress) is fun at Grade 2, but sadly then deposits you on an escalator of quartzite scree. More esoterically, go up north-east from the mouth of Coire Mhic Fhearchair to reach a shelf going round onto the north flank of Ruadh-stac Mòr. Use deer tracks to slant up this to the broken sandstone crags at NG 949 619. Wind a way up leftwards through these using short ribs and bits of gully, Grade 2, quite loose and vegetated in places but with superb views. At the top quartzite boulders lead up to short outcrops and the summit plateau. This has the benefit of avoiding the notorious scree couloir on the usual ascent, but is quite serious.

78 — East Ridge, Stùc Coire an Laoigh — Grade 1

◯ NG 970 592   🏃 1HR 40   ◿ ARÊTE   ⊤ +100M

Although the scrambling doesn't amount to much, this sandstone ridge provides an enjoyable alternative to the eroded path slogging up the headwall of Coire an Laoigh.

Approach
Follow the path up from the small wood at NG 977 578 to the 650m contour. Bear up left to reach the ridge.

The Route
The ridge is broad at first, with boulders and walking-angle slabs. Halfway up it narrows, and here a steeper slab is climbed centrally by a short groove. An exposed step down just right of the arête then leads to broken ground and mossy slabs. Follow these airily along the narrow ridge to the pointed summit of Stùc Coire an Laoigh. Continue round the ridge to rejoin the path at the col.

79 — North Ridge, Spidean Coire nan Clach — Grade 2 ✶

◯ NG 970 603   🏃 3HRS   ◿ SLABS   ⊤ +250M

Easy-angled quartzite slabs with overlaps in a great wild setting. Much of this could be walked up by the confident, but it is quite smooth in places and the overlaps add exposure. The described line is just one among many choices, and all difficulties are avoidable.

Approach
The ridge rises above Lochan Uaine (unnamed on the 1:50,000 map) on the saddle south of Ruadh-stac Beag (NG 968 605). This is best reached from Kinlochewe, either over Ruadh-stac Beag or up the corrie between it and the east end of Beinn Eighe using the Old Pony Track starting at NH 022 628 (more parking at the visitor centre 300 metres north). From Lochan Uaine go leftwards below steep cliffs to reach broken slabs and scree right of the stream descending from the upper corrie between Spidean Coire nan Clach and Sgùrr Ban.

The Route
Link together minor slabs until the rock becomes more continuous. Keep to the main rib-line until it reaches overlaps coming in from the left. Climb a delicate slab right of a right-facing corner, then bear right to a smooth slab below a larger overlap. Traverse right across the bottom of this and climb its right-hand edge, then the narrower inset slab above. Go up left of a cairn and through shattered overlaps. Head for a short steep band on the skyline and go through a notch in it, then easy slabs lead up the ridge, with a pleasantly narrow arête leading to the summit.

80 Toll Bàn Headwall — Grade 2

 NG 978 600	 2HRS 45	SLABS	+70M

A scenic approach into one of the area's wildest corries leads to a short but sound scramble up quartzite slabs. Inward-dipping strata give sharp positive holds.

Approach
From the parking place just off the road at NH 022 628 (more parking at the visitor centre 300 metres north) the Old Pony Path leads up to the saddle between Meall a' Ghiubhais and the main Beinn Eighe group. Head up southwards and follow the stream up to Loch an Tuill Bhain at NG 978 603 (unnamed on the 1:50,000 map). Go up broken rock and scree to the lowest point of the slabs below the col between Sgùrr Bàn and Sgùrr nan Fhir Duibhe.

The Route
Climb two corners and a blunt rib to a grassy niche. From the top of the niche go straight up to reach a bigger steeper nose. Climb a smaller nose to its right. Either finish easily above or go 10 metres right to nice slabs finishing just below the col.

81	**The Black Carls (Bodaich Dubh)**		Grade 1 *	
◯ NG 983 603	🚶 2HRS 30	⊿ ARÊTE		⊤ +50M

An airy clamber along a narrow shattered arête, quite loose but great positions and setting.

Approach
Usually reached by the path from Cromasaig (NH 025 610). Follow this up to the fork in the Allt a' Chuirn then go straight up the ridge ahead to the summit of Creag Dhubh. Follow the ridge south-west to reach the pinnacles.

The Route
Either climb the first tower steeply, or pass it on the right. Weave in and out of smaller pinnacles and down to the next col. Go up a corner, then follow an easy narrow ridge. At the next notch either climb steeply just left of the arête or take an easy path on the left. At the final notch either climb direct or use a broken path on the left before regaining the crest by a short gully.

Ruadh-stac Beag 896m

Hidden away behind Beinn Eighe, Ruadh-stac Beag is quite an independent summit – steep and rocky all round. Most of it is very shattered, but the clean quartzite slabs at the north-east corner give a couple of excellent scrambles.

 PAGE 171
 OS LR 19
 EAST
 QUARTZITE

Access avoiding hard start

82	**Long Stroll Slab**	Grade 3 ✶✶✶
◯ NG 977 617	🚶 2HRS 10	◿ SLABS ⊺ +100M

Sustained, committing and intimidating but not at all hard. More direct versions are feasible but they are around Very Difficult.

Approach
As for Route 80 to the saddle between Meall a' Ghiubhais and the main Beinn Eighe group. Head up south-west and cross the Allt Toll a' Ghiubhais. The 100m triangular slab is obvious, at the north-east foot of the mountain. Start centrally, at the lowest point.

Long Stroll Slab, Ruadh-stac Beag (Route 82, Grade 3).
Scrambler: Noel Williams. © Iain Thow

The Route

Go up to a right-facing corner and follow this and its left-hand arête. Below and left of the main overlap is a smaller shattered overlap stretching leftwards. Traverse left below this until it eases, then go back up right into the centre of the slab above the overlaps. Now go up direct, keeping right of the blanker part of the slab, delicate in places. When the slab ends at a scree shoulder go left up juggy ribs to broken ground. A few more minor outcrops can be found on the way to the summit. The strange metal cage close to the summit is to protect a rare moss.

83 Overlooking Rib — Moderate or Grade 2 ✷

◇ NG 977 616   🏃 2HRS 10   ⊿ SLABS   ⊤ +100M

This is the rib overlooking the left-hand edge of Long Stroll Slab. The start is steep and sustained, but can be avoided by a diversion left, returning across loose scree. The top half is nice and airy. There are some awkward moves and some exposure, but not together.

Approach
As for the previous route. Start at the bottom of the rib bounding the slab on its left.

The Route
Climb the rib just right of the crest to reach a grassy ledge. Go up left from this to gain the crest (crux). Follow the crest up over another steepening, easier than it looks, to reach ledges leading up right to the edge overlooking Long Stroll Slab.

An easier start (Grade 2) is to begin at the left-hand end of a scree shelf below the rib and go up broken slabs, heading up leftwards below steeper slabs until you meet the screes on the left. Climb a short tier to scree above the first level of cliffs. Traverse right across this (horrible) to reach the edge overlooking Long Stroll Slab.

Climb the airy rib above. Gradually the angle eases before a final flourish up a blocky nose of knobbly Pipe Rock. Minor outcrops can be found above on the way to the summit

Beinn a' Mhùinidh — 692m

Although the summit of the hill is anonymous moorland, the line of cliffs wrapped around the north-west and south-west flanks provides plenty of character, culminating in the steep clean face of the Bonnaidh Donn.

🌐 PAGE 171
⟁ OS LR 19
✥ WEST
⛰ QUARTZITE

84 Bonnaidh Donn, Route One Difficult **

◇ NH 022 655   🚶 1HR 45   ◿ BUTTRESS   ⊤ +120M

Steep clean quartzite ribs, exposed in places, but with good positive holds.

Approach
From the car park at Incheril (NH 038 624) follow the track north-west for 3km as far as the stream descending from the large waterfall. Head up steeply to reach the main rock band at a beak of rock seen on the skyline as you approach (this is not the beak of rock mentioned in the *Northern Highlands* climbing guide). A goat track leads left below the cliff and in a few hundred metres you reach another beak of rock where the face bends right. This is the first point at which you can see all the way up Gleann Bianasdail.

The Route
Start just left of the beak and go right up a slab to the skyline. Carry on up the crest to easier ground. Go up right to climb a steep face, starting at a large block. An easy rib on the left leads to a steeper thin rib on the right. Carry on easily to another steep rib, which is started on its left, then climbed on the right-hand side of the arête. Where the next rib curves over rightwards go left to an intimidatingly steep rib, the crux of the route. Climb it by a groove just left of the arête, stepping right onto the skyline near the top. Above this a small overhang and an easy rib lead to the plateau. A steep 10m outcrop en route to the summit adds more fun.

Bonnaidh Donn, Route One (Route 84, Difficult).
Climber: Pete Pollard. © Scott Muir

Slioch 981m

The square-cut tower of Slioch dominates the east side of Loch Maree, its ascent from Kinlochewe being a classic walk. The north-west buttress provides an enjoyable way of turning this into a loop.

 PAGE 171
 OS LR 19
 WEST
SANDSTONE

85   North-West Buttress   Grade 2 or 3 ✱✱

◇ NG 999 691   🚶 2HRS 50   ⟋ OUTCROPS   ⊤ +350M

Open scrambling with much variation possible in a splendid situation. Not particularly exposed and a good choice for a mixed-ability group. The bedrock is clean sound sandstone but the ledges are scattered with small stones, easily knocked off. If the lowest buttress is avoided it is only Grade 2.

Approach

From Incheril (NH 038 624) follow the track north-west and along Loch Maree to the bridge at the foot of Gleann Bianasdail. Carry on north-west to the waterfall and deserted settlement at NH 003 670. Head up north-west following the stream to a prominent boulder on the watershed below the north-west corner of Slioch's cliffs. The scramble takes the ridge directly above, avoiding the initial steep section.

The Route

Above the boulder are twin buttresses. Either start right of the right-hand one and traverse onto it at 5m, then climb the ridge above on good holds (Grade 3), or go up the gully between the buttresses and right onto the top of the steep section at 30m.

From a grass ledge go up right and up the right-hand side of a spur, then the right-hand side of the prow above. Carry on up clean outcrops to an open slope. Above this go up left of two rounded pinnacles, then up left to the skyline. Climb clean slabby rock, go right of a prow, then up the slabs behind it and stacked blocks above. Carry on up the crest, climbing a short steeper wall by a groove.

The buttress now becomes a sharp ridge, and a short exposed descent leads to two easy pinnacles. A steep path with small outcrops now leads to the summit, or alternatively an exposed ledge leads left again across the far wall of the gully to the skyline of Main Buttress, which provides a spectacular finish (Grade 2).

The route finishes at the North Top, which is the highest but only by a metre, so Munro baggers would be advised to visit the trig point too in case of future reversals of status.

Those coming up the usual route from Gleann Bianasdail can find some easy scrambling on the way up Sgùrr Dubh. From the two lochans beyond this go left to climb an easy-angled broken rib to the main summit area (Grade 2). Alternatively the slabs low down on the north side of the east ridge of Sgùrr an Tuill Bhain at NH 026 687 provide some entertainment with a remote atmosphere.

North-West Buttress (Route 85, Grade 2 or 3).
Scrambler: Mark Robson. © Adrian Camm

Gairloch

The excellent little peaks behind Gairloch have huge amounts of exposed rock, much of it solid Lewisian gneiss. As well as hundreds of short rock climbs, there is scope for any amount of scrambling, the routes included being merely a sample of the many possibilities available. Their accessibility makes them ideal for an evening or a short day. In addition, as the weather around Gairloch is markedly better than in the bigger hills nearby, linking scrambles here can often provide a good day when it's wet in Torridon. One mountain scramble on Baosbheinn is also included here – really part of Torridon, but most easily accessed from Gairloch.

1.	Baosbheinn	Route 86	P.206
2.	Meall Aundrary	Route 87	P.207
3.	Sìthean Mòr	Route 88	P.210
4.	An Groban	Routes 89–91	P.211
5.	Creag Mhòr Thollaidh	Route 92	P.215

Baosbheinn 875m

A superb hill with a long ridge traverse and numerous sandstone cliffs. Most of these are very vegetated, but there is one excellent route.

 PAGE 204
 OS LR 19
 NORTH
 SANDSTONE

86	**Oidhche Spur**		**Grade 3** ★★
⌀ NG 877 655	🏃 2HRS 30	⊿ BUTTRESS	⊺ +250M

Sustained rock steps, generally clean, with some exposure and a hard but avoidable crux.

Approach

Take the track south-east from the barn at NG 857 721 to Loch na h-Oidhche. The new plantations at Bad an Sgalaig are part of the campaign to regenerate the native Caledonian Forest, with ash, rowan, birch, oak, scots pine and hazel all planted. Just before the loch leave the track and go right to cross the outlet stream. Go up south-west to the foot of the face below the south-east peak of Baosbheinn. Start at the right-hand end of the lowest tier of rock in the centre of the face.

The Route

On the right-hand end of the tier is a corner. Start up its left arête then move right to climb the right-hand branch when the corner divides. The arête above leads to easy ground. Go up grass and minor outcrops to a steeper tier, then go left below an overhang and up blocks leftwards to more open ground. Carry on up minor outcrops to a small steep tier, passed by going up left from a rock platform in a central niche. The next tier is hard, but on its extreme right-hand edge a superb rough slab leads to the top of the first section of the spur.

Go up scrappy outcrops, then up right to the skyline, where things get tricky for a few metres. Start on the left and climb an exposed and delicate arête. This can be avoided by an easier rib and corner 5 metres right. Climb the corner above, finishing on the left arête, then go up blocks to an easing of angle. Carry on up the easy ridge, with the odd outcrop, to a vertical prow. Go right of this up greasy steps until it is possible to step awkwardly left onto the prow. Go up the arête and a short step to easy ground. A pleasant ridge with more short steps carries on past a pinnacle to the summit.

There is more scrambling on the north-west ridge just beyond the main summit (Grade 1). Keep to the crest over the pinnacles, then avoid the steepest descent on the right. If doing this section in reverse the lower arête is excellent, starting at a steep crack on the left, then along the wildly exposed crest.

Elsewhere on the mountain some scrappy scrambling can be found on the end of the north-east ridge, while the left-hand edge of the main face of Creag an Fhithich has some short steep outcrops leading to a narrow ridge. The right-hand rib of the face impresses from a distance, but flatters to deceive.

Meall Aundrary   327m

Accessible scrambling ideal for an evening. The south-east side has many easy-angled slabs which link to give a pleasant Grade 1, but the best route is on the north end of the steep west face.

 PAGE 204
 OS LR 19
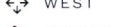 WEST
 GNEISS

---

 87   **North-West Buttress**   Grade 2/3 ★★

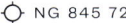 NG 845 729    20MINS    BUTTRESS   +70M

The right edge of the buttress is a clean rib of rough gneiss, with positive holds making it much easier than it looks. Quite sustained in the middle section and exposed at the top.

Approach
Park at the start of a track by a right-hand bend near a small loch at NG 841 721 (not much space). There was a bad fire here in 2018 and the scars are still visible. In summer deep bracken makes the direct approach hard work, so after going through the gate go along the right-hand side of the piled stone, then go up left over a small hump to reach a traversing track. Follow this left to a gate, and just before this go right up the fence to another gate. Go through this and over another hump (currently with lots of scorched trees) to get a view of the cliff. The scramble is the almost separate buttress on the far left end, so contour around the top of a small valley to reach it. Start on the right-hand corner of the buttress, by an isolated boulder of Torridonian sandstone.

Before the bracken grows up it is quicker to go left of the piled stones and take minor tracks directly up to the top gate.

The Route
Climb the rib to a shoulder below a steepening. The groove in the centre is much easier than it looks, but beware the odd loose hold. Carry on to the top of the buttress. Climb a slabby knoll by a Y-shaped groove, then more slabs lead to the skyline. The summit is up on the right, with a couple of steep boulder problems on the way.

North-West Buttress, Meall Aundrary (Route 87, Grade 2/3).
Scrambler: Noel Williams. © Iain Thow

Sìthean Mòr — 384m

Another of the spiky gneiss peaks behind Gairloch, this consists of an east-west ridge with a steep rocky northern flank. Ascents from other directions are possible but are complicated by recent planting and deer fencing. Flowerdale's Sitka spruce plantations have been felled and replaced by native species, part of the attempt to bring back the native Caledonian pine forests.

 PAGE 204
 OS LR 19
 NORTH
GNEISS

88 North Face — Grade 2/3

○ NG 834 746   🏃 45MINS   ⊿ INTRICATE   ⊤ +230M

A series of disjointed ribs giving good situations. The grain of the rock dips awkwardly, so the scrambling tends to be harder and less satisfying than on its neighbour An Groban.

Approach
From the Old Inn at the south end of Gairloch (car park just north of the river at NG 811 752) follow the path beside the private road to Flowerdale House, then the signed path right then left to rejoin the main path up Flowerdale. Keep ahead where the large track goes steeply uphill to reach Flowerdale Waterfall. Go up left of this, then at the top bridge bear left on a rough path to a stile. Go down and cross to the south bank of the stream. Start at the end buttress on the right, the closest to the stream, with a black wall at its top right.

The Route
Easy slabs lead to a steeper buttress. In dry conditions tackle this direct to a halfway shelf, otherwise climb over large pointed blocks to the left, then dodge a steep wall on the left to reach the shelf. An awkwardly grained slab leads to the top of the buttress. Go up two short steep steps, the second either by vertical jugs in the centre (Grade 3) or by an easy left-to-right shelf on the left.

Go left up heather below an overhanging wall to a wet gully. At the mouth of this go left along a shelf, then follow more heather up left to a large bay. At the back of this climb a shallow rib just right of a wet slot, quite insecure at the top. Go left across a shelf to the crest and up to a steepening. Go left to the skyline, then follow a ramp back up right below a block. Keep going right to reach a vertical wall, where steps lead back up left to the ridge again. Follow this up to easy ground. The left-hand summit is the higher, and has a splendid view of the Torridon hills.

An Groban   383m

One of the best small peaks in Scotland, this striking pointed summit feels like a proper mountain despite its diminutive stature. Both flanks are very rocky, giving endless scrambling possibilities on mainly excellent gneiss, surprisingly long given the size of the hill. Routes 90 and 91 have lots of positive holds so are not affected too much if wet and are in the Gairloch sun belt so a good Plan B if it's raining in Torridon.

⊕ PAGE 204
◁ OS LR 19
✥ SOUTH-WEST
⌂ GNEISS

Remainder of route down and round to left

89   North-West Face   Grade 2/3 ✶

| ⌖ NG 834 751 | 🚶 40MINS | ◿ BUTTRESS | ⊤ +230M |

Really two separate scrambles, but they are easily linked to make a good route up the hill. The sloping grain of the rock makes it awkward in places.

Approach

As for route 88 to the stile, then follow the far side of the fence up left. Head up rightwards, aiming for a grass slope between two buttresses. The right-hand buttress has two vertical walls. Start on the left-hand edge of the left-hand wall.

The Route

Go up the ridge on the left edge of the wall. At the top keep up left on steeper juggy rock to a minor top. The main peak is up right and easily reached directly, with some very minor scrambling, but down and left of this is a large steep grooved wall, home to several rock climbs. Go left to pass under this to the next buttress, which has a steep start and slabs above.

Gain the lowest slab at its bottom left-hand corner and work right across it to the far edge. Move up right onto the higher hanging slab and go up to a niche on the edge of the buttress. Climb the rib above to blocks then go up left to a ledge. Climb the slab above moving left, delicate but always escapable, then climb a gentler slab on the right to easy ground. Various outcrops can be added in on the way to the summit.

90 Humpback Buttress   Grade 2 or 3 ★★

NG 837 747   45MINS   BUTTRESS   +230M

A string of outcrops separated by grassy/heathery shelves, mostly slabby with the odd steeper wall on positive holds, ending on a sharp summit with a great view. The first buttress is quite loose but easily avoided, making the route Grade 2. Lots of possible variations, with everything avoidable, so a reasonable choice for a mixed ability party.

The next buttress left also makes a pleasant Grade 2 scramble, but is not as good a line.

Approach
As for Route 88 as far as the stile. Keep ahead up the valley to reach a steep grey wall low on the left-hand slope, leading up to a prominent humped buttress with slabs on its left. Start at the right-hand end of the grey wall, at its lowest point, about 100 metres before the low drystone wall.

The Route
Go up right of a large block, then bear left (loose) to the top of the first buttress (Grade 3, easily avoided on the right). Bear left up heather, boulders and short steps to climb a greasy corner right of a clean rounded nose. Go up left again and climb a steep wall to a large boulder, then easy slabs. Another short steep wall and more slabs lead over the 'Humpback' to a saddle. Straight ahead a shallow gully splits the buttress centrally. Follow slabs right of this past a sandstone boulder, with harder moves if desired. Above these easy steps lead to a short steep wall below a brownish band with a small overhang. Climb this by steep steps from the lowest point on the left (the crack direct through the overhang is Severe). More short outcrops lead up to the summit.

Right-Hand Slabs, An Groban (Route 91, Grade 2).
Scrambler: Iain Thow. © Noel Williams

91 Right-Hand Slabs — Grade 2 ✶✶✶

◇ NG 838 747   🏃 50MINS   ◿ BUTTRESS   ⊥ +230M

This is the buttress just right of Humpback Buttress, a sweep of slabs with no strong line but numerous possibilities. The slabs have both incut holds and good friction, so are usually easier than they look. There are plenty of breaks but neither grade nor quality ease off till almost the top.

Approach
As for Route 90, but carry on to the drystone wall and up its far side. Just right are two short chimneys/gullies, just left of a grey vertical wall.

The Route
Go up the left-hand chimney/gully left of the vertical wall and carry on up steep steps to a grassy terrace. Link sets of slabs above, delicate in places, until the angle eases. Climb a steepening by an easy left-to-right ramp, then numerous slabs lead up to a large grass shelf below a band of steep red rock. Above a group of small blocks climb a wide stepped weakness between two steeper buttresses to more broken ground. Either work up and left linking minor outcrops directly to the summit or go up rightwards to climb the left edge of an airy but juggy buttress to reach the skyline ridge further right.

Creag Mhòr Thollaidh 343m

A very rough gneiss hill with lots of short rock climbs on its flanks, including the idyllic Tollie Crags. There is less scrambling than you might expect, as much of the rock is very steep. A superb viewpoint.

 PAGE 204
 OS LR 19
 NORTH-WEST
 GNEISS

North-West Rib, Creag Mhòr Thollaidh (Route 92, Grade 3).
Scrambler : Iain Thow. © Noel Williams

92 North-West Rib — Grade 3 *

NG 860 780 | 20MINS | BUTTRESS | +200M

A short accessible route ideal for an evening. The rib itself is a good line, but short hard sections force deviations.

Approach
Follow the Tollie to Slattadale path from NG 859 790 past the steep craglet of An Leth Chreag to the foot of the main cliffs. The lowest crag has a steep orange chimney/crack at the bottom. Start just right of this.

The Route
Climb the right-hand edge of the buttress on jugs, then steep slabs to its top. Go horizontally left to climb a steep wall with reddish bands on small positive holds, then slabs above lead to an easing. The undercut groove on the right has large loose flakes in it, so avoid it on the left, then climb a rib just left of a heathery groove, above a steep drop on the left. Go up right easily and follow a level heathery ridge to an overhanging nose. Bypass this on the left by steep heather and a traverse right to rejoin the rib.

Climb a groove in the nose above for a few feet until cracked slabs on the left lead to easy ground. Go up to a shelf, climb a broken tier, then bear up left to climb lovely rough slabs crossed by a prominent brown band. Small outcrops lead to the skyline, then go right to twin ribs leading up to the north summit. The main summit lies south-east across a broad saddle. There are easy slabs beyond this on the left-hand side, or alternatively you can go 200 metres right (south-west) from the saddle, descending to reach a clean slabby rib. This is sustained Grade 3, on small holds but with excellent friction, quite exposed near the top.

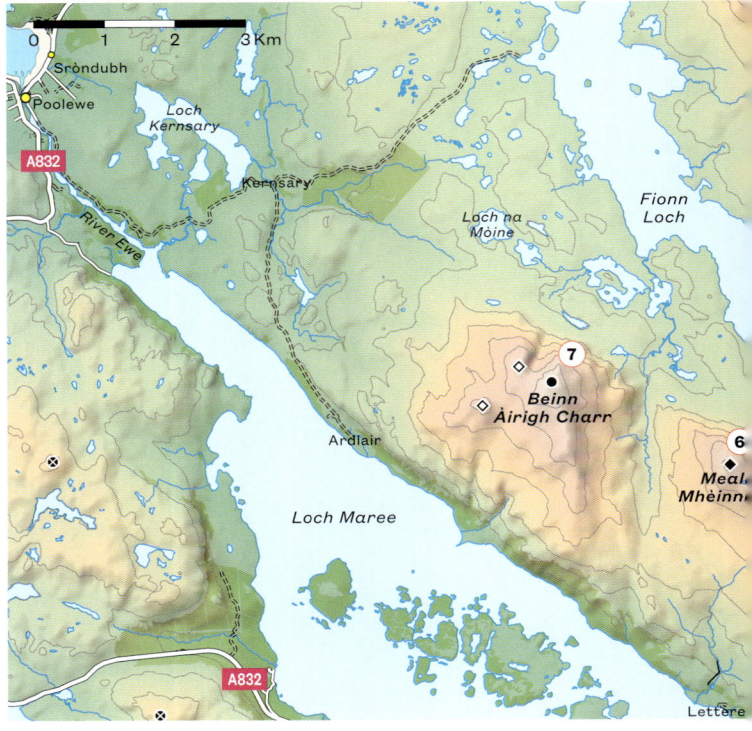

Carnmore is a scrambler's heaven, with several lifetimes' worth of rock. A ring of rocky peaks surrounds the basin of the Fionn Loch, those on the north-east side being largely gneiss and those on the south-west being hornblende schist. The gneiss provides mainly slabby routes on perfect clean rock, while the schist gives more broken routes of over 300 metres on largely inward-dipping holds. Most of these routes are too far from the road to do comfortably in a day, and with so many excellent routes close together it is far better to plan a trip with at least a couple of overnight stays. The barn at Carnmore is open and free (outside the stalking season), while there are many excellent camping spots nearby.

From Poolewe (parking NG 858 808) follow the private road southwards, forking left on the estate road to Kernsary. At Kernsary cross the bridge and go up past the keeper's cottage, then 0.5 km beyond this turn right

Carnmore

into the wood. Keep on the forest track to a stile
(NG 910 789). A good path leads past Loch an Doire
Crionaich and crosses the stream at the mouth of
Srathan Buidhe (more directly than the map shows).
It then continues for some 3km before crossing the
causeway between Fionn and Dubh Lochs. Reach
Carnmore Lodge soon after, and continue to the barn
about two hundred metres further west.

1.	Beinn a' Chàisgein Mòr	Routes 93–94	P.220
2.	Càrnan Bàn	Routes 95–98	P.223
3.	A' Mhaighdean	Routes 99–102	P.226
4.	Beinn Tharsuinn Chaol	Route 103	P.230
5.	Beinn Làir	Routes 104–106	P.231
6.	Meall Mhèinnidh	Route 107	P.234
7.	Beinn Àirigh Charr	Routes 108–109	P.235

Beinn a' Chàisgein Mòr 856m

An unimpressive hill from a distance, but on the south side are the rocky tor of Sgùrr na Laocainn and the superb Carnmore Crag, home to some of the finest mountain rock climbs in Scotland. The two scrambles described use the flanks of these on immaculate gneiss.

- PAGE 219
- OS LR 19
- SOUTH
- GNEISS

93 Grey Ridge   Grade 3 ✶✶✶

NG 981 772 | 20MINS (CARNMORE) | BUTTRESS | +250M

Originally recorded as a Moderate rock climb, but removed from the modern guidebook because the frequent ledges made it a poor roped climb. This route gives excellent slabby scrambling with the odd steeper move, and only one optional Moderate section. Quite sustained despite the ledges and less escapable than it looks from below.

Approach
From Carnmore Lodge go up beside the stream between Carnmore Crag and Sgùrr na Laocainn. On the right edge of Carnmore Crag is a narrow gully, Grey Ridge being the broad rib right again. Start at a quartzy rib in the centre.

The Route
Go up the rib, then up right to climb a steeper slab by an ill-defined juggy crack. More slabs lead to a vertical wall. Start at the right-hand end of the overhang or at a steeper crack just left (Moderate), then follow

the crack up superb slabs, steepening slightly at the top. Move left to the skyline and climb easy ribs to open ground. Above are a few boulder problems, notably a steep pinnacle (Difficult), with a step (or fall!) across to the main cliff.

94 Sgùrr na Laocainn Right-Hand — Moderate ✱

NG 988 768   25MINS (CARNMORE)   BUTTRESS   +250M

Sustained and committing, on good rock but with some vegetation. The finish is good but disjointed.

Approach
From Carnmore Lodge take the path up rightwards below Sgùrr na Laocainn (Torr na h-Iolaire). Right of the main face is a small pale face low down, then right again is a grassy gully, then another small face. Right of this are two prominent gullies, the right-hand one very deep at the top. The route climbs the buttress between these, starting just left of the left-hand gully, at a small rib.

The Route
Climb the left edge of the rib, which is steep but positive, then move right and go up a vegetated rib, quite steep at the top. A little higher cross the gully on the right to the bottom of the main buttress. Go up the centre of this until it steepens, then move left and up a ramp. Traverse back up right with a vertical wall above. Break through this by a chimney, which is hard to enter (crux). At its top step right and go up slabs to vegetation. Easier slabs lead to heather, bypassing an overhang on the left. Then follow more slabs on the left edge, with good cracks at steeper sections, until a final bulge is passed by an airy step right onto the lip of the overhang.

The buttress now peters out, so cross the gully on the left and either follow easy slabs on its far edge or go up left to more sustained rocks in the centre of the buttress. Go up these on contorted juggy rock, with much variation possible. Finish up shattered boulders.

Càrnan Bàn 650m

A minor summit overshadowed by its famous neighbours, but with excellent scrambling on perfect gneiss, escalating into easy rock climbing in places.

🌐 PAGE 219
✈ OS LR 19
↔ SOUTH-WEST
⛰ GNEISS

95 Pocket Slab — Moderate

○ NG 997 763 | 🚶 1HR (CARNMORE) | ◿ SLABS | ⊥ +150M

Steep slabs with nice moves but not much of a line. Often wet, but worthwhile in the dry for the amazing contorted rock, scattered with pockets ranging in size from fingerholds to ones you could sit in!

Approach
From Carnmore Lodge take the Shenavall path up eastwards for 1.5km until it flattens out around NG 995 767. Cross the stream at an obvious bouldery area just above the gorge and follow deer tracks round south-eastwards to below the outlet of Fuar Loch Beag. Where the stream from this emerges from the boulders below it head left. High up and facing west is the large mass of Barndance Slabs, with a steep base and an overhang at the bottom right. Pocket Slab is right of these and faces north-west, with two grass rakes slanting up left and pocketed rock above.

The Route
Follow the lower rake up, then where it ends carry on in the same line on juggy pocketed rock to reach a long grass ledge below an overhang. Go up from the left end of this on even bigger pockets until eventually an overhang forces you rightwards to the top of the crag. There are many easy slabby craglets above on the way to the top of the hill.

© Kinley Farmer — Càrnan Bàn

Start hidden

Fuar Loch Beag

| **South-East Face** | **Grade 2/3** |

○ NG 997 762   ⚡ 1HR (CARNMORE)   ⟋ OUTCROPS   ⊤ +200M

Excellent gneiss but quite a bitty scramble, escapable after each section.

Approach
As for the previous route but carry on past the main slabs to the foot of a small north-west facing steep cliff just left of the stream, with easier rock to its left. Start about 50 metres left of the steep cliff, in the corner where the face swings round from west to north-west, at the start of a grassy ramp leading up left. There is a much steeper buttress down and left and a bouldery streamlet just right.

The Route
Zigzag up broken steps to another grass rake, then move right and climb a lovely well-defined groove. Easier slabby rock then leads to the top of the knoll. Just right is a grassy ramp running up left above steep rock. Go up this and near its top break through the steep band above, with easier rock beyond. The steeper finish to the right is Moderate.

 **97 Cakewalk (Maiden Buttress)** Difficult *

 NH 001 762   🚶 1HR 10 (CARNMORE)   ◁ BUTTRESS   ⊤ +80M

Mostly pleasant slabby cracks, exposed in places, but with a short steep crux.

Approach
As for Route 95 to the outflow from Fuar Loch Beag, then follow the northern shore of the loch to the 100m high Maiden Buttress above its north-east corner. This contains several excellent Severes, while Cakewalk climbs the far right-hand edge. Start just before an open gully (descent), below a narrow reddish slab which starts at about the same level as the big overhang.

The Route
Climb cracks just right of a small overlap, then the slab above until the cliff steepens. Follow a gangway on the right, then pass large detached blocks and climb a thin crack to a shelf. On the left is a steeper thin crack, quite hard but only for a couple of moves. This leads to a platform from which easy but nicely positioned slabs continue slanting rightwards up the edge of the buttress to the top.

98 Doddle   Grade 3 ✶✶

| ⌖ NH 002 762 | 🚶 1HR 10 (CARNMORE) | ◿ SLABS | ⇕ +75M |

A slabby rib of perfect gneiss, fairly escapable and with a definite crux.

Approach
As for the previous route. This is the separate line of slabs just right of the descent gully on the right-hand side of Maiden Buttress.

The Route
Start up easy-angled slabs below and right of the start of Cakewalk. Transfer to steeper slabs on the right and go up centrally, pulling through a small overlap at a crack (crux). Go up to another steepening and pass this on the left arête. Finish direct on excellent slabs.

A' Mhaighdean 967m

Probably the most remote Munro, A' Mhaighdean throws down a long stepped ridge to the north-west, with cliffs on both flanks. The ridge itself has a couple of short easy scrambling sections, while more serious routes can be found on the faces either side.

🌐 PAGE 219
➤ OS LR 19
✧ VARIOUS
⌂ GNEISS & SANDSTONE

© Kinley Farmer

99 Bivouac Rib — Grade 2

◯ NH 012 755   🏃 2HRS 30 (CARNMORE)   ⊿ BUTTRESS   ⊤ +250M

A blunt spur of slabby gneiss outcrops, not as continuous as it looks from a distance but in a great wild setting.

Approach
From Carnmore Lodge follow the approach as for Route 95 but instead of crossing the stream stay on the path for nearly another kilometre. At a small cairn turn right on a smaller stalkers' path and cross the outlet from Lochan Feith Mhic-illean. Follow the path up to a shelf above Fuar Loch Mòr, where it becomes a rougher path traversing above the loch. At around NH 015 758 the path drops slightly and about 100 metres beyond the lowest point head off right along a grass shelf. Follow this round to the head of the corrie, cross one stream and slant up to a knoll at the foot of the spur, crossing another stream on the way. The bluff below the knoll is craggy but too steep for scrambling, although some slabs can be found on its right flank to add a little more scrambling if desired.

The Route
There are quite steep slabs ahead and left but these are too hard for scrambling, so climb slabs with right-slanting pinkish markings right of these. Carry on up mossy boulders and slabs, then easier slabs just left to reach grass left of a leaning wall. Go up right to the top of a knoll with a great view. Pass two big boulders, then what looks like a slabby rib turns out to be more boulders. Carry on up these, with the spur becoming more defined, to clamber on to the top of a rock eye. Enjoyable slabs on the left lead up to grass, then an easy airy ridge takes you over a minor top to the grassy plateau of A' Mhaighdean's north top. This seems oddly out of place amid all the rock, but on its far side the craggy summit upthrust is perched above a huge drop, with a classic view out over the Dubh Loch.

100 North-West Ridge — Grade 1 or 2 ✱

◯ NG 997 761   🏃 1HR 10 (CARNMORE)   ⊿ OUTCROPS   ⊤ +300M

A superb way up the hill, but only minor scrambling, first on gneiss slabs, then around sandstone pinnacles.

Approach
From Carnmore Lodge follow the approach as for Route 95 as far as the outlet of Fuar Loch Beag. Cross the stream below the boulders and go up right to the ridge, with optional easy slabs on the way.

The Route
Follow the broad ridge, with more easy slabs. As it narrows go up slabs below a prominent perched block. Above this go up a left-slanting slab below a nose. The ridge now broadens, although still with easy slabs possible. Where it steepens either go up a slab direct at Grade 2 or avoid it on the right. The rock now changes to sandstone, and at the next

saddle an open gully descending right from a perched block marks the approach to Red Slab (Route 101).

From the saddle two short steps are easily climbed centrally, then walk up stony slopes to another steepening and go up steps in this. As the ridge narrows cross a neck, then a few metres later cut down left, then go right through a notch. Pass right of a small pinnacle and then a much larger one to reach broken ground and the top. The pinnacle can be traversed at a loose and exposed Difficult by climbing a steep groove in the left-hand arête, then descending the east arête and a vertical corner just right.

101	**Red Slab**		**Difficult** ✶✶✶	
⬦ NH 002 755	🚶 1HR 45 (CARNMORE)	⊿ SLABS	⌶ +90M	

A sustained and wildly exposed route on amazing rock – a solid conglomerate consisting entirely of holds. One of the best routes of its grade in Scotland.

Approach
The route woud be masochistic to approach from below so it is far better to access it from the North-West Ridge of A' Mhaighdean (Route 100). From the top of the open gully just after the start of the sandstone descend the gully and follow the bottom of the cliff leftwards (looking out). Pass underneath the first buttress (Conglomerate Arête, Very Difficult), then cross the next gully, going up slightly to join a grass ramp above more broken rock below. Continue under the first part of the next buttress to reach the Red Slab, which has a very undercut right arête.

The Route
Start as far right as feasible and go up bearing right to a small ledge. Traverse right on this to the edge, then go up to a terrace with huge blocks above. Go diagonally right to a block on the skyline. Climb the arête in a mindblowing position on small but positive holds to reach a terrace below the top. You can walk off left here but it would feel like a cop-out. Climb onto a block and up a final steep wall on good holds.

102 Kids' Ridge   Grade 3 or Difficult ✱✱

NH 005 743   1HR 30 (CARNMORE)   OUTCROPS   +450M

A succession of gneiss outcrops leads to good clean slabs with steeper sections, quite intimidating from below. A long route with much variation possible.

Approach
From Carnmore Lodge go down to cross the causeway and turn left to follow a rough path along the south shore of the Dubh Loch. Carry on up the valley to Gorm Loch Mòr. 200 metres east of the outflow from the loch a deep gully comes down with a steep red right-hand wall. Left of this is a black niche down which a stream sometimes dribbles. Start at a rib down left from this, at the top of a boulder field.

Looking down Red Slab, A' Mhaighdean (Route 101, Difficult).
© Grahame Nicoll.

The Route

Climb vegetated slabs to grass, then more slabs to a clamber over boulders. Pass right of a large red boulder, then climb blocky slabs above it. At a vertical wall go left until it gets less steep, then climb it past a large pocket. Go up grass to a clean outcrop, gained from the left. Go up the crest to boulders. Above these go right onto a red rib (starting this direct is Difficult). Go up the rib and grass above, then climb a steep awkward red wall to reach more sustained rock.

Follow slabs up to a steepening (Difficult direct), then take a ramp right and climb a steep corner. More slabs lead to a steeper red nose. Climb the left edge of this, then go up pocketed slabs and a corner. Work up right to the crest, with steeper clean slabs off to the left (these can be taken direct at Difficult). Climb the crest and a juggy groove above, then a steeper nose by rightward-running cracks. The angle now eases, so go up left and follow the slabby crest, passing a superb pocketed slab, until the rock peters out just before reaching the main ridge.

Beinn Tharsuinn Chaol 652m

An intermediate ridge between A' Mhaighdean and Beinn Làir, this well hidden hill is very craggy, particularly on its north side. The prominent Ghost Slabs above the Dubh Loch are impressive, and provide some scrambling up behind their right-hand edge, but the steeper buttress above the west end of the Gorm Loch Mòr is better.

⊕ PAGE 219
⊲ OS LR 19
✣ NORTH-EAST
⌂ GNEISS

103 Gorm Loch Mòr Spur   Grade 2 *

◯ NG 995 743   🏃 1HR 30 (CARNMORE)   ◢ BUTTRESS   ⊤ +180M

Clean slabby ribs on the usual perfect gneiss, but a bit short on character.

Approach
As for Route 102 until 0.5km beyond the head of the Dubh Loch, then go south-west up a stream to reach a bowl west of Gorm Loch Mòr. The spur rises directly above the west end of the loch, on the lip of the corrie.

The Route
Go up a delicate slabby rib until it peters out. Go left and up slabs and a short nose, then move right onto more slabs and go up these rightwards. Continue linking slabs until a steeper band crosses the buttress. Climb this left then right. At its top go left to another slabby rib and climb this to the top. The summit is well off to the right across a narrow col.

Beinn Làir   860m

A mountain of two contrasting faces. On the south-west flank grassy slopes run down to Loch Maree, while the north-east face is huge, dropping in complex 400m cliffs to hidden Gleann Tulacha. Over 20 buttresses stretch for 4km along the glen, with the best climbing being at the west end, notably the classic Severe, Wisdom Buttress. Further left the ridges are mostly scrambling angle, although generally with the odd harder section. The best scrambles are concentrated around the north summit on inward-dipping hornblende schist. All are serious undertakings with escapes ranging from tricky to impossible. The cliffs are quite vegetated and become very greasy when wet, so allow a couple of days of good weather for the cliff to dry out.

🌐 PAGE 219
🧭 OS LR 19
✢ NORTH-EAST
⌂ HORNBLENDE SCHIST

104 Tower Ridge   Difficult *

◯ NG 978 740   🏃 1HR 45 (CARNMORE)   ◢ BUTTRESS   ⊤ +350M

A serious and scary route with a sting in the tail. Most of the route is Grade 3, but the crux is exposed and gymnastic, although a one move wonder. The only route in this book where heel hooking is useful!

Approach
From the southern corner of Fionn Loch (NG 968 754) take the path up towards Bealach Mhèinnidh. After 200 metres or so head south-east and pick up a vague path heading through the pass below the north-

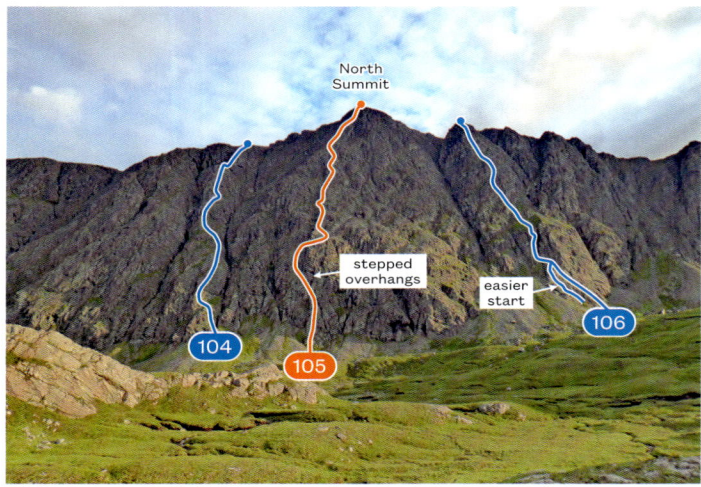

facing Creag na Gaorach, emerging into the head of Gleann Tulacha (NG 976 746). Beinn Làir dominates the glen, with the broad North Summit Buttress coming lower down the slope than the others. Tower Ridge is the next ridge left, just across a deep gully, with a broad base and a narrow top. Start on the right-hand edge at a stream/gully.

The Route
Go up easy slabs leftwards to grass, with cleaner slabs to the left. Take a grass ledge left onto these (or swing left lower down and climb a pocketed slab, harder). Climb the crest, passing a tower on the right. Where the rib peters out climb a rough outcrop on the right, then slabs and a small crest to the left. A couple of short slabs lead to easy ground level with the foot of a huge leaning tower across the gully to the right.

Go up left to climb clean slabs on the left edge, then grass and more slabs, becoming vegetated at the top. Now move left to broken outcrops on the left arête, with a long low overhang to the right. Zigzag up an awkward steepening, then slabs lead to broken ground below a steep loose wall. Follow a grass ledge right until the overhang stops, then work back up left (greasy) to regain the crest. Broken outcrops and easy slabs lead to a level ridge.

Things now get more serious, and although the next section can be avoided on the left, this is on scarily steep grass and is not recommended. At the neck in the ridge pull up strenuously on overhanging jugs, then follow the exposed arête to another narrow saddle. Go up right of the crest, then cross it and go up a slab to the left skyline. Follow this, bypassing a pinnacle on the right, then cross another pinnacle to a third saddle. The final pinnacle is a dead end, so slant down right from the saddle to an exposed grassy ramp leading into the gully. Regain the ridge, which leads easily to the plateau.

105 North Summit Buttress Grade 3 ✽✽

◯ NG 977 741   🚶 1HR 40 (CARNMORE)   ◿ BUTTRESS   ⊤ +350M

An exciting expedition up a big, serious, intimidating face. Steep at times, but the inward dip of the strata produces numerous good holds. Although the route winds around to avoid the steepest rock it feels a logical line once embarked upon it. Some loose rock in places but spectacular situations.

Approach
As for the previous route to the head of Gleann Tulacha. The described route follows the centre of North Summit Buttress, the lowest on the face, dodging the stepped overhangs at 50m on the left. At the bottom right of the buttress is a steep clean face. A small path traverses left immediately below it and about 100 metres along this the ground opens out. Start here, at a juggy rib, with a big stepped overhang 50m up.

The Route
Climb the rib until steeper rock forces moves left into a minor gully coming down from the big overhang. Go left out of this and up vegetated rock left of the overhang into another minor gully. Go up this (loose), then bear right as soon as possible up onto a grassy step above the big overhang.

Go up left on rough juggy slabs and up an arête. Climb a small overhanging wall on big jugs (or avoid it on the right) to broken ground at half-height on the buttress. Dodge the next overhang on its left (loose and grassy), then climb a nice spiky rib to easier ground. Climb the right-hand side of the next buttress, finishing by moving left up a pocketed slab onto the nose of the overhang. A shattered arête now leads to more open ground. Go up scrappy rock and grass to reach the left arête of the buttress. Climb this, mostly on jugs, bypassing a steep tower near the top on the left, to arrive at the nicely positioned North Summit.

106 Left Wing, Butterfly Buttress Moderate

◯ NG 975 742   🚶 1HR 35 (CARNMORE)   ◿ BUTTRESS   ⊤ +350M

Steep in places, with a rather indirect line, but nice positions on juggy rock.

Approach
As for the previous two routes as far as the head of Gleann Tulacha. Butterfly Buttress is the double buttress right of North Summit Buttress, between it and the recess of the Amphitheatre. Start on easy slabs below and right of the Left Wing.

The Route
Climb the slabs, steeper at the top (easier start on left). Go up left to a broken buttress just left of a deep gully with a steep face on its right. Climb the broken buttress, finishing up juggy black slabs (often wet) to open heathery slopes. Trend left up juggy ribs, aiming for a small steep buttress topped by a prominent perched block. Climb to the block, starting in the chimney down right from it. This takes you to the left arête of the

buttress. Carry on up the arête, steep and exposed at first, then easier and quite grassy. When the arête broadens move right and climb the left edge of a central groove, then more jugs above. A central crest now develops as the buttress narrows. Climb this to a pinnacle, dodged on the left (Difficult direct), then an easy ridge leads to the plateau.

Meall Mhèinnidh 722m

Another mountain of two contrasting flanks, easy on the south-west but with a steep craggy north-east face. This is about 250m high at its maximum and made of hornblende schist with plenty of incut holds.

 PAGE 218
 OS LR 19
 NORTH-EAST
 HORNBLENDE SCHIST

107	**North-East Face**		**Grade 2**
◇ NG 957 752	🚶 2HRS 40	◿ INTRICATE	⊥ +200M

A fairly easy but serious way up a big face. Indirect and vegetated in places, but with some excellent scrambling too. Most sections are avoidable but you are committed to the general line. Less exposed than you might expect from the size of the face.

Approach
From Poolewe follow the Carnmore approach described in the introduction until 1km beyond the crossing of the Srathan Buidhe stream. Slant up southwards to reach the face. There is a steep lower tier, and near the far end of this are two streamlets (just damp streaks in dry weather) with steep rock to their right.

The Route
Start just right of the two streams and follow a weakness slanting left across them. Cleaner rock on their left leads to the terrace above the lower tier (better accessed from the left if the lower tier is wet). Follow this right for 100m or so until it narrows to a sheep track. Climb slabs above this, then go up left and climb ribs to grass. Carry on up more easy slabs, finishing up a spiky rib. The ground now becomes more broken, with a rake going up left and rows of short ribs right of it. Climb vegetated ribs above, bearing slightly right, with steeper rock up left. Move left onto this when it becomes less steep and go up the slabs. Carry on slightly left and go up a lovely rib on the edge of a gully. More slabs above lead to easy ground. A rib on the right provides a nice finish. A few minor outcrops can be included on the way to the summit.

Beinn Àirigh Charr   791m

The western sentinel of the Carnmore area, this superb viewpoint has a north summit, Martha's Peak, from which spectacular 400 metre cliffs fall towards Loch an Doire Crionaich. The largest buttress directly above the loch is taken by Ling and Glover's Route, which has a scrappy and vegetated lower half and a steep and serious finish. Left of this and starting much lower down, above the south-east end of the loch, is Bell's Route which links two lower buttresses with the left edge of the summit tower. Left again is a section of huge boulders topped by the sharp arête of The Beanstalk (HVS), and left again the shorter Square Buttress, above the smaller lochan at NG 940 766.

 PAGE 218
 OS LR 19
 NORTH-EAST
HORNBLENDE SCHIST

---

108 Square Buttress **Difficult**

NG 938 764   2HRS 10    BUTTRESS   +250M

A steep start leads to slabs of sound juggy schist and an easy finish. Not recommended in the wet.

Approach
Follow the approach from Poolewe described in the Carnmore introduction as far as Loch an Doire Crionaich (NG 936 770). Half a kilometre

beyond this is an unnamed lochan, with Square Buttress above. Start at its right-hand edge, where a steep slab leads up leftwards.

The Route

Take the steep slab up left, with the strata sloping unhelpfully. Just to the left a short awkward chimney leads to a grass ledge crossing the buttress. Go right along this, two-thirds of the way to the right-hand edge, then go up steeply on jugs to follow slabs leftwards into the centre of the buttress. When the angle eases move right and follow the next ramp up to the top of the main buttress. Go up easy steps above until they run out into the hillside. Easy slabs continue for another 100m or so before petering out to grass.

109	**Bell's Route**		**Grade 3 or Moderate** ✶✶	
⬡ NG 935 767		🏃 2HRS	⊿ BUTTRESS	⊤ +400M

Slabby, positive and intricate, the longest line on the mountain. The top and bottom sections are exposed and worth Moderate, but both can be avoided and the route is not sustained. The schist gets very slippery in the wet so pick a dry spell.

Approach

As for Square Buttress to Loch an Doire Crionaich. The route begins above the south-east end of the loch, and initially ascends a feature called Lower Buttress. Start near the left edge of this, at the lowest rocks, below and left of an overhanging wall.

The Route

Go up the left-hand edge of the lowest spur, then move right onto the front and up an easy slab. Go up left and then right to a ledge below an overhanging wall. Follow a very narrow ledge left and ascend delicately to the skyline and easy ground. All this lower section can be easily avoided on the left.

Follow easy slabs up right to the crest of the buttress. Climb excellent sharp-edged slabs just left of the crest, then easy ground to a steepening. Climb this right then left on sloping holds, then go up left to the skyline. Continue up easy slabs, then move left and up a steeper rib to arrive on top of Lower Buttress.

Walk across the neck to the main hillside and link together easy slabs to reach an arête with a deep gully on its left. Follow the arête up right, with a nice step off a block, then climb a short vertical wall. Dodge the steeper bits until the arête becomes slabby again and runs out into the hillside.

Cross the gully on the right (Staircase Gully) and climb delicate slabs, gradually easing. Carry on up to a steeper section. This can be avoided on the left, but a much more spectacular finish can be taken by following a grassy ramp leading right. Then step right onto the main face in an amazingly exposed position. Thankfully big holds lead up to regain the arête, from where easy rocks lead up to the summit of Martha's Peak.

High up on Bell's Route (Route 109, Grade 3 or Moderate).
Scrambler: Robin Chalmers. © Noel Williams

The Fisherfield Forest, sometimes called the Great Wilderness, comprises a horseshoe of predominantly sandstone peaks around Gleann na Muice. The scrambles here involve long days and feel quite remote. The western fringes of the area are best approached from Poolewe and were described in the previous chapter, while this chapter deals with those routes usually approached from the north and east. The dominant peak of the area is the mighty An Teallach, a range in itself. The traverse of its pinnacled main ridge over Corrag Buidhe is one of the best days out the Scottish hills can offer. Although this is closer to the road, it is still a big day and should not be underestimated.

Further east lie the Fannaichs, predominantly grassy hills with wild open corries. Here a few buttresses offer scrambling approaches to the main ridges, adding interest to a day spent linking the summits. The routes are sometimes quite vegetated but the rock is satisfyingly juggy.

Fisherfield & the Fannaichs

1. **Mullach Coire Mhic Fhearchair**	Route 110	P.242
2. **Beinn Dearg Mòr**	Routes 111–112	P.244
3. **Allt a' Ghiubhsachain**	Route 113	P.246
4. **An Teallach**	Routes 114–116	P.246
5. **Beinn nam Bàn**	Route 117	P.252
6. **Sgùrr nan Clach Geala**	Route 118	P.253
7. **Sgùrr Mòr**	Route 119	P.255

Mullach Coire Mhic Fhearchair 1018m

The highest point of the main Fisherfield horseshoe, this rocky peak throws out a long ridge eastwards into the remote country at the head of Loch a' Bhraoin, giving a grand expedition.

 PAGE 240
 OS LR 19 & 20
  EAST
  GNEISS & AMPHIBOLITE

110	**East Ridge**		Grade 2 **
NH 076 728	2HRS	OUTCROPS & ARÊTE	+450M

Really two scrambles in one, the first being steep rough amphibolite slabs, not sustained but with some tricky moves, generally avoidable, while the second is a sharp ridge with shattered pinnacles, easy but quite exposed. A longish day if done from the road.

Approach
From the road at NH 162 761 take the track to Loch a' Bhraoin, then follow the path along the north shore and up the valley until it turns northwards towards Loch an Nid. The East Ridge is directly ahead,

On Sgùrr Dubh – the second section of scrambling, East Ridge, Mullach Coire Mhic Fhearchair (Route 110, Grade 2). Scrambler: Fiona Reid. © Mike Watson

starting as a steep broad spur (Tom an Fhiodha). On the right-hand side of this are vegetated vertical cliffs, while the left-hand side has more broken outcrops. Halfway along is a pink slab at the foot, just above the end of a broken wall. Start about 50 metres left of this at a narrow buttress between two short gullies.

The Route
Either start up the left-hand side of the buttress (hard), or traverse in from the right. Carry on up easier slabs until the two gullies converge. Go into the right-hand one briefly, then up slabs on the left to the top

of the buttress. Follow broken slabs and heather above, passing left of a larger cliff. Once above this go right across the gully and up knobbly outcrops until the easy ground to the left finishes. Go left and up steep rough slabs, then climb two easy outcrops. Go up left again and climb a steep pink slab, then further left to a steeper buttress. Start this by a thin pink rib on the right-hand edge, then move left and up an exposed ramp. Easier outcrops now lead to the top of Tom an Fhiodha.

Walk up over Sgùrr Dubh to a narrow arête, then descend a shattered ridge. The pinnacles can be crossed or dodged on the left. Go up a blunt tower and the ridge swings right airily. Follow it down to an overhang, avoided on the left. The final pinnacle can be crossed or avoided on the left before a sharp arête leads to easy ground. A pleasant narrow ridge continues over a minor top to the summit.

Nearby, the huge quartzite slabs on the east flank of Sgùrr Ban are mostly walking angle, apart from the lower right section which is marginally steeper. They make a fun way up though, or a descent for the confident. A detour to the lovely perched top of Meallan an Laoigh is well worthwhile.

Beinn Dearg Mòr — 910m

Not being a Munro, this splendid peak gets somewhat neglected, being best known as the backdrop to the usual view of Shenavall bothy. Although mostly quite vegetated sandstone, it provides a couple of good ridge scrambles, the South-East pinnacles and the steeper East Buttress.

- PAGE 240
- OS LR 19
- SOUTH-EAST & EAST
- SANDSTONE

---

111 South-East Ridge — Grade 1/2 *

| NH 034 791 | 4HRS | ARÊTE | +200M |

A narrow ridge with some easy pinnacles, generally Grade 1, but with a couple of sections that deserve Grade 2 if at all wet. The approach is quite steep and rough.

Approach
From the road at Corrie Hallie (NH 114 849) take the track south-west up Gleann Chaorachain, then fork right to reach Shenavall bothy (the route can be shortened by 7km by using the bothy for an overnight stay). Cross the river and take the rough path south-west to another river crossing at Larachantivore. In wet weather both these crossings can be tricky, sometimes impossible.

Slant south-west up rough pathless ground. A band of vertical cliffs blocks direct access into Beinn Dearg Mòr's south-east corrie, so go up steeply before reaching this, then traverse left into the corrie. A strange

rock crevasse runs across the mouth of the corrie, crossable at either its right-hand end or its highest point. Go up left to the start of the ridge.

The Route
At first the crest is rocky but easy, up short steps and over two minor towers. When it bends right and becomes narrow stay on the crest until just before the first pinnacle, then cut down left through a cleft into a gap between the pinnacle and slabs beyond. Go through the gap and up a shallow groove on the right (care needed in the wet). Cross a broad pinnacle and descend just left of the far end, then another short drop leads to a col. Walk up to another pinnacle, descending first on the left, then on the crest. The last step down to the col is steep and slippery. There are several more short steps on the ridge before it merges into the broad summit slopes.

112 East Buttress — Grade 3 ✶✶

| ○ NH 044 801 | 🚶 3HRS 10 | ◿ BUTTRESS | ⬍ +550M |

Sustained scrambling on clean rock, mostly Grade 2 but with a couple of harder sections. Quite steep and occasionally exposed, but also very juggy. The lower sections are avoidable but the top part isn't.

Approach
As for the previous route to Larachintivore (with the same potential river crossing problems). Slant rightwards up rough heather and boulders to the foot of the buttress.

The Route

The lower part of the buttress is poorly defined. Pick a way around several steep walls, mostly on heather but with some blocky scrambling. As the outcrops start to coalesce into a ridge a steep thin pillar of blocks provides a good introduction. Climb the next tier centrally on big boulders, starting with an awkward mantelshelf. A short tier above turns out to be a detached boulder, quitted on the right. Go left and clamber up what can only be described as gigantic scree. Tackle the more sustained rock above by flakes in the second niche from the left, then climb the wide crack above, finishing on the right arête. Go up the left arête of the next tier, then the slab above, then move left and do the same again. All these difficulties are avoidable on the left.

The arête gradually becomes heathery, with easy pinnacles. Climb a steeper prow on its right arête to boulders, then descend steeply, easiest on the left. Above the col take a very exposed grass ledge out right to blocks on the arête, then ascend easy slabs and go up right to the crest. From the lowest point of the next tier follow slabs up right to a steeper tier. The chimney ahead is squalid, so go left and up a grassy ramp to easy ground. Ledges lead back right to the crest, which leads to the south peak.

An Teallach   1062m

A massive mountain with many summits, An Teallach would be many people's choice as the best hill in Scotland. The pinnacled main ridge is a superb scramble, hard or easy according to choice. There are also a few nearby routes, but fewer than you would expect from the amount of rock, as the massive horizontal bedding of Torridonian sandstone mitigates against good vertical lines.

- PAGE 240
- OS LR 19
- VARIOUS
- SANDSTONE & QUARTZITE

---

113   **Allt a' Ghiubhsachain**   **Grade 2**

NH 110 857   5MINS   STREAM   +100M

The slabs in the lower part of this stream can be used either as a roadside evening scramble or combined with the next route as an approach to An Teallach. Low water conditions are essential.

Approach

From the road follow the true right (south) bank of the stream through rhododendron jungle to enter the stream at easy slabs just below a ruined hut on the far bank.

The Route

Go up the slabs and follow the left-hand side of the stream round below steep clifflets. Just above the hut cross the stream and go up to a small gorge, where an escape up the right wall is necessary. Regain the stream as soon as possible and use a rib in the centre, then the left wall to boulders. Cross to the right bank and exit up a steep corner above a large pool, a little way back from the fall. Above the falls follow shelves on the left wall, then round a corner and go up left of a larger fall (serious), escaping left at the top. The falls above are discontinuous (and sometimes impossible), so cross back over and join the path.

Ghiubhsachain Slabs (Route 114, Grade 3).
Scrambler: Iain Thow. © Noel Williams

114 Ghiubhsachain Slabs — Grade 3

| NH 100 842 | 1HR | SLABS | +50M |

Short but fun slabs covered with incut quartzite holds. If starting the ridge traverse from Corrie Hallie it can easily be incorporated into a direct return to the car from Toll an Lochain.

Approach
From the top of the previous scramble continue up the path into Coir' a' Ghiubhsachain. Quartzite cliffs line the east side of the valley, and the described route is at the far end of the initial section, roughly opposite the corrie of A' Ghlas Thuill and 100 metres or so before a wide break in the cliffs. They are the lowest slabs on the right-hand end of this lower scarp.

The Route
A short steep tier leads to a ledge, then climb open smooth slabs with delicate incut holds. A second steeper tier is climbed direct up a ladder of larger incuts.

115 Corrag Bhuidhe Traverse — Moderate ***

| NH 065 832 | 4HRS | ARÊTE | +200M |

One of the best ridges in Scotland, with lots of exposure (even on the easier options) and one pitch of Moderate, which most people rope up for. Best tackled south-east to north-west as the harder bits are then climbed up not down, but if going the other way beware of descending the end of the ridge directly. This is steep, exposed, often slippery and has been the scene of numerous accidents. Cut down right well before this, at the open gully mentioned below.

Ascending the flake-crack on the Corrag Bhuidhe Traverse (Route 115, Moderate). Scrambler: Noel Williams. © Iain Thow

Fisherfield & the Fannaichs

An Teallach

On the Corrag Bhuidhe Traverse (Route 115, Moderate).
Scrambler: Ewan Ingram. © Finlay Wild

Approach
From the Corrie Hallie car park (NH 114 849) follow the path up Gleann Chaorachain, forking right onto the path to Shenavall, then leaving it after about 1.5km to go up right. A path soon develops, leading up to the summit of Sail Liath. Go steeply down and up over Stob Cadha Gobhlach, with a minor pinnacle in between. A broad ridge then runs down northwards before steeper rockier ground leads up to the top of the South Buttress of Corrag Bhuidhe. This latter section is Grade 2 if all the outcrops are taken direct (there is a path on the left). From the top of the buttress follow the ridge along and up, with some very easy scrambling. A small pinnacle marks the start of the serious stuff, with the Bad Step prominent above.

The Route

The Bad Step can be tackled direct, but this is steep, greasy and exposed (Difficult). It is better to take a path running left below the cliff to reach a steep clean slab with a flake-crack on its left. The lower branch of the path bypasses all difficulties (and all the fun?), carrying on round two projections to go up an open gully to the ridge. Climb the flake-crack (awkward to start), moving right onto the slab as soon as possible, then go up left onto a shoulder. Climb a short corner on the left and follow polished steps up left to grass and the ridge. Follow this left to a col above the open gully where the easy route comes in.

From here all difficulties can be easily bypassed by a path on the left, although still with some exposure. More interesting is to go up the next top just right of the arête and follow the skyline. Descend either via an easy gully on the left or by the delicate and wildly exposed end. Pass two minor pinnacles and climb the ridge up ahead over tottering blocks, then a narrow level arête leads to another steep and exposed (but juggy) descent at the far end. The next top has an awkward rounded start and leads to the summit of Corrag Bhuidhe. After an easy descent simple scrambling takes you over the airy perch of Lord Berkeley's Seat and on to Sgùrr Fiona. The usual circuit carries on over Bidein a' Ghlas Thuill and descends the path to Dundonnell.

A good alternative descent from the latter which avoids most of the road walk is to take the ridge running south-east, then at the saddle before Glas Mheall Liath cut off right and descend steep grass to Loch Toll an Lochain and a classic view. From the north-east corner of the corrie a small path leads down into Coir' a' Ghiubhsachain and the road (very wet in the rhododendron jungle at the end). From Toll an Lochain it is also possible to cut down and across Coir' a' Ghiubhsachain, climb Route 114 and follow the north side of a small gorge to Corrie Hallie. The stream crossing at the end is not usually problematic.

116 Sgùrr Ruadh — Grade 1

◯ NH 040 854   🏃 2HRS   ⊿ OUTCROPS   ⊤ +200M

Easy steps add interest to an unusual way up An Teallach.

Approach
Follow the path up the east side of Ardessie Falls from NH 054 896, then a rougher path along the Allt Airdeasaidh. Cross the mouth of Coire Mòr to the foot of the ridge, at the left-hand side of which are a few bouldery outcrops, starting at a bent fence post.

The Route
Climb the bouldery outcrops, then a few small faces to reach the ridge proper. Go up a flaky rib, then the next outcrop either by the easy gully in the centre or the ribs on either side. More ribs follow, then go up left of a steeper outcrop on the skyline to an easy narrow ridge and the first top. There is another minor outcrop on the way to the main top of Sgùrr Ruadh, and a few more can be found further along the ridge, which has stunning views out over Loch na Sealga.

Beinn nam Bàn 580m

A steep-sided and unfairly neglected hill with a superb view. The described scramble takes the right edge of Badrallach Crag, which has several fine rock climbs at around VS.

🌐 PAGE 240
⊲ OS LR 19
↔ WEST
⛰ SANDSTONE

117 Windy Ridge — Grade 3 ✶

◯ NH 104 911   🏃 25MINS   ⊿ BUTTRESS   ⊤ +100M

A steep blunt arête of rough sandstone, with more isolated outcrops above. Quite exposed in places, with lots of possible variation.

Approach
Take the minor road starting 2.5km south of Dundonell towards Badrallach and park at a large layby (NH 098 916) about 300m south of the sharp bend above Allt na h-Airbhe. The crag is up right but its lower tier is vegetated so head up the north shoulder of Beinn nam Ban then traverse right once above the messy lower crags. There are lots of good outcrops on the way up, especially a long line of 10m slabs low down, generally Moderate to V Diff. Start at the lowest rocks on the right edge of the crag, 15 metres right of a block leaning against its foot.

The Route
Go up steps to ledges, then up a rib right of a groove (the groove is Moderate). A steepening can be avoided on the right by a right-to-left ramp to reach the large halfway ledge. Go up a short open corner (or a rib to its right – Diff), then climb ribs above in the same line to the top of the main cliff. There are lots of options above, the best being a

steep juggy rib projecting slightly forwards. This soon eases, with short steps above leading to the plateau. The summit of Meall nam Ban is a few minutes away up right.

Sgùrr nan Clach Geala — 1093m

The Fannaichs are often thought of as grassy hills with broad ridges, but Sgùrr nan Clach Geala has a dramatic east face of towering buttresses. A set of lesser bluffs next to this gives a scenically-sited scramble.

 PAGE 240
 OS LR 20
 EAST
 PSAMMITE

118	Slanting Buttress		Grade 3 ✱	
◯ NH 191 718	🚶 2HRS 30	◿ OUTCROPS	↕ +250M	

Steep tiers of psammite climbed on big positive holds in a superb situation. The two biggest tiers are both easier than they look but can be avoided on the right.

Slanting Buttress, Sgùrr nan Clach Geala (Route 118, Grade 3).
Scrambler: Marco de Man. © Iain Thow

Approach

Best approached from the north by crossing the saddle of Am Biachdaich, starting from either Loch a' Bhraoin (NH 163 761) or Loch an Droma (NH 254 755). From the saddle drop down leftwards at first, then traverse southwards below broken clifflets to the crag. Slanting Buttress is the inclined buttress starting below and right of the main buttresses. Start at the bottom left-hand corner, at the mouth of Slanting Gully, which bounds the main cliff on the right. It is possible to just do the top half (and best) part of the route by traversing in along a higher shelf, starting at the first steep tier.

The Route
Go up right onto the buttress and up easy steps. As the gully on the left narrows go up crinkly slabs on its edge (awkward) or avoid them on the right. Reach a large sloping grassy shelf below a steep tier. Climb brown slabs near the left-hand end, then go up to an overhang on positive holds. Go up right below the overhang and back above it on a ledge, then up to another terrace. Climb the first clean rib from the left, which is steep but juggy. At the large overhang traverse airily right and go up the next rib. On the next tier climb the left-hand rib and go up to another terrace, with the buttress now opening out. Climb an easy rib ahead and another up left to more ledges. Go up left to another juggy buttress and the top.

Sgùrr Mòr 1110m

The graceful cone of Sgùrr Mòr is a prominent feature of many northern highland views, the highest hill north of the Kyle railway line. Most ways up are grassy but the following scramble is worthwhile.

- PAGE 240
- OS LR 20
- NORTH-EAST
- SCHIST

---

119 North Spur **Grade 2**

NH 205 722 | 2HRS 30 | OUTCROPS | +100M

A scatter of schist outcrops coalesce into a sharp ridge leading to the highest summit of the Fannaichs. The route looks impressive from a distance, but is very mossy and broken on close acquaintance. All difficulties are avoidable if desired.

Approach
From the west end of Loch Droma (NH 254 755) take the vehicle track up to and along Allt a' Mhadaidh. A smaller path continues to Loch a' Mhadaidh. Go up left on grass to the foot of the North Spur, which is quite broad at the bottom. Start at the lowest clean rib on the left-hand side.

The Route
Go up the juggy rib to a big boulder, then continue directly up moss and boulders to the left-hand side of steeper rock above. Climb mossy slabs with big quartz crystals, then a steeper buttress with big flakes to arrive on a blunt ridge. Mossy outcrops with a few optional harder problems lead to a grassy platform. Above this the ridge narrows but eases and steep airy walking leads to the summit.

Another route nearby
Worth including if climbing Meall a' Chrasgaidh from the north-east is the broken rib at NH 187 733, mostly Grade 1 but with a short Grade 2 section. It's a bit loose in places but with nice positions and lots of jugs. A rough path zigzags around all the outcrops.

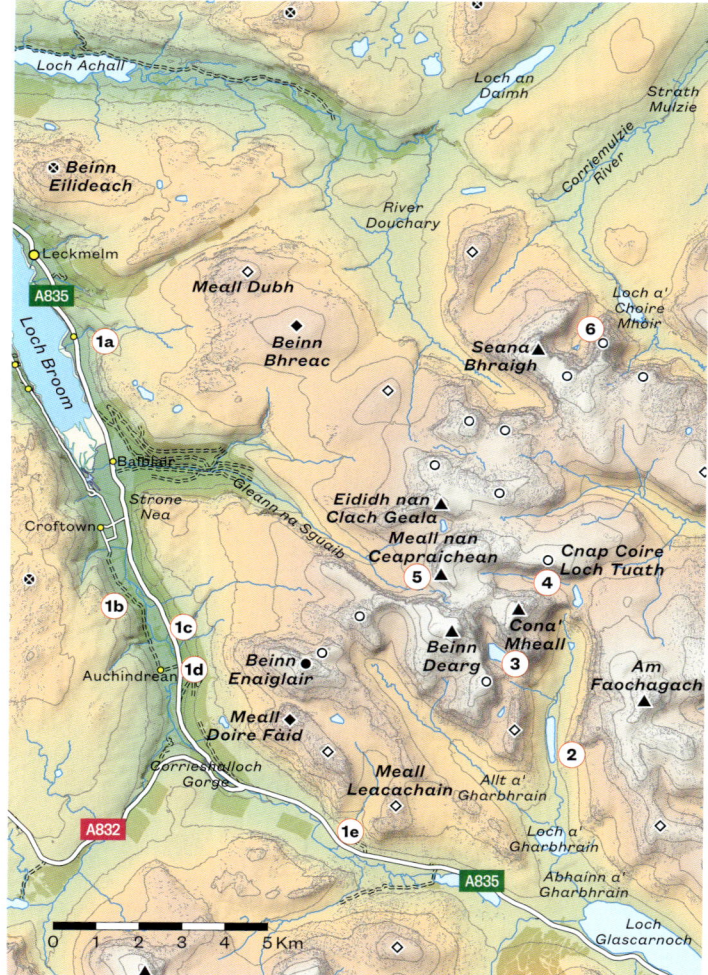

1.	Ullapool Gorges	Routes 120a–e	P.258
2.	Am Faochagach	Route 121	P.260
3.	Cona' Mheall	Routes 122–124	P.262
4.	Cnap Coire Loch Tuath	Route 125	P.265
5.	Meall nan Ceapraichean	Route 126	P.266
6.	Seana Bhraigh	Routes 127–128	P.268

Inverlael & Easter Ross

This is the vast sprawling range north of the Ullapool road, culminating in Beinn Dearg and Cona' Mheall. Most of the area is an extensive upland plateau, rimmed to the west by a semicircle of higher summits and cut by deep craggy-sided valleys. The rock is mainly schist, often vegetated, but in places it runs to some long buttresses and clean slabs. Cona' Mheall and Seana Bhraigh provide the best routes. In addition to the areas described, the south flank of Càrn Alladale (NH 410 895) is a pleasant easy scramble up huge boulders, while the area around Glenbeg Bothy (NH 314 835) has a scatter of mainly slabby crags, but the scrambling is scrappy relative to the effort involved in reaching it. The Alladale Slabs (NH 375 872) give a choice of steep blank quartzite or equally steep heather, while the long flank of Beinn Dearg above Gleann na Sguaib is mostly too steep for scrambling, although an excellent winter climbing venue.

Ullapool Gorges

Around the head of Loch Broom are a number of gorges, of which the spectacular Corrieshalloch Gorge is the best known. In dry weather this can be waded up as far as the falls. Just to the west is the equally impressive Cuileig Gorge, but the central section of this involves swimming. Several steeper gorges come down the hillside into the lower glen.

- PAGE 256
- OS LR 20
- VARIOUS
- SCHIST

120a Ardcharnich Gorge — Grade 2

NH 174 885 | 2MINS | STREAM | +150M

The lower gorge is easy but very overgrown, while the upper gorge is extremely impressive, but blocked by impassable falls. It also has very loose walls and is difficult to swim out of while wearing boots and a rucksack! The right branch starting at the mouth of the upper gorge is quite long and pleasant.

120b Allt a' Gharbhain — Grade 2

NH 182 824 | 30MINS | STREAM | +250M

Probably the best of the bunch, deep-cut and narrow, with more sustained scrambling than its neighbours.

Approach
From the crossroads north of Inverbroom Lodge follow the minor road and track to Garvan. Go past the buildings to reach the bridge over the stream.

The Route
The stream is easy at first, with one awkward step on the left at a smooth slab. The first large fall is started wetly on the right and finished up a stepped rib in the centre (quite exposed). Go right into a small gorge, climbing another fall on the left, then crossing right just below the top. An obviously impassable fall comes in from the left and it is best to escape right here up steep vegetation. The upper gorge can be reached by a steep loose slimy gully on the right and an exposed grass traverse, but the small falls above are not worth the nervous energy expended in reaching them.

120c Allt a' Bhraighe — Grade 1

NH 198 816 | 15MINS | STREAM | +200M

A deep gorge of no great difficulty, but it would be hard after heavy rain. Two impassable falls are easily avoided.

Approach
Park opposite the Wood Turning Centre at NH 195 811 and follow the path up from the left-hand side of the car park entrance. Cross a wider track and slant up leftwards to a sharp bend, where a steep muddy pathlet slants down into the gorge.

The Route
A few small pitches lead to an impassable fall avoided by steep scree on the left. The shelf across to the top of the fall is very loose, so go over the top of the spur to rejoin the stream. More level stream bed follows, then the final fall is avoided by grass on the left.

120d Allt na h-Ighine   Grade 1

○ NH 200 813	🏃 15MINS	⊿ STREAM	⊤ +150M

Another easy but scenic gorge, unfortunately with an impossible finish.

Approach
Follow the previous approach as far as the sharp bend, but continue rightwards up the path to a bridge.

The Route
Descend into the stream on the left and pass the stream gate. Lots of boulder hopping with fallen trees and the odd minor pitch follows. Crossing a conglomerate boulder on the right by a little fall is the best bit. A larger fall appears on the left, climbable at Grade 3, as is the next small fall above, but the next (hidden) fall is not, and the escape there is loose and exposed, so best to go up the open gully on the right just before the large fall.

120e Allt Leacachain   Grade 2

○ NH 233 764	🏃 5MINS	⊿ STREAM	⊤ +70M

A more open stream scramble, with all difficulties avoidable if desired.

Approach
From parking at NH 236 759 follow the track north-west alongside the pipeline to the small dam.

The Route
The stream largely consists of easy slabs, with the odd steeper step. The highlight is a short shuffle along horizontal cracks on the left, followed by a long step across the stream onto the lip of an overhang.

There are pleasant continuations up onto Meall Leacachain (618m) by its north ridge or onto Meall Doire Faid (730m) over Meall nan Doire-achain, or doing both via the Corbett Beinn Enaiglair.

Allt Leacachain, Ullapool Gorges (Route 120e, Grade 2).
Scrambler: Simon Fraser. © Noel Williams

Am Faochagach 954m

A rounded plateau summit, not one of the more inspiring Munros, but the described scramble adds some interest. The river crossings make this a poor choice in wet weather.

- PAGE 256
- OS LR 20
- WEST
- PSAMMITE

121	Cnoc na h-Iolaire		Grade 2
◯ NH 286 784	1HR 30	OUTCROPS	+150M

A blunt spur crossed by lines of broken psammite slabs, not exposed or serious but with the odd awkward move.

Approach
From the parking at the head of Loch Glascarnoch (NH 277 743) take the initially inconspicuous boggy path starting opposite the car park to the Abhainn a' Gharbhrain. In dry weather this is crossable around NH 282 753 but it isn't unusual to have to go round the north side of Loch a' Gharbhrain. This involves crossing both the Allt a' Gharbhrain

and Allt Lair, both of which can still be tricky. Once on the far side of the water head northwards to gain a grassy spur curving up north-eastwards towards Cnoc na h-Iolaire. The odd outcrop can be found lower down, then the spur flattens out at around 450m. Pass a small vegetated outcrop to another smaller flattening then go up right to much more continuous rock.

Cnoc na h-Iolaire (Route 121, Grade 2).
Scrambler: Doug Hall. © Iain Thow

The Route
Climb tiers of rough slabs separated by heathery ledges, mostly easy and with a wide choice of route. Occasional harder sections can be found but everything is avoidable. The best slabs tend to be on the right. After 100m or so the spur curves over into easy ground with just the odd outcrop, then grass leads to the summit of Cnoc na h-Iolaire. A grassy slope runs up to the broad ridge of Am Faochagach.

Cona' Mheall   980m

Beinn Dearg's smaller and more graceful partner has a rocky ridge running north-west to south-east, with psammite buttresses falling 300m into Coire Ghrannda.

 PAGE 256
 OS LR 20
 VARIOUS
PSAMMITE

122. Twisted Rib — Moderate *

○ NH 269 809   🚶 2HRS 45   ⊿ BUTTRESS   ⊤ +300M

There are huge amounts of feasible scrambling on this face, the buttresses generally getting harder northwards, the final ones being more climbing than scrambling. Twisted Rib is fairly central, directly above the head of the loch and just right of the most prominent gully. Steep outcrops with lots of route choice lead to a better-defined slabby buttress, exposed at the top and tricky in the wet.

Approach
From the A835 just west of Loch Glascarnoch (parking NH 277 743) take an initially inconspicuous path starting opposite the car park to the Abhainn a' Gharbhrain. Stay on the near side and head north past Loch a' Gharbhrain to the Allt a' Gharbhrain. Go up this until it can be conveniently crossed, then go up the opposite slope to Loch nan Eilean. Continue past this on a shelf leading into the mouth of Coire Ghrannda. Follow the east side of the loch to crags above the north end. Start at the third buttress from the right, with a long low overhang at its foot.

The Route
From just right of the overhang climb slabs up left to a nose. This is steep, so go a long way left to a ramp leading up left to pass the main cliff. Go right and slant right up slabs, then more slabs and small outcrops lead to a big terrace.

Climb the right-hand side of a vertically grooved nose, then go up to the next tier, easily climbed by a rib on the left. On the next crag step right from boulders onto a nose and go up. The next band is steeper. Climb a square groove, with a hard move left at the top to a ledge. Go up detached blocks at the left-hand end of this, then easy slabs. Go left and up a broad shattered rib, which becomes the left edge of the buttress. Carry on up this to the top. The last section involves an exposed move up right on large flakes just left of the arête.

From below the last steep section it is possible to traverse right across the gully onto the next buttress and climb its slabby arête. This is sustained Moderate, but less exposed.

123. South Ridge — Grade 1 *

○ NH 275 804   🚶 2HRS 30   ⊿ SLABS & ARÊTE   ⊤ +250M

Easy slabby outcrops lead up to a narrow ridge. A great way up the hill, but with only minor scrambling.

Approach
As for the previous route to the mouth of Coire Ghrannda. Above the outflow from the loch is a broad slope with numerous slabby outcrops.

The Route
Link together outcrops (generally Grade 1 but harder moves can be found) until the buttress coalesces at a scree fan. A path now runs up directly ahead, but the ribs to the right are worth including. Join the

main ridge and follow it up. This is mainly narrow and grassy but with a short steep descent to a col and a couple of rock steps beyond. After two minor tops the ridge broadens and runs up to the main summit.

124 North-East Slab — Moderate ✶✶

| ⌖ NH 280 820 | 🏃 3HRS | ⊿ SLABS | ⊤ +120M |

A single curving psammite slab, easy-angled but with some fairly blank sections and one quite hard overlap. A confident scrambler on a dry day will find it mostly almost walking with one tricky step, but for the nervous it will be gripping and in the wet it is lethal. A serious and committing route in a remote situation.

Approach
Loch Tuath at the foot of the face can be reached by following the path up Gleann na Squaib from the head of Loch Broom (parking NH 183 854) and descending eastwards from the saddle at its top. A shorter but rougher approach is to walk in up Coire Lair, starting as for Route 122 and then continuing up past Loch Coire Lair and Loch Prille (brief scrambling on a deer track right of the falls) to reach Loch Tuath. The slab is high above the south side of the loch.

The Route
Start up the right-hand side of the central groove and go up to two-thirds height, where a short curving overlap completely crosses the slab. Climb this left of centre where there is an intermediate step. There is only one hard move, but it makes the exposure of the sweep of slabs below very noticeable. Carry on up the narrowing recessed slab, funnelled between the steeper areas either side, with a few delicate sections before it runs out into the hillside. Minor changes in angle drastically alter the difficulty, but the main thing is to avoid wet areas. There are a couple of minor rock steps at the top of the east ridge.

Cnap Coire Loch Tuath 884m

This minor summit at the end of Meall nan Ceapraichean's east ridge has a large south face with extensive patches of slabby psammite. The described route climbs the leftmost and largest of these, directly below the summit.

- PAGE 256
- OS LR 20
- SOUTH
- PSAMMITE

---

125 South Face Grade 3

○ NH 283 824   🏃 3HRS   ◿ SLABS   ⊤ +270M

A slabby wander up a large face. Quite intimidating, but a lot easier than it looks and with plenty of route options. Best avoided in the wet.

Approach
Loch Tuath at the foot of the face can be reached from the head of Loch Broom as for Route 126, going up Glean Sguaib and over the col at its head, long but mostly on a path. It is easier going to pass south of Loch Tuath and cross the stream just below the small lochans beyond it. The route starts just above, aiming for a prominent clean slabby nose.

  A shorter but much rougher approach is from the head of Loch Glascarnoch (parking NH 277 743) as for Route 121 then continuing past Loch Coire Lair and Loch na Still. Go up the right-hand side of the head of the corrie on a deer track just east of the stream, cross the stepping stones at the mouth of Loch Prille and continue west of the loch. Cross the stream below the small lochan just east of Loch Tuath to arrive below the slabby nose mentioned above.

The Route

Climb a scrappy slab, then the clean slabby nose. Dodge a vertical wall on the right and go up left to the large area of slabs in the centre of the face. Climb the right-hand edge of these, passing just right of a prominent dark overlap. When the slabs steepen escape right to grass (this is possible at several levels). Go up the grass then traverse left to boulders above the slabs. Climb a grooved rib with squarish overlaps to grass and boulders. Up right is a clean rib with a steep juggy start. Climb this then a choice of minor outcrops to the top.

Meall nan Ceapraichean   977m

A grassy plateau with a rocky west face, this is often linked with Beinn Dearg to give a fine day out. Good stalkers' paths make the access easy.

 PAGE 256
 OS LR 20
 WEST
 PSAMMITE

126 West Face — Grade 2

◯ NH 256 832   🚶 3HRS   ◿ BUTTRESS   ⊤ +200M

Small buttresses lead up to a psammite slab prominent from the approach up Gleann na Sguaib. The first half consists of avoidable outcrops, while the top half is more sustained and briefly exposed.

Approach
From the parking at Inverlael (NH 183 854) take the forestry road eastwards, first south of the stream, then north. At the forest edge go out into Gleann na Sguaib and continue up the path, forking left at NH 234 835. Just before reaching Lochan a' Chnapaich leave the path and bear right to the lowest point of the screes. Go up right to broken outcrops, the lowest on the slope.

The Route

Climb the outcrops, then move right to a wavy slab. Climb this left to right on sharp quartz holds. Start the next rib on the right and go up the nose to grass. A rock band now crosses the slope, climbed on the right, then go up left to a spur. A steeper cracked nose is climbed airily on the arête and leads to delicate slabs. Go up these to pass left of the top overhang and reach easier ground.

Seana Bhraigh 927m

One of the most remote Munros, Seana Bhraigh is rimmed by large vegetated cliffs which provide superb winter routes. The spike of An Sgùrr projects northwards from the plateau and is one of the few mainland summits only reachable by scrambling. The west face consists of well-defined ribs, one of which gives an excellent long scramble.

- PAGE 256
- OS LR 20
- NORTH & WEST
- PSAMMITE

127 An Sgùrr Ridge — Grade 1 or 2

◯ NH 298 887 🏃 2HRS 30 ◿ BUTTRESS ⊤ +450M

A blunt ridge with schist and psammite outcrops leading to a sharp peak in a remote situation. The crux is reaching the 'mainland' from the summit.

Approach

A long way from any direction! Loch a' Choire Mhoir is reached by a private vehicle track up Strath Mulzie, and outside the shooting season it is possible to drive to the Schoolhouse Bothy at Duag Bridge. A mountain bike is still useful for the remaining 8km up to Loch a' Choire Mhoir. Alternatively another private road leads up Glen Achall to Loch an

Daimh. From there fork right to take a stalkers' path up alongside Allt nan Caorach and across a saddle to reach Loch a' Choire Mhoir.

In either case, from the foot of the loch cross the stream and head up south-west into the mouth of Luchd Choire, where the route starts up to the left.

The Route

A small outcrop above the moraine at the corrie mouth is Grade 2, easily avoided. Where the steep wall on the left finishes go left onto the ridge and climb it on blocky rock (Grade 2 direct, easier on the right). Carry on up the skyline, zigzagging up two steeper vegetated sections to reach a level shoulder. Short outcrops lead to a pink slab, climbed on the arête, then more broken ground leads to walking as the ridge narrows.

Keep to the bouldery crest until a steeper prow forces a move right (loose). Carry on up the crest to another steepening. A path zigzags up this (or Grade 2 direct). The angle now eases and short steps lead to the top. Descend via an exposed path just left of the crest (not obvious to start). From the saddle two short easy steps lead to a grassy ridge and the plateau.

---

128 Corriemulzie Rib **Grade 3 or Difficult ★★**

| ○ NH 295 882 | 🚶 3HRS | ⟋ BUTTRESS | ⊤ +300M |

A spiky rib, quite steep at first, with an exposed crux, then a much easier top half. The inward-dipping psammite is quite juggy and positive but some parts are fairly mossy. Most sections are avoidable but this is often on extremely steep grass.

Approach

As for the previous route as far as Luchd Choire, then continue to the lochan. The face consists of six ribs, of which the left-hand two are short and the right-hand one is grassy. The described route is the left-hand of the remaining three, which starts lowest on the face, directly above the outflow of the lochan. Go up broken ground to the first steep rock, starting by a rock table.

The Route

Climb slabs to a ledge, then go up the right-hand edge of a V-shaped recess, steep and juggy. Climb a steep crack, then a slab above, starting at a quartzy block. Vegetated slabs and broken ground lead up left to more sustained rock. After a short slab climb a groove with an awkward start to break through steeper rock. Now climb tiers of slabs on the crest, some quite steep but all with good holds, to reach a huge perched block.

The clean slabs above are the crux. Start with a flake-crack trending right, then when it bends left either go straight up and over an airy bulge on good holds (Difficult) or bear up right to climb an easier crack above the gully. Both ways lead to a mossy ledge with easier slabs above. Go up these and blocks to a saddle halfway up the ridge. A well-defined ridge of easier mossier rocks leads to the main ridge just north of the summit of An Sgùrr. Reach the plateau as for Route 127.

Coigach & Assynt

The twin peninsulas of Assynt and Coigach are a magical landscape where isolated rocky peaks of Torridonian sandstone dominate a crumpled carpet of Lewisian gneiss. All the main peaks have scrambling about them somewhere, and in Stac Pollaidh and Suilven the area boasts two of the finest and most distinctive peaks in Scotland. Inland, the area is bounded by the more rounded but still rough ridges of Ben More Assynt and its satellites.

1.	Ben More Coigach	Routes 129–130	P.272
2.	Beinn an Eòin	Routes 131–132	P.275
3.	Stac Pollaidh	Route 133	P.277
4.	Cùl Beag	Route 134	P.281
5.	Cùl Mòr	Routes 135–136	P.283
6.	Suilven	Route 137	P.287
7.	Conival	Route 138	P.290
8.	Ben More Assynt	Routes 139–142	P.291
9.	Quinag	Route 143	P.294

Ben More Coigach 743m

A complex of steep-sided sandstone peaks rather than the simple ridge that is usually first seen, the main ridge is narrow but easy, with the west end and south face providing the scrambling.

 PAGE 270
 OS LR 15
 WEST & SOUTH
 SANDSTONE

129	**West Ridge Direct**		**Grade 3** **
NC 082 034	1HR	BUTTRESS	+150M

A minor diversion from the path, short but on sound rock in good positions, high above the sea. Quite technical in places but the hard bits are not too exposed and easily avoided if required.

Approach
Park at Culnacraig (NC 064 041). Take care not to block the turning space – there is a bigger parking area a few hundred metres back up the road. Go up the path just right of the bridge. At the first shoulder traverse right and go round to cross the Allt nan Coisiche a little above the waterfall. Go up right to a shelf to see three buttresses on the end of the ridge, just right of the path. The left-hand one is a broken Grade 1, the central has a vertical finish, the right-hand one is the route described. A few easy rock steps lead up to it.

High up on West Ridge Direct, Ben More Coigach (Route 129, Grade 3).
Scrambler: Phil Williams. © Peter Woolnough

The Route

Start with a short crack, then a wide steep crack above (or an easy groove to the right). Another crack/groove follows, finishing just left of a prow. From a niche on the right go up the crack above for a few metres, then step left and climb the left arête, with one delicate step halfway up. An easy-angled ridge now leads to a steepening, climbed by another delicate slab (homesick gritstone climbers will enjoy the jamming crack on the right). Go left up easy ground into a bay and climb the tower on the left. A few short steps lead to the ridge, where some added excitement can be contrived by following the crest (path on left). About 1km further along the ridge the main summit is off left and in mist it is easy to miss this.

130 Isle Martin Buttress   Grade 2/3

| ⌖ NC 087 033 | 🚶 1HR 15 | ◿ BUTTRESS | ⊤ +300M |

This is the second major buttress along the south face. It is technically easy for the grade, but serious and exposed, with a messy vegetated start leading to nicely positioned easy scrambling above.

Approach
Follow the approach for the previous route to the shelf, then continue right to follow a good sheep track along below the main South Face. Pass over a lower buttress and cross a gully, then a few metres beyond is a left-slanting heathery groove. Start here.

The Route
Climb the groove, avoiding the steepest bit on the left to emerge on the left skyline above the main gully. Zigzag up heather to boulders perched on the left arête below a steeper face. Traverse right past a leaning block and bear up right on more open heather. All this is very exposed. Climb a right-slanting slabby groove, finishing on the right to reach a terrace. Go up left to a small undercut slab below a larger tier. Climb the slab from the right, then traverse left below steeper rock to a short groove. Climb this, then bear right up better rock to reach a shoulder and easier ground.

Go up the ridge ahead, including problems as desired. Near the top the ridge is split by a minor gully. The right-hand branch has better rock, with a steep finish up juggy flakes, while the left-hand branch requires a devious route around leftwards to start. Where the ridges rejoin a steep chimney in the tower ahead is a Difficult variation, or go round to the right. A few easy steps with optional problems lead to the summit ridge.

Beinn An Eòin 618m

This twin-peaked sandstone hill is often thought of as part of Ben More Coigach, but is actually separated from it by a 300m gulf. The saddle between them is dominated by the huge prow of Sgùrr an Fhidhleir with its classic HVS rock climb up the Nose, but the blunter rib opposite provides good though disjointed scrambling, and the ridge between the two summits also has its moments.

 PAGE 270
 OS LR 15
SOUTH-WEST
SANDSTONE

| 131 | South-West Flank, Sgòrr Deas | Grade 3 ** |

 NC 100 062   1HR 30   BUTTRESS   +300M

Problems on small outcrops to start, with a superb sustained finish.

Approach
From the east end of Loch Lurgainn (NC 138 067) a boggy path leads south-west up the Allt Claonaidh. Where this reaches the deer fence go right and follow the fence around the north side of Lochan Tuath. About 300 metres beyond the loch the path descends slightly and you start to see along the west face of Sgòrr Deas. Start on the small slabby buttresses on the right, at a triangular slab with a steep start.

South-West Flank, Sgòrr Deas, Beinn an Eòin (Route 131, Grade 3).
Scrambler: Noel Williams. © Iain Thow

The Route

Swing left onto the slab (hard but avoidable) and climb it, continuing up several short walls on good holds, bearing slightly left to an easing of angle. Two more short walls can be taken in before the ground flattens out.

Above is a deep gully on the left, with steep grass right of it and steep outcrops right again. Work a way up these outcrops, easier than they look, to reach a steep rock band running across from the gully on the left. Climb the right-hand end of this on good holds, then bear left up more grass to reach the nearest outcrops.

Climb a small corner, then a flake right of a larger one, escaping left at the top. Go up a series of slabby flakes on big rounded holds, very sustained but with a wide choice of route. As the rib becomes more defined the flakes lead into a groove just right of the skyline. Climb this, then a short steep crack. After one minor outcrop the ground eases, with the summit not far away.

132 · South-West Ridge, Sgòrr Tuath — Grade 2

| ◇ NC 105 073 | 🏃 2HRS 30 | ⊿ OUTCROPS | ⊤ +60M |

A series of short problems, avoidable and not exposed, give a pleasant way of climbing the ridge.

Approach
Almost invariably approached over Sgòrr Deas, taking the easy ridge northwards then descending more steeply rightwards to the col.

The Route
From the Deas/Tuath col go up to a wall on the left and climb its left arête on big holds. Carry on up more outcrops on the ridgeline to reach a steep wall at the top. The best line is left of centre, just left of the steepest section. Climb a groove leftwards to finish on the arête.

Stac Pollaidh — 613m

An amazing mini-mountain, little more than 600m high, but as craggy and spectacular as you could wish. Its pinnacled summit ridge provides excellent scrambling at a variety of grades, with many possible variations. The sandstone is clean and rough, but sometimes quite shattered.

- 🌐 PAGE 270
- ⊲ OS LR 15
- ↔ VARIOUS
- ⌂ SANDSTONE

133 East-West Traverse — Grade 1 to Difficult

◇ NC 110 105   🏃 45MINS   ◿ ARÊTE   ⊤ +150M

An easy and a harder line are described, but variations are legion. The true summit lies at the westernmost end of the ridge. This is guarded by an unavoidable small tower, which involves a move or so of about Moderate. Many parties are content to visit a cairned summit a little to the east of the true summit. The direct route to the true summit from the west is given Difficult in climbing guides, but is severely undergraded.

Approach
From the car park at Loch Lurgainn (NC 107 095) take the good track uphill through newish planting, bearing right at the fork just before the fence. Carry on up to go round the east end of the hill. For the East End Direct leave the path at around the 400m contour, just after it starts to go up steeply leftwards. For the other options continue on the path around the northern flank and then ascend steeply to a saddle on the summit ridge.

The Routes

a) East End – Grade 2 or 3
From the 400m contour bear up left to minor rocks. Follow these rather scrappily to the eastern summit (steep at the top). Descend to a notch, then climb awkward grooves on rounded steps to another top (briefly Grade 3). An easy descent leads to the main saddle. If reaching the eastern summit from the saddle the descent into the notch feels very insecure – the notch can also be reached directly from the main path by traversing left just before reaching the main saddle (not obvious). This traverse can be used to avoid the awkward grooves, making the route Grade 2.

b) West End Easier Route – Grade 1 ✶✶
From the saddle pass left of the first wall, the first steep gully and two more open ones. Regain the ridge via the third open gully, with a steep move at a short jammed boulder (awkward but not exposed), then either go left up slabs or cross over to the north side of the ridge to join a path up to the next broad col. Even easier is to go up the next wide gully along (quite loose) to the broad col.

From the broad col head west and go rightwards up easy ground, crossing a transverse barrier to where the ridge flattens. Keep right of boulders on the crest to a short awkward sidle along an overhung ledge above a gully. Climb slabs beyond and follow the ridge leftwards to the cairned summit. Access to the highest top is blocked by a short vertical tower, with all routes at least Moderate. Return the same way.

c) West End Harder Route – Grade 3, Moderate or Difficult ✶✶✶
From the saddle pass left of the first steep wall. If in search of challenge you can go a short distance up the first gully and climb the right-hand of two corners in its left wall, with an obvious flake crack at the top (an exposed Diff), then follow the ridge. Alternatively, go up the next gully along to reach the ridge, making the route Grade 3 (to the cairned

Reaching the ridge of Stac Pollaidh, West End Easier Route (Route 133b, Grade 1). Scrambler: Marco de Man. © Iain Thow

On the crux of Stac Pollaidh, West End Harder Route (Route 133c, Moderate).
Scrambler: Gary Mooney. © Iain Thow

summit). Just before the ridge go left up a slab, then follow the ridge along to the next pinnacle, dodge this on the right and go up a gully to regain the ridge. Follow this to a short drop with an airy step across. Go up a short steep problem and along to a short delicate descent to a broad col (easy gullies either side). From the col go up slabs and the ridge becomes easy, with minor problems if desired, until it flattens out. Keep right of boulders on the crest to a short awkward sidle along an overhung ledge above a gully. Climb slabs beyond and follow the ridge leftwards to the cairned summit. The best return route from this summit is by the Grade 1 route described above.

Access to the highest top is blocked by a short vertical tower. The direct route has suffered a rockfall and is now V Diff. By far the best and most popular route is to go down left and squirm up into a deep groove, which is easy once you're in it (Moderate). The summit is easily reached from its top. Return the same way, which, unusually, most find easier in descent.

Cùl Beag 769m

This isolated and quite rough sandstone peak has a steep and damp north face and a west face that contains one superb scramble, with more possible.

- PAGE 270
- OS LR 15
- WEST
- SANDSTONE

Lurgainn Edge, Cùl Beag (Route 134, Grade 3).
Scrambler: Adrian Camm. © Mark Robson

134 Lurgainn Edge — Grade 3 ★★★

◯ NC 138 087　　🏃 45MINS　　◿ BUTTRESS　　⌶ +250M

An outstanding route, traditionally graded Difficult but more of a scramble if you avoid the two overhangs on the direct line. The positions in the top half are tremendous, making up for the purgatorially steep approach. The upper part can be avoided in the gully to the left, but this misses the best part of the route. This section is committing once embarked on it and the steep grass in the avoiding option would be nasty in the wet. A good summer evening route for the energetic.

Approach
Park by Loch Lurgainn just east of Linneraineach (NC 126 089) and start up the path to Loch an Doire Dhuibh. At the top of the trees leave this and head up direct across pathless moorland and steep heather, aiming for the right-hand side of the prominent central Y-shaped gully. Go up steeply to the first rocks on the right-hand side of the gully.

A more technical start can be found using the right-hand edge of the steep wall about 300 metres right to gain the mid-height shelf, then walking left to the top half of the route. This is cleaner but much more indirect and feels somehow unsatisfying.

The Route
Climb three short stepped outcrops, then go up into a minor gully, where a path develops. Follow this up to more rock and an open scoop. Go up the left-hand arête of this (loose at the top), then up right below a jutting nose. Go up left to broken ground, then up right to cleaner rock. A vegetated groove left of this leads to the top of the tier. Things now improve.

From the lowest point of the next tier climb flake-cracks to heather. Carry on up easier rocks, climbing little ribs on big rounded holds. A steeper wide flake-crack is interesting (easier to the left). When the ridge narrows climb a steep tower with a thin crack, then keep on direct up the crest to easy ground and a narrow neck. Either climb the overhang direct (Difficult, but only one move) or dodge it by a gully to the left. The next rounded overhang is harder, but easily avoided by an exposed ramp on the right, then cutting back left to the top. A short walk leads to the summit.

Cùl Mòr　　849m

The twin peaks of Cùl Mòr are an easy walk up from the east, but the other sides are steep and rocky, though the sandstone is mostly too broken for quality rock climbing. The distinctive pinnacles on its north-west end provide the best route, but Table Rib is in an impressive setting on the south face, finishing on Coigach's best picnic spot.

🌐 PAGE 270
➤ OS LR 15
↔ VARIOUS
⛰ SANDSTONE

135   Table Rib   Grade 3 *

◯ NC 156 114   🚶 1HR 30   ◢ INTRICATE   ⊤ +250M

A good line and excellent positions, but the actual scrambling isn't as good as it looks from a distance. The start is quite serious, although not too exposed. An alternative start further left avoids this, but it is not as good a line.

Approach
Either walk in from Loch Lurgainn (NC 126 089) via Loch an Doire Dhuibh and scramble up the Allt Lochan Dearg (avoid the two main falls on the right) or traverse west from the usual path to Cùl Mòr from Knockan Cliff (parking at NC 189 094) to go down past the dramatically situated Lochan Dearg a' Chuil Mhoir. Take a shelf north-west from here, then slant up to the face. Table Rib is the left-hand rib on the main steep face, before the cliffs break down into open slopes. Start in the steep gully to its right.

The easier start (Grade 2) is reached by carrying on along the shelf below the cliffs until the third gully comes down (Longstaff's Gully). Go up the near edge of this, mostly on a zigzag deer path. Once above the steep cliffs go up right to join Table Rib at a grassy col.

The Route
Go up the gully and its left-hand branch to slimy slabs with a columnar vertical cliff up to the right. Start left of the centre of the slabs and work up left (crux) until it is possible to traverse left to reach the skyline at a block. Climb the crack behind this to a larger block. Bridge up behind it, then climb a crack left of a steep nose. An easy ridge now leads to a saddle at the top of the initial slabs.

Broken ground with occasional problems leads to a steep wall crossing the ridge. Climb this by a grassy gully on the right, gained by a rounded groove right again. The ridge now opens out and the easier version comes in from the left. Climb stepped prows ahead to a pinnacle and a larger nose. Grovel onto a boulder left of the overhang and go up, then more easy steps lead to a level ridge. The sting in the tail is a hard little overhang (avoidable), emerging on the Table.

136 Pinnacle Ridge — Moderate *

NC 155 129 — 1HR 30 — BUTTRESS — +200M

Not as good a line as it looks from a distance, but parts of the scrambling are excellent. Has a definite delicate crux, which isn't where you expect. Coire Gorm, crossed on the approach, is a much used red deer hangout so the route is best avoided during the stalking season.

Approach
From the parking just north of Knockan Cliff (NC 189 094) take the path leading north. After 2km leave it to traverse rightwards into Coire Gorm on the north side of the summit. Pinnacle Ridge is the right-hand skyline, but once below it the 'ridge' breaks up into several buttresses. The described route starts up the left-hand low-relief one. There are plenty of easier variations, mostly on the left.

The Route
Climb two short steep walls, then the front of a vertical tower by big ledges. The buttress ends after a couple more steps, so cross right and climb the next one past a sharp prow to easy ground. Traverse right under towers to the skyline ridge. Gain this by a slabby ramp on the left and follow the easy flaky ridge. Climb a steeper tower by a grimy chimney (or avoid it on the left), then go up cleaner steps. Climb a vertical corner right of a big prow, then bear up right to the next ridge.

This buttress is the crux, avoiding it on the left makes the route Grade 3. Climb a nose by steep flakes, then mossy ledges and a delicate step up lead to the first pinnacle. Hop the gap and descend ahead to a col. Go up the left-hand side of the ridge on excellent clean rock, then up easier ground to say hello to 'the Old Man' (about VS?), who is more properly called *Bòd a' Mhiotailt*. Cross the next col and go up broken ground, then up another clean slab on the left-hand side of the ridge. At the next steep section pass the first wall on the left, then a steep slab leads to an easy ridge and the top.

High up on Pinnacle Ridge, Cùl Mòr (Route 136, Moderate), with Suilven in the background. Climber: Richard Merryfield.
© Noel Williams

Suilven 731m

Although a contender for Scotland's finest peak, Suilven has less scrambling than a distant view might lead you to expect. The ridge traverse is a classic for its views and situations, but other routes are either too hard or too vegetated for enjoyment. The obvious weakness right of the nose of Caisteal Liath is a steep and verdant Moderate (Pilkington & Walker, 1892), thoroughly unpleasant but it does allow a complete traverse of the mountain.

- PAGE 270
- OS LR 15
- VARIOUS
- SANDSTONE

137 Ridge Traverse Grade 2 or 3 ★★

| NC 157 181 | 3HRS | RIDGE | +300 & -300M |

One of the best mountain days in Scotland with superb positions and scenery. Even the easiest options are often very exposed but the scrambling itself is fairly minor and all the harder bits are avoidable if Meall Bheag is omitted. The clean rough sandstone isn't too affected by rain but strong winds make the hill a poor choice.

Approach
The shortest approach is to park at a small parking space 1km west of Glencanisp Lodge (NC 107 220), after which the road becomes private. Follow the road past the lodge and take the track up Glen Canisp. After 5km this crosses the river and about 400 metres later a recently

Looking east towards Meall Mheadhonach with the stone wall in the foreground.
© Noel Williams

repaired path goes up right, eventually rising very steeply up the gully to the saddle (Bealach Mòr).

An alternative is to start from Inverkirkaig (NC 085 194), from where a good track leads up past Kirkaig Falls (well worth the short detour) to Fionn Loch. A boggy path heads up from halfway along the loch and another from just before its east end, and these eventually meet and steepen into an eroded route to the saddle (Bealach Mòr). Although this approach is 1.6km longer and much rougher it has the advantage of being in the sun and the return route from Meall Bheag at the eastern end is of similar length to the northern one.

The Route
The ascent from the col to the main summit, Caisteal Liath, is easy with the odd rocky step and some exposure (Grade 1). The path early on passes through a gap in an amazing stone wall which traverses the crest of the ridge. Return the same way.

From Bealach Mòr to Meall Mheadhonach is similar, but with more problems and two unavoidable scrambling sections. Just after the first notch an optional steep wall is Grade 2, then the start of the descent into the second notch is on sloping steps (Grade 1). The other side of the col is another steep wall (Grade 3 but easily avoidable on the right). Just before the summit of Meall Mheadhonach is a more sustained Grade 2 section. Start up right to a large block, then go back left to the skyline and up to a hollow tower. From the top of this make an awkward step right and go up to the top.

From Meall Mheadhonach many will return to Bealach Mòr and descend from there. A slightly more challenging option is to continue the traverse and descend from the lesser peak, Meall Bheag, at the south-eastern end of the mountain. For this option, from the summit of Meall Mheadhonach, descend a small step and then zigzag very steeply down on grass to the col below the huge leaning prow of Meall Bheag.

Meall Beag

Step up and make an awkward move left (crux, Grade 2) to a ledge. Follow this further left and climb a groove, then continue left to a terrace below the upper wall. Go up left then right (or direct, slightly harder), then climb a short slab and easy steps to the summit. After negotiating one short narrow section where a cleft crosses the ridge the rest of the descent is easy.

In reverse the descent from Meall Bheag can be hard to find. Start well right and zigzag down well-used rock to reach grassy ledges. Follow these left (looking out) to the saddle.

Those returning to Glen Canisp can join the track past Loch na Gainimh after 1.5km, making a convenient loop. Both return options from here seem a long way at the end of a day (12km), and the northern one always seems to have more uphill than you remember from the walk in.

Conival 808m

This summit and its neighbour, Ben More Assynt, are the culmination of a vast sprawling range separating the distinctive peaks of the west from the rolling moorlands of the east. The south ridges of both hills are narrow and rocky, though not particularly difficult.

- PAGE 270
- OS LR 15
- SOUTH-EAST
- SANDSTONE & GNEISS

138	South Ridge	Grade 2 or 3 ✷
◯ NC 307 191	🚶 2HRS 20	◿ OUTCROPS & ARÊTE	⊤ +350M

A bit disjointed, but with several enjoyable sections. Quite exposed in places. The initial gneiss outcrops are all avoidable, but the upper sandstone ridge is not (Grade 2).

Approach
There is a large car park near the Inchnadamph Hotel at NC 251 217. Cross the bridge and take the good track up into Gleann Dubh. After 2km this becomes a smaller path up the glen. Stay with the River Traligill, forking left along the stream up Gleann Dubh. Where the path goes up left out of the gorge go up right to reach the saddle between Conival and Breabag Tarsuinn. Go through this and take a shelf on the left to two small pools. Slant up bearing right to the lowest rocks on the skyline. Start on the right edge of the right-hand vertical face.

The Route
Climb steeply to a shelf slanting left, which leads to easier ground. Walk up right, linking together small outcrops as desired. As the ridge starts to become better defined climb a steep slab just left of the skyline, then another a little higher, both delicate. Walk up to the towers now visible above.

The first tower is preceded by conglomerate boulders, then climbed on lovely rough slabs to reach more boulders. The second and third towers are climbed easily on the crest, then the ridge becomes mainly walking, although still narrow. A step across a gap is quite exposed, before more broken steps lead to the summit.

A more sustained and steeper start can be found further left, but this is quite loose and has a foul approach up steep scree.

Ben More Assynt   998m

This is the highest peak in Sutherland. It is linked to its western neighbour, Conival, by a shattered quartzite ridge, then the south ridge has some nicely positioned easy scrambling on flaky gneiss. The final spur of the south ridge, Sail an Ruathair, has some lovely slabs for anyone coming in that way.

- PAGE 270
- OS LR 15
- SOUTH-EAST
- GNEISS

139 South Ridge — Grade 1

◯ NC 320 199　　🏃 4HRS　　⊿ ARÊTE　　⊤ +100M

Mostly narrow but easy, though a couple of awkward bits are quite exposed.

Approach
Usually approached via Conival and done in descent from the summit of Ben More Assynt, however, the scrambling is better south to north. If not including Conival the approach from remote Glen Cassley is excellent and not much longer, with gabbro slabs low on the east ridge worth including.

The Route
Descending from Ben More the first scrambling met is an easy but exposed slab, descended just right of the crest, then a short narrow arête follows. Just before the lowest point a rocky knoll has to be crossed, either directly (delicate start) or on the right (big holds but very exposed). The ascent to the South Top is narrow but easy after a short rock step. Many will return the same way, but a more aesthetic return is to carry on over Carn nan Conbhairean before descending south-west to Dubh Loch Mor, where a grassy shelf leads back to the Conival/Breabag col. Direct descents to Dubh Loch Mor from the ridge are very steep and loose.

Also worth a look if you are in the area are the quartzite slabs on the west flank of Breabag at NC 281 163. These make a fun diversion on the way up the hill (Grade 2/3), and are easily escapable. The prominent slab right of the lowest outcrops is better than the one with a steep left-hand wall further left. Protruding 'pipes' give better friction than usual for quartzite.

140 South Slabs, Sail an Ruathair — Grade 3 **

◯ NC 334 140　　🏃 1HR 20　　⊿ SLABS　　⊤ +100M

Quite sustained scrambling on rough syenite slabs with lots of possible variation. Short but excellent.

Approach
A good (cycleable) private road leaves the A837 at NC 296 083 (plenty of space but several 'no parking' notices, possible to get a car off the road just opposite). This runs for 6km past Benmore Lodge, then a smaller path branches right up the Allt Sail an Ruathair. 1km up this cross the stream and go up to the foot of the cleanest and most continuous part of the obvious slabs. A steep left-slanting grass rake separates them from the easier and more broken slabs to the right (which start slightly lower down the hill). Start about 10 metres left of the foot of the rake.

The Route
Climb the clean slabs, with excellent friction and a scatter of comforting holds. Bear up left past occasional minor steepenings to reach the grass

rake. Cross this and climb slightly steeper but more broken slabs to the top of the main face. The route can be extended up rather mossier slabs by moving right 20 metres or so. The shallow corners just left of the lower part of the route are the same grade and the steeper prow above the top of the rake is Moderate.

141 South-East Slabs, Sail an Ruathair — Grade 2

◯ NC 335 141   🚶 1HR 20   ◿ SLABS   ⊤ +100M

Much easier slabs split by grassy ledges but still on excellent rock. Makes a good plan B if you don't fancy the more sustained route or have a mixed ability group.

Approach
As for the previous route but start at the lowest slabs further right, just beyond the grassy rake.

The Route
The slabs are almost walking at first but gradually steepen. There are sometimes moves where you are glad of the good holds but easier options are always available. They naturally run into the mossier slabs mentioned in the previous route, which are still Grade 2.

142 East Flank, Sail an Ruathair — Grade 3 *

NC 332 146 — 2HRS — SLABS — +70M

A good continuation to either of the previous routes.

Approach
From the top of the previous routes go up over the Far South Top of Sail an Ruathair (408m) and descend to the saddle beyond. Slant down right below the next top on an intermittent deer track to the lowest point of the reddish slabs on the east flank (tiny cairn).

The Route
Go direct up the slabs, with occasional small overlaps to add interest. The rock isn't quite as perfect as on the previous scrambles but is still delightfully rough.

Quinag   808m

A range in itself, this many-topped hill culminates in two huge buttresses overlooking Kylesku. The western face throws down a long line of broken ribs, but the rock is very loose and the faces much steeper than they look from below.

- PAGE 270
- OS LR 15
- NORTH-EAST
- SANDSTONE

143 East Buttress, Sàil Gharbh — Grade 3 *

NC 217 299 — 1HR — BUTTRESS — +350M

Sàil Gharbh is the left-hand of the two summits in the classic view from Kylesku. Its left-hand buttress is the least steep, consisting of sandstone tiers with good holds. The route is technically quite hard in places, but without much exposure. The lower part is often wet, making easier options advisable.

Approach
From the top of the Kylesku to Inchnadamph road (NC 232 274) a good path leads towards Quinag. After a little over 1km leave it and contour northwards. Go round below the lowest (wet) tier of Sàil Gharbh until this starts to break up. Reach a rocky shelf with a cubic block (cairned), and the sandy beach at the head of Loch Airigh na Beinne visible below.

The Route
Climb a steep clean rib directly above the cairn, with slabbier but mossier ribs to the right, then go left up wet steps to a large grass terrace. Climb a short clean rib just left of a minor gully (or the gully) to reach a second grass terrace. Slant up left to a triangular slab with a small overlap at its foot and climb the left edge of this into a wet bay with steep rock above. Grovel onto a huge boulder on the right and go up further right to easy

ground. The tier above the second terrace can be avoided by starting further left and zigzagging up a deer path left of the main cliff.

Walk up right to the skyline and up easy slabby steps to the next and largest tier, which starts with two short stepped buttresses. The next two sections are the hardest, but can be avoided by grass on the right. Start at a waist-level shelf right of centre and climb direct, then up right, with an awkward step right below a nose. Go up left and just left of the skyline work left up two cracks to a terrace. The avoiding route comes in here. Climb an obvious central weakness on the next tier, steep at the top. Now climb numerous bands of easy steps until the ground eases to walking. There is a final tier where the buttress runs into the main hill, climbed easily by a gully left of centre.

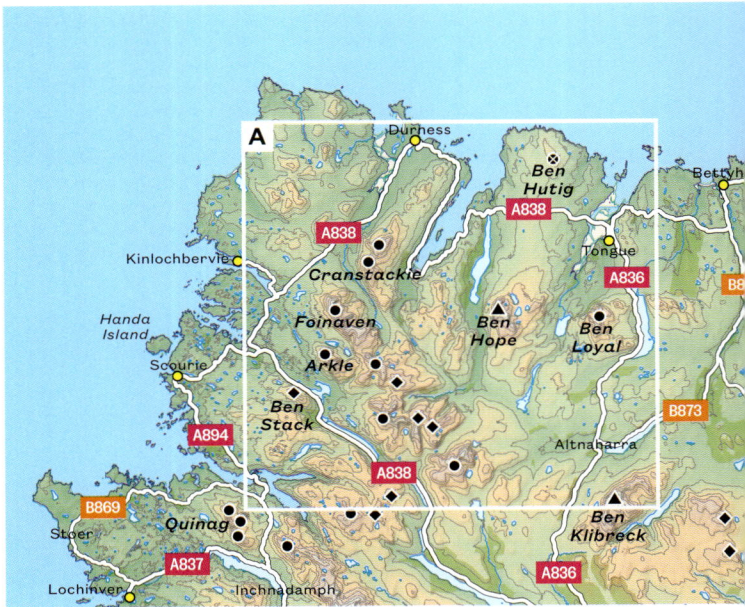

This area includes everything north of the A838 Lairg to Laxford Bridge road, plus Ben Stack just south of it. In the east the Old Red Sandstone hills of Caithness rise sharply from endless moorland, while in the centre the isolated peaks of Ben Loyal and Ben Hope dominate the north coast. The west is the best, however, where the sweeping crests of Foinaven and Arkle and the prominent spike of Ben Stack look out over miles of contorted gneiss.

All these peaks provide wild rough walking, often with the chance to have a whole mountain to yourself. In places there are long mountain rock climbs, with the 300m high Creag Urbhard on Foinaven taking pride of place. In addition the fringes of the area contain large numbers of short outcrop climbs, on both the sandstone sea cliffs of Caithness and the peerless gneiss of western Sutherland, with scope for many more in both cases. The coast itself is also well worth exploring, with dramatic sea cliffs and perfect sandy beaches.

A.	**North-West Sutherland**	Routes 144–157 P.298
B.	**Caithness**	Routes 158–159 P.321

The Far North

© John Fleetwood

North-West Sutherland

The heartland of the area is the convoluted range of the Reay Forest, coming to a climax with the quartzite peaks of Foinaven and Arkle. Foinaven in particular is one of the best scramblers' mountains, with a concentration of good long routes on both gneiss and quartzite. Stretching away eastwards from these is a chain of unfrequented summits which eventually finishes overlooking the empty moorlands of the Flow Country. Off to the north, Ben Hope and Ben Loyal are well separated from the main range, the latter having a quirky character quite unlike any other Scottish summit.

1.	Ben Stack	Route 144	P.299
2.	Ben Screavie	Route 145	P.301
3.	Arkle	Route 146	P.302
4.	Foinaven	Routes 147–152	P.304
5.	Cranstackie	Route 153	P.315
6.	Ben Hope	Routes 154–155	P.316
7.	Ben Loyal	Routes 156–157	P.318

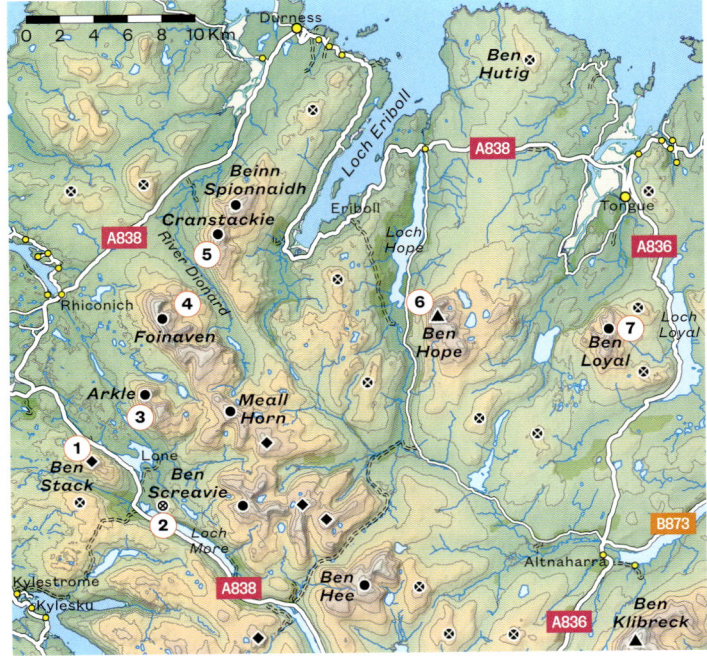

Ben Stack 721m

A steep-sided ridge running north-west to south-east, this peak is separated from the rest of this section by the A838 road, but is included here because the easiest access is from this road. The north side has two bands of shaggy cliffs separated by a terrace, with the upper one offering some scrambling.

- PAGES 296 & 298
- OS LR 9
- NORTH
- GNEISS

144   North Flank   Grade 3 ✱

| ⌖ NC 268 426 | 🏃 1HR | ◿ BUTTRESS | ⊺ +250M |

The inward-dipping stratified gneiss gives a not-too-intimidating scramble on small positive holds with good friction and little exposure. Only the early parts and the separate finish are Grade 3 and all outcrops are avoidable so a reasonable choice for a mixed ability party.

Approach

Park by the farm building at NC 265 437 and go up the path just west of this to Loch na Seilge. Just before crossing the stream running into the loch turn left up a broken fence. Follow a rough path alongside this until the fence turns right. Leave the path here and traverse up left until below the north face. Ignore the lower broken section and start at a clean slab with a thin blind crack directly above Loch Stack Lodge. This is the skyline seen on the approach and the largest clean mass of rock visible.

North Flank, Ben Stack (Route 144, Grade 3).
Scrambler: Iain Thow. © Noel Williams

The Route

Climb the slab, then another slab above and a hanging rib on the left. Broken ground and more ribs then lead to a roof. Traverse in above this from the left and climb the rib above. Move left to go up an easy rib, then another long easy rib on good rock, then more outcrops until they end. Traverse 20 metres left to find more rock and string together more ribs until these run out into easy slopes. A few more minor outcrops can be found to reach the ridge west of the summit.

At this point a glance over the other side of the ridge reveals an obvious slabby rib. Traverse across to this and climb it, moving right at the top to finish up another shorter rib.

Ben Screavie   332m

A minor but quite independent hill with a steep but quite broken quartzite face above Loch More.

- PAGES 296 & 298
- OS LR 9 & 15
- SOUTH-WEST
- QUARTZITE

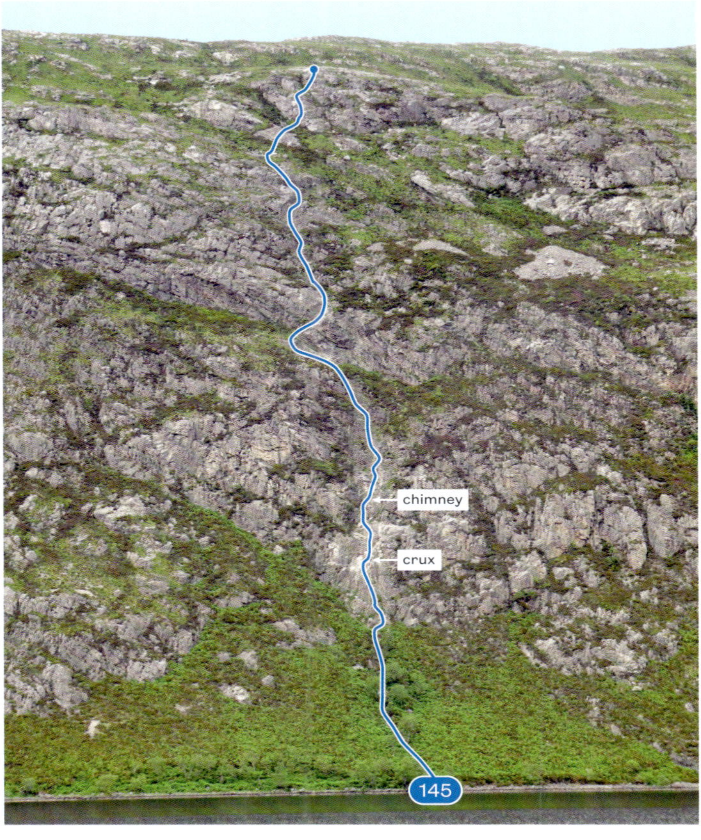

145 Allt Screavie — Difficult

◯ NC 309 387   🚶 40MINS   ◿ STREAM   ⊤ +200M

Although a stream in wet weather this line dries out quickly and once dry gives a sustained climb on mostly clean quartzite. The lower half is steep and sustained and although only Moderate technically it deserves a Difficult grade for its intimidating and committing nature.

Approach
The rickety bridge that once crossed the outlet from Loch More has now been demolished so approach from the bridge at NC 297 401 (parking by road and by bridge). Cross the bridge and turn right immediately to cross the bog past Loch nan Ealachan to Loch More. A rough deer track contours along just above the loch, but it gradually becomes easier to follow the stony shore (except when the loch is high, but then you probably shouldn't be doing this route in those conditions). It is easy to miss the start of the stream, as it is tiny and enclosed between high heathery banks, so keep an eye out for the more prominent line above, identifiable by a large distinctive white area where the cliff steepens.

The Route
Go up the easy stream bed, with occasional small steps, to reach the foot of the main cliff. Climb either the groove on the right with one steep move, or the more open rib to its left, to reach an easing below the crux. Move up and climb steeply just right of a vertical prow (which is right of the obvious smooth white slab). Go up and left to climb a short left-facing chimney to easier ground. Continue up the stream bed over another minor step then bear up left below a large overhanging wall. Traverse right above this to regain the stream bed and follow this easily for much further than you expect. Once it slackens off walk up right past a triangular scree patch to climb broken outcrops to easy ground. The summit is up left, with an excellent view.

Arkle — 787m

Another gem of a hill, whose dramatic quartzite ridge curves around a wild corrie and gives brief easy scrambling. The huge sunny south face offers long though quite broken scrambles, of which the following is the best.

🌐 PAGES 296 & 298
✈ OS LR 9
↔ SOUTH-WEST
⛰ QUARTZITE

146 South Rib — Grade 3

◯ NC 310 437   🚶 1HR 30   ◿ BUTTRESS   ⊤ +200M

A nice line and airy positions, but much of it quite loose. Technically easy for the grade but serious and inescapable, although not sustained and with plenty of choice in detail.

Approach
Cross the bridge south of Loch Stack (NC 297 401) as for Route 145 and follow the track to Lone. Just beyond this turn left to reach a small wood below the Allt Horn. Cross bog on the left for about 1km until steep heather and scree lead up to the first deep-cut gully (not the more open stepped groove visible from Lone, which gives a scrappier scramble). The route is the right-hand edge of this, very prominent from a distance.

The Route
Start on the right edge of the gully and climb a crack left of the rib. Climb a steep tower (or an easy rib to its left) to heather, then go up broken rock to a steepening. Climb this direct, then more broken ground. At the next steepening climb an easy stepped slab on the left, with the gully dropping away below. Go up to and climb a groove on the left edge, then shattered ground leads to heather, with the biggest tier ahead. Climb directly up the skyline until an overhang forces you left into grooves. A couple of easy ribs follow before the ground begins to ease off. A slab capped by a striped boulder on the gully edge is worth including before a final tier leads to the shoulder.

South Rib, Arkle (Route 146, Grade 3).
Scrambler: Pete Pollard. © Scott Muir

Foinaven 911m

One of the finest hills in Scotland, Foinaven consists of a long crest of quartzite with a complex of corries and lateral ridges running off north-east. The main ridge offers some brief easy scrambling at Lord Reay's Seat, but the little-visited Dionard side gives some of the most atmospheric scrambling in the area. The northern routes are mainly slabby gneiss, while further south are quartzite slabs fringing the enormous verticalities of Creag Urbhard. The gneiss routes can be easily linked together to give a superb day out.

- PAGES 296 & 298
- OS LR 9
- VARIOUS
- QUARTZITE & GNEISS

---

147 Second Dionard Buttress Grade 1

◯ NC 359 485   🚶 2HRS 30   ◿ SLABS   ⊤ +300M

Easy slabby scrambling in a wild situation.

Approach
From a small car park (NC 308 566), on the north side of the road 300m north-east of Gualin House, cross the road and follow the track up Srath

Dionard for 10km to the north end of Loch Dionard. Carry on along the west side of the loch (quite rough), then 200 metres beyond it a wide heathery ramp slants back up right, with broken rock below and a long vertical tier above (the main part of Second Buttress). This is not the shattered ramp which starts above the head of the loch and leads into more serious ground. Second Buttress has a smaller tier above, then a higher tier up and left again contains the Third, Fourth and Fifth Buttresses. Start on the right-hand edge of the heathery ramp, at a thin tongue of slabs.

The Route
Go up the walking-angle slabs, then up right on heather to the broader slabs which form the top half of the ramp. Go up these, mostly walking but with the odd harder section, to reach a scenic perch on the top of the impressive First Dionard Buttress. A deer track now zigzags up heather on the crest of the buttress, passing a couple of short steep walls. The buttress then broadens, with a few easy outcrops en route to the minor summit at the top of the cliffs.

148 Upper Slabs, Creag Urbhard — Grade 3 **

| NC 353 486 | 2HRS 45 | SLABS | +120M |

A large sweep of smooth clean quartzite slabs, sustained and serious. There are no real lines and a vast choice of route. Some areas are quite blank and having been caught out in the middle by a thunderstorm I can vouch for them being desperate in the wet.

Approach
Follow the track up Srath Dionard as for the previous route, then the pathless west shore of the loch below the huge face of Creag Urbhard. Above the south end of the loch is the huge overhanging prow of First Dionard Buttress. Go rightwards up a grassy rake immediately beneath it into the corrie behind Creag Urbhard. On the right the broad South Ridge forms the top edge of the main cliff. This has some easy slabs, but far better is to go further into the corrie to the prominent slabs up on the right, with steeper rock to their left.

The Route
There are so many route options that any line can only be a suggestion. Generally the further right you go the easier it gets (but there are exceptions). Easy-angled broken slabs lead to a bouldery easing at half-height. Above this a broken line of overlaps extends across from the steeper rock up left. The best route goes up right to bypass these, then heads back up left to pass under a higher set of overlaps. Once beyond these the angle soon slackens to broken slopes.

149 Twin Caves Ridge, A' Chèir Ghorm — Moderate

| ⌖ NC 330 502 | 🚶 3HRS 10 | ◿ BUTTRESS | ⬆ +120M |

A' Chèir Ghorm is a narrow quartzite ridge running north-east from the main Foinaven Ridge. It has a stepped north face broken into a dozen or so ridges. Unfortunately these are very loose, but the situations are impressive. The bottom 30m is steep, then the angle eases. The face is highly confusing, and several of the ridges make reasonable scrambles, the described one being the easiest to identify.

Approach

Approach up Srath Dionard as for the previous routes. Either leave the vehicle track at around NC 353 505 and follow the stream up or cut across from Cnoc Duail after Route 150. At the north-east end of the A' Chèir Ghorm ridge the rock extends the whole height of the face. Near the right-hand edge of this is a deep gully with a scree shoot issuing from it. On either side of this there are small outcrops below the main face. Twin Caves Ridge is the right arête of the gully, with the brownish twin caves at its foot. Start left of these, just inside the gully.

The Route

Go up steeply (loose) and pull up into a minor gully using a jammed block. Climb rightwards onto the arête, where the angle eases and the arête breaks up into short steps. Climb these following the skyline to arrive on the ridge just left of the summit. The A' Chèir Ghorm ridge itself has a narrow section with easy scrambling just before the steep rise onto the main ridge.

150 North Face, Cnoc Duail — Grade 3 ✶✶

◯ NC 337 518   🚶 1HR 50   ◿ SLABS   ⊤ +300M

A long slabby route on perfect gneiss. The lower section is easy-angled with the odd steeper step, the upper half steeper and more sustained, with an intimidating crux.

Approach
Follow the track up Srath Dionard as for the previous routes for 6km to the stream coming out of Coire Duail. Turn right up this until it steepens at slabs. These give a nice prelude, then the main scramble is up left. The left-hand side of the buttress is pinker and steeper. Start at gentle slabs below and right of this, at the left-hand of two main slabby areas.

The Route
Follow walking-angle slabs up left, gradually steepening into a more defined rib. At the top move left and climb the next rib, then steeper knobbly rock. Go up to another steepening and climb it (the nose on the right is Difficult). Easy slabs and heather now lead to the base of the upper buttress.

Avoid the steep wall at the foot on the right (the groove at the right-hand end of the wall is Difficult). Easy steps lead to another steep nose. Go left under this to a long slabby rib, which widens into superb delicate scrambling, sustained and serious. Finish up a well-positioned groove on the right-hand edge (crux). At the top go left and up another short rib. An awkward start leads to a slab and another rib, then short steep walls lead up left to more slabs. The ground now eases off, but more slabby problems can be found on the way to the summit.

151 Coire Duail Slabs — Grade 2 or 3

◯ NC 323 512   🚶 2HRS 45   ◿ SLABS   ⊤ +120M

Enjoyable slabby scrambling on excellent gneiss but with no real line. Conveniently included between Cnoc Duail and the Ganu Mor Slabs. There are two main sets of slabs, the left-hand ones being steeper.

a) Left-Hand Route – Grade 3 ✶✶

The harder of the two variations, more sustained but still with lots of breaks.

Approach
If doing Cnoc Duail first then from its summit descend south-westwards to a grassy col, then slant down north-westwards (deer track) to pass along below the cliffs and head up a minor valley to reach the slabs.
If starting with this route follow the track up Srath Dionard as for the previous routes to the stream coming out of Coire Duail. Follow this up to the lochan and then take a small valley up right just below the cliffs (not the one with the main stream in it). The slabs are just above and the left-hand route starts at the lowest rock, a steep wall with a slab above, about 20 metres left of a small stream.

The Route

Climb sloping steps at the right-hand end of the wall to reach walking-angle slabs and grass. Pass a long red overhang by steeper slabs to its left. When these run out move left to more slabs and a grass terrace. Above this pass a long steep band by steps below a reddish prow, then work up left to grass below a patterned slab. Climb this and slabs above, easing in angle to walking. Climb a steeper red slab on the left, then move right and climb slabby blocks to grass.

Broken ground now leads to the summit of Ganu Mor, but more scrambling can be found by traversing off right, slanting down a grass ramp below a steeper cliff, then heading right across the top of slabs. This takes you into Coire Ghrannda a little higher up than the lochan, with Ganu Mor Slabs up left.

b) Right-Hand Route – Grade 2

The easier alternative, much of it walking angle but with a steeper start and finish. Still pleasant enough.

Approach

As for the previous route but go about 100 metres further up the valley, at the left-hand edge of the last slabs before it opens out.

Route

Climb the left edge of the slabs then move right once the angle eases. Clean easy slabs continue for some distance, gradually easing to walking. Bear right to more slabs, then when these become steeper and more broken go more sharply right to arrive on easy slabs above the lochan in Coire Ghrannda. Carrying on up the steeper slabs takes you to easy slabs, then through steeper outcrops and up steep grass onto the east shoulder of Ganu Mor, never more than Grade 1 but quite hard work.

Left-Hand Route, Coire Dubh Slabs, Foinaven (Route 151a, Grade 3).
Scrambler: John Fleetwood. © Iain Thow

152 Ganu Mor Slabs — Grade 3 ★★★

NC 318 513 | 3HRS | SLABS | +120M

low-angled ramp

152

A mass of gneiss slabs, quite sustained and serious, but with lots of route choice. The slabs dry fast after showers but weep for a while after prolonged rain.

Approach
These form the south side of Coire Ghrannda above the lochan. Approach either from the previous route as described above, or by slanting up the north flank of lower Coire Duail to arrive on the right-hand lip of the upper corrie, right of the slabs guarding the entrance. If doing the latter then the walking-angle slabs at NC 336 525 are worth including. From the lochan walk up the south side of the corrie for 200 metres to a steep slab on the left with a wide grassy rake running up leftwards from its foot and a pink tongue coming down to boulders on its right. Go 50 metres up the rake to a moss patch below quartz blotches (a smaller grass rake goes up right from here).

The Route
Climb the slab past the quartz, aiming for a vertical pink dyke. At the base of this take a ledge rightwards onto a big slab. Climb this about 10m right of the pink band, carrying on up the line of a hairline crack.

Ganu Mor Slabs, Foinaven (Route 152, Grade 3).
Scrambler: Iain Thow. © Noel Williams

At a grass patch go left and up more slabs, starting at a small left-facing riblet and passing left of a red overlap. The slabs end at a grass terrace with short steep walls above. Take a low-angled, red ramp left, and above its end climb a steep pink dyke. Where this splits take the right branch and carry on up the right-hand arête. Above this boulder problems lead to grass, with the summit of Ganu Mor 150m higher.

On the left-facing riblet, Ganu Mor Slabs, Foinaven (Route 152, Grade 3).
Scrambler: Iain Thow. © Noel Williams

If the main slab is wet a less serious route is to start from the same place but head up right to follow the right edge of the slab (Grade 2/3) then avoid the steeper ground above on either left or right (left extends the scrambling better but is more serious and exposed).

Dionard Rib, Cranstackie (Route 153, Grade 3).
Scramblers: Simon Fraser and Robin Chalmers. © Noel Williams

Cranstackie

800m

Although Cranstackie is usually climbed along with its neighbour Beinn Spionnaidh in a short horseshoe from Rhigolter to the west, the mountain's most interesting side is the west flank of the long south ridge. This throws down a row of buttresses offering some good short rock climbs and several scrambles. In a less isolated setting they would be popular, but here only the most continuous one is described.

- PAGES 296 & 298
- OS LR 9
- SOUTH-WEST
- GNEISS

153 Dionard Rib — Grade 3 ★★

| ○ NC 346 533 | 🏃 1HR 30 | ◿ BUTTRESS | ⊤ +200M |

Excellent clean gneiss slabs, with a few steeper moves. Quite sustained but not particularly exposed.

Approach
From a small car park (NC 308 566), 300m north-east of Gualin House, follow the track up Srath Dionard for 5km and ford the river about 100 metres beyond the first fishermans' hut. If the river is high it will be necessary to contour round the slope from Rhigolter. Above the fording place is a grassy bowl with a steep cliff well above it. To the right are a gully, then broken ground, then a clean rib jutting forward with a steep left-hand face halfway up. This is the route. Right again is a steep reddish cliff, then more ribs, some of which also have good scrambling potential. Steep slopes lead up to the rib, just left of a minor gully.

The Route
The first clean rock starts with an awkward move onto boulders, then follow the right-hand edge to heather. Clean slabs lead to easy ground, then go up heather and small slabs until the rib becomes more definite. Make a hard move onto it, then go up easy slabs to a ledge with a deer path. Another slab leads to a second deer path. Follow the rib on the left in a good position, then go right below a bulge and climb a juggy crack to a heather ledge.

Climb a crack right of centre (hard to start) or an easier crack further right. Now follow the centre of the rib to heather below a steep wall. Dodge this by boulders on the right edge, then go up left to regain the crest. Easy slabs lead to a leaning wall. Pass this by a ramp slanting up right (harder than it looks). An easy rib then leads to a steeper rib up left, started on jugs. A lovely central groove follows, with either a hard and exposed exit on the left or an easier one on the right. Easy slabs run up to broken ground a short way below the ridge.

Ben Hope — 927m

The northernmost Munro is flanked on its western side by a large and complex psammite cliff with at least six major ridges and numerous minor ones. The two most prominent are at the northern end, separated by a wide gully. Brown's Ridge is the left-hand one, while Bell's Ridge, which is Severe, is the right-hand one. Right of Bell's Ridge a grass rake runs up right above a lower steep section to a col on the next major ridge further right (Tower Ridge). Petticoat Ridge runs down into the rake halfway between Bell's Ridge and Tower Ridge.

- 🌐 PAGES 296 & 298
- ⌖ OS LR 9
- ↔ WEST
- ⛰ PSAMMITE

154 Brown's (Myles's) Ridge — Grade 3 ✶✶

◯ NC 476 508   🏃 2HRS   ◿ BUTTRESS   ⊤ +400M

A steep grass approach leads to sustained and exposed scrambling on good holds, then an airy but easy ridge. Almost all difficulties are avoidable, but this usually involves very steep grass. For a long time the only ascent recorded in guidebooks was Hamish Brown's winter one (1969), hence the name, but there was an earlier one in summer by Doug Myles (1933).

Approach
Start at the usual approach to Ben Hope, from the barn at NC 462 477. Go up the path as far as the first shelf, then follow the shelf northwards to Dubh-loch na Beinne. Beyond this two gullies run down the upper cliffs, the right-hand being the start of the rake mentioned above. Start just left of the left-hand gully.

The Route
Go up steep grass left of the first buttress, then more steep grass before cutting through a rock band by a left-to-right rake. Go up left via a short juggy wall and more grass to a bigger buttress with overhangs. Left of the overhangs go left up steps and a short wall to more grass. Go left to a grassy bay, then right up this to the skyline and the start of the better scrambling.

Climb a juggy arête and a wide crack, then another steep crack, finishing with an awkward and exposed step right and a hard pull up onto a ledge. Go up just left of the arête, then move right onto it. This is very exposed, but big jugs lead up it to an easing of angle. Follow the arête to the top, easy at first, then with lots of juggy steps and little problems.

Where the ridge becomes less defined head up left to clamber up blocks, then more short walls lead to the main north ridge.

A steep nose blocks the way to the main summit. This can be passed at Difficult via delicate and exposed ledges on the right. It is much easier to dodge it by way of a gully on the left, returning back right as soon as possible to enjoy the blocky arête beyond.

---

155 **Petticoat Ridge**   **Grade 2 or Difficult**

○ NC 475 505   🏃 2HRS 30   ◢ BUTTRESS   ⊤ +100M

A short juggy ridge, quite exposed, with a purgatorial approach. The latter can be avoided by an intricate and serious descent from the summit.

Approach
The direct way in is to slog up the rake mentioned above, avoiding the steep lower section by traversing in from well to the right. A far more pleasant but serious and exposed alternative is to descend the first major ridge south of Tower Ridge (not the minor ridge dropping from the narrow point of the plateau). Go down about 50m to grass, then slant down right (facing out) on a deer track into the top of a basin. Continue right to a col on Tower Ridge, which is at the top of the rake. Petticoat Ridge starts about 60m down the rake.

The Route
Avoid the first rocks on the right and start either by a slabby rib leading up left to a steepening, dodged by an awkward gully on the right (Difficult), or by coming in by the second grass rake on the right. Either way leads to a vertical tower on the crest. Traverse right below this on small ledges to an easy pull up. Continue up the ridge on huge blocks. Near the top it broadens and steepens, with big holds leading up to the main north ridge above its rock step.

Ben Loyal   764m

This isolated mountain consists of a series of rocky summits linked by grassy saddles, with the northern end dominating the Kyle of Tongue in a large vegetated cliff. Views range from Orkney in the east along the whole of the north coast to Cape Wrath. The hill is made of an intrusive igneous rock called syenite, similar to granite but with very little quartz. Metamorphic reworking has caused some of the crystals to line up, making it very slippery in places.

⊕ PAGES 296 & 298
✈ OS LR 10
⇅ VARIOUS
⌂ SYENITE

156 Sgor a' Chleirich Ridge Grade 2

| NC 569 492 | 2HRS 15 | INTRICATE | +150M |

Nice positions, but not great scrambling.

Approach
Walk in from Ribigil south of Tongue (NC 584 547) and follow the track to the cottage at Cunside, with Sgor Chaonasaid towering ahead. The stream just before the cottage can be hard to cross after rain. Go up towards the peak then leave the path to follow a shelf slanting up right through a beautiful birch wood below the cliffs. Continue along the top of the woods until a steep ascent can be made into the corrie between Sgor a' Bhatain and Sgor a' Chleirich. Go up right to the ridge.

The Route
Avoid the initial slabs, then go up boulders and a groove in an easy-angled nose. At steeper rock climb mossy slabs on the left from right to left. Easier ground then leads to a steep clean rib. This is more than scrambling, so go up the gully to the left or the mossy rib left again. Just below the top of the rib traverse delicately left onto the main ridge and go more steeply up this. Finish up either a wide crack (Moderate) or a stepped gully to the left.

157 Sgor Chaonasaid Spine Grade 2 (and a jump!) ✶

| NC 579 499 | 2HRS 15 | ARÊTE | NEGLIGIBLE |

The northern peak of Ben Loyal has an impressive north face, unfortunately disappointing from a scrambling point of view, but the spine running south along the ridge is entertaining. It forms a jaggy ridge in three sections, once described as 'like climbing along the back of a Stegosaurus'. The first section is split by a deep notch which has to be jumped. This is scary but downhill if you are going north to south.

Approach
Start as for the previous route but stay on the path going up leftwards below Sgorr Chaonasaid to the 300m contour. A scrappy scramble can be made up the left-hand edge of the north face, starting up isolated slabs at the foot, but a lack of friction on these forces you largely onto steep grass. Better is to go round further left (still quite steep and often wet), passing the wreckage of a Hampden bomber from 1943. One of the four crew (C A Faulks from Sheffield) survived and was carried off the hill the next day by the shepherd from Ribigill and the local doctor. This slope takes you to a grassy shelf at around 530m, then cut back up rightwards to pick up the path running below the unmistakable Chaonasaid Spine, with Sgor Chaonasaid summit further right.

The approach can also be made from anywhere along the road alongside Loch Loyal to the east. This is shorter but much boggier and rather dull.

The Route

Reaching the actual summit of Sgor Chaonasaid involves an awkward step up. Return down the step, then down left to the col between the summit and the Spine. Go up steeply onto the arête running south. Follow this to the scary jump over the gap. This is about 1.5 metres across and 2 metres down, with a good landing, but the penalty for failure is high. Carry on until a steep drop ahead forces a delicate descent right, then make a long step across a gully to a ledge. Go down the arête, then cut back left to a col. Pass the next pinnacle on the right (or detour up it), then pull up steeply at a jammed flake to follow another arête. Where this ends drop down right, then down left easily to an escape. Cross slabs and a rock bridge ahead, then at the end go down right then left to easy ground.

Other Areas

There are many other crags scattered over this huge area which can provide scrambling. Beinn Ceannabeinne (NC 423 646) has lots of fun outcrops but no real lines. Creige Riabhaich on Beinn Direach (NC 409 377) has a 50m slab which is a good Grade 2 direct (finish left of the wet upper groove). Below this the waterfall on Allt an Aslaird (NC 422 376) has some superb slabs at its top, but they are cut off from the lower stream bed by an overhanging wall. The north-west corrie on Ben Hee has lots of rock but the lower slabs are mainly walking and the upper outcrops mostly too steep. Meallan Liath Bheag (NC 523 510) has some brief fun on its south-west shoulder.

Caithness

Most of Caithness is a vast sprawl of peaty moorland scattered with innumerable lochans, but its southern corner holds a group of largely sandstone hills which can provide a little scrambling. Morven is the most prominent of these, a distinctive feature of the view from many parts of north-east Scotland, but the delightful little peaklet of Maiden Pap has the best scramble.

| 1. | Maiden Pap | Route 158 | P.322 |
| 2. | Morven | Route 159 | P.323 |

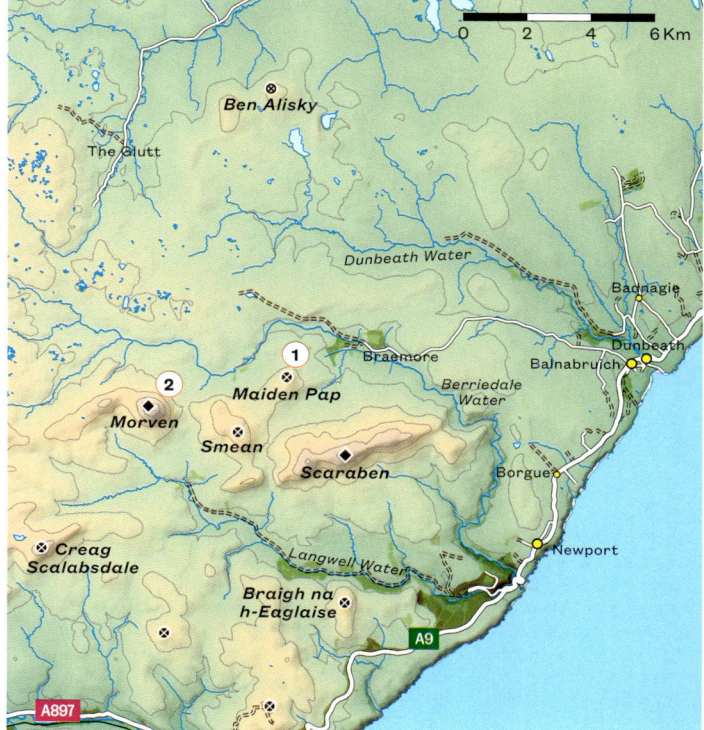

Maiden Pap — 484m

This prominent spike east of Morven is a great little summit.

- PAGES 297 & 321
- OS LR 17
- NORTH-EAST
- CONGLOMERATE

158 — North Flank — Grade 2 or 3 *

ND 048 295 | 1HR 10 | OUTCROPS | +130M

Entertainingly delicate conglomerate slabs and juggy walls with a variety of interchangeable problems.

Approach

From the end of the public road at Braemore (ND 073 304) cross the bridge and take the track running west along the river, turning left to avoid Braemore Lodge and left again to avoid Braeval cottage. Beyond the cottage rejoin the main track and follow it through the first wood and along to the next one. Turn left up the wood edge towards Maiden Pap, then continue in the same line up a sketchy path to a grassy strip ending about 50m below the crags. Slant up left to two slabs at the foot of the face, the right-hand one with a small rowan halfway up.

The Route
The right-hand slab is a delicate Grade 3, the left-hand is Grade 2. Slant rightwards up easier slabs and heather to reach a band of steeper rock. There is a little prow on the left (Grade 3) and a slab to its right (Grade 2), but the best line is the steep but extremely juggy crack on the right (Grade 2). Another steep but easy crack and a smaller outcrop lead to an easing. Climb the right edge of the foresummit ahead, starting at a little pinnacle. On the way to the main summit there is a short rib on the left just above the saddle.

On the far side of the summit the north-west rib provides a very short but excellent scramble, steep but on big juggy holds (Grade 3).

Morven   706m

This conical sandstone hill is the highest of a compact group in the southern corner of Caithness. On a good day views range from Assynt to the Cairngorms.

- ⊕ PAGES 297 & 321
- ⊲ OS LR 17
- ↔ NORTH-EAST
- ⌂ SANDSTONE

---

159 **North-East Ribs**   **Grade 1**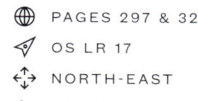

◯ ND 006 287   ⚘ 2HRS 40   ◿ OUTCROPS   ⊤ +80M

Morven is a steep pull from any direction, but these ribs add some interest to the top part.

Approach
These are most easily approached from Braemore (ND 073 304) following the path to Corrichoich bothy (passing left of Braemore Lodge and Cottage), then continuing directly towards the mountain. Looking up from the north-east three ribs can be seen high up. Go steeply up heather to the left-hand of these.

The Route
Climb the left-hand ridge (the others are similar but with a few harder sections). At the top traverse right to the skyline rib and climb it. There are more similar ribs to the right and the tor to the south of the summit has some boulder problems.

Well worth a visit while in the area is the Smean (ND 033 277), the prominent tor between Morven and Scaraben, which turns out to be a complex of rock tors reminiscent of Dartmoor. A keen boulderer could spend hours here.

Rùm

Rùm has the largest complex of gabbro outside Skye, and the traverse of its main ridge is one of the great days out. As well as the one-pop big day there are several excellent scrambles on the subsidiary ridges and faces. The routes on the south flank of Barkeval are particularly good, on delightfully contorted peridotite. The island is worth a visit for the wildlife alone, with both Golden and Sea Eagles and Britain's biggest colony of Manx Shearwaters. The bizarre legacy of the Bullough family in the extravagant Kinloch Castle and the Harris Mausoleum adds another layer to the island's attractions.

Kinloch has both a bunkhouse and a basic campsite, and there are bothies at Dibidil and Guirdil, the former handy for the southern part of the Rùm Cuillin. All of these can be booked through www.isleofrum.com/accommodation/.

1.	Barkeval	Routes 160–164	P.326
2.	Askival	Routes 165–169	P.332
3.	Trollabhal	Routes 170–173	P.335
4.	Ainshval	Routes 174–176	P.338
5.	Sgùrr nan Gillean	Route 177	P.341

Barkeval 591m

This often neglected summit is the true start to the main ridge traverse and has the best scrambling on Rùm on its south face. The peridotite of which it is composed has some of the juggiest holds you could desire. Please note that there may be nesting raptors. Check for access restrictions on the Mountaineering Scotland website before visiting, www.mountaineering.scot/campaigns/safeguarding-access/birds-and-nesting.

- PAGE 324
- OS EXP 397
- SOUTH
- PERIDOTITE

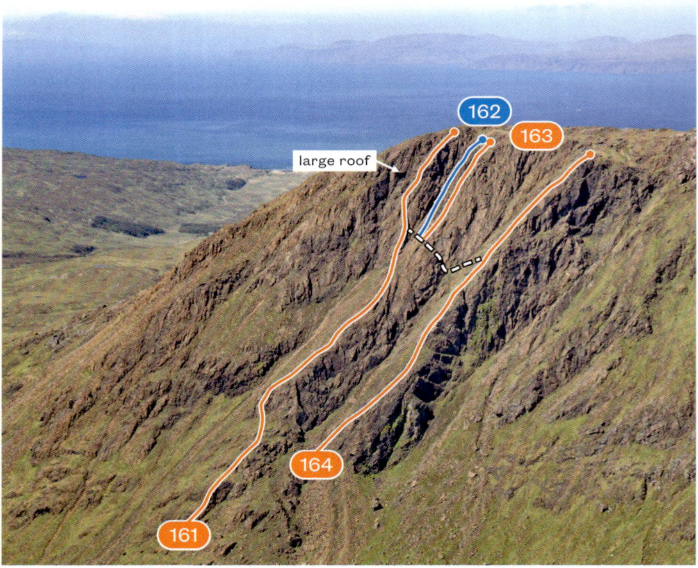

large roof

160	**North-West Flank**		Grade 1 or 2	
◇ NM 375 975	🚶 1HR 40	⟋ OUTCROPS	⊺ +100M	

Quite broken but very rough slabs, with avoidable steeper parts.

Approach
Take the path south of the castle (signed 'Rùm Cuillin') and turn left over the bridge. Follow this path up into Coire Dubh. Once into the corrie take a smaller path slanting up right, not obvious at first, to cross the

col south of Meall Breac. Carry on in the same line to a small lochan at NM 377 978, then cross the shallow corrie to the south to reach walking-angle slabs facing down towards Kilmory.

The Route
Ascend the slabs and go up left to climb a cracked slab with steeper rock to its right. More slabs lead up right, with a steeper square tower climbed right to left (Grade 2 direct). Reach a wide grassy rake and walk up right to slabby outcrops on the skyline. These lead up to the summit, often only walking but finishing with a lovely 'crazy paving' wall just below the top.

161 Broad Buttress — Grade 3 or Moderate ★★★

| NM 374 969 | 2HRS | BUTTRESS | +280M |

Stepped tiers to reach a half-height easing, then a more sustained steep headwall with superb holds.

Approach
The route is the left-hand of the two right-slanting ribs that make up the right half of the face, Descent Spur being the right-hand one. It is most easily approached by descending the latter (see Route 164), but alternatively slant down from Bealach Bairc-mheall for about 1km. Cross the gully beyond Descent Spur and keep slanting down westward until there is no more rock beyond.

The Route
Start up a steep knobbly wall, then several more short walls lead to a bigger face. Climb a cracked rib near its left end on excellent holds (sustained and airy, but avoidable on the left). Where it eases move right across a minor gully, where more outcrops lead up right towards the steeper headwall (the biggest outcrop has a lovely central juggy crack).

Arrive at the headwall just left of a minor scree gully, with Honeycomb and Narnia Arêtes starting just off to the right. Climb a juggy rib left of the gully and where this merges into the steeper ground climb direct on huge holds. At the top a nearly vertical rib on the right skyline provides an exposed variation (Moderate), but beware the wobbly block halfway up. This section is easily and more logically bypassed on the left, then the ground eases as you approach the summit.

162 Narnia Arête — Moderate ★★★

| NM 375 971 | 2HRS 30 | BUTTRESS | +100M |

The left-hand and sharper of the two arêtes starting from halfway up Broad Buttress. One of the best easy climbs in the country, sustained and exposed but on amazing holds.

Approach
Start by climbing Broad Buttress (Route 161) as far as the foot of the headwall, then move right across the minor gully to the foot of the left-hand ridge.

Broad Buttress, Barkeval (Route 161, Grade 3).
Scrambler: Jo Roberts. © Noel Williams

Narnia Arête, Barkeval (Route 162, Moderate).
Scrambler: Davie Austin. © Noel Williams

Honeycomb Arête, Barkeval (Route 163, Grade 2).
Scrambler: Jo Roberts. © Noel Williams

The Route
Climb the exact crest on some of the best holds you could ever hope to find. Try to refrain from whooping too much! If you haven't had enough at the top a short tower off left gives a steep finish on yet more jugs.

163 Honeycomb Arête — Grade 2 **

| ○ NM 375 971 | 🏃 2HRS 30 | ◢ BUTTRESS | ⊤ +100M |

The right-hand of two arêtes starting from halfway up Broad Buttress, with a distinctive honeycomb effect on its left flank.

Approach
Start by climbing Broad Buttress (Route 161) as far as the foot of the headwall, then move right across the minor gully to the foot of the right-hand ridge.

The Route
Use a combination of the crest and the left flank, sustained but on excellent holds. Finish all too soon.

164 Descent Spur — Grade 1, 2 or 3 *

| ○ NM 375 969 | 🏃 1HR 50 | ◢ BUTTRESS | ⊤ +280M |

Descending this from the summit is a good way of reaching the harder routes on the face, but it makes an enjoyable route in its own right.

Approach
The route is the rightmost buttress on the face, slanting up rightwards with very steep rock on its right flank. Approach as for Route 160 into Coire Dubh but continue straight ahead over Bealach Bairc-mheall and slant down right to the foot of the buttress, about 1km beyond the bealach and 150m lower. The steep right flank mentioned above is a good landmark.

The Route
Start in the gully left of the spur. The superb rough groove up the front is Grade 3, with an easier line just right. Above this the best rock is on the left at first. Zigzag up (or go direct at Grade 2) to where the buttress eases. Dodge stepped overlaps on their left and continue up the crest above, never difficult but occasionally exposed.

In Descent
About 200 metres east of the 591m summit of Barkeval a minor top projects southwards. This is the top of Descent Spur. It is in line with Hallival from the summit cairn. Descend the crest, zigzagging in places, then keep right (facing out) in the lower section to finish in the gully.

Confident climbers can link all five Barkeval routes going up North-West, down Descent Spur, up Broad Buttress, down Honeycomb Arête and up Narnia Arête.

Askival   812m

A dramatic pointy peak of mostly excellent gabbro with four good ridges perched high above the sea. A tremendous viewpoint.

 PAGE 324
 OS EXP 397
 VARIOUS
GABBRO & PERIDOTITE

165	**North Ridge via Askival Pinnacle**		**Moderate** ✶✶
⌖ NM 394 955	🏃 2HRS	⟋ ARÊTE	⊺ +120M

Quite grassy in places but the positions are superb. The main section is serious and inescapable, with a definite crux. Shearwaters nest in burrows at the foot of the ridge and in spring the burbling of underground chicks adds a spooky quirk.

Approach
From Kinloch follow the path up into Coire Dubh as for Barkeval, then continue more steeply up to the Bealach Bairc-mheall. Head southeast up the broad shoulder and either clamber over Hallival with minor scrambling or traverse round it on the west. From the col between Hallival and Askival a narrow grassy ridge leads towards the latter, then at the first rocks the path goes left.

The Route
The minor pinnacle at the foot of the ridge can be climbed direct, but it is quite loose and harder than it looks. It is easily avoided on either side (most go left), returning to the crest at a small col beyond it. Clamber over a minor spike to another small notch, then step up right off a block to a slab on the right flank. Traverse right a few metres on a grass ledge then climb the main slab on good but spaced holds (crux). A short arête leads to an awkward step up, then traverse left and up two short steps before regaining the crest. Pass left of a big pinnacle then the crest becomes easy. After a short descent bypass a steep wall by a bouldery groove on the left, then more crest leads to a broad gravel area. From here to the top is easy.

166 North Ridge, Easy Route — Grade 1

| NM 394 955 | 2HRS | INTRICATE | +120M |

Not great scrambling but the easiest way up the highest peak on the island from Kinloch.

Approach
As for Route 165 to the first rocks.

The Route
Follow the path leftwards, gradually rising but staying below the cliffs. Zigzag up just before reaching a short steep black wall with a slanting overhang on its right. Keep left under another short black wall, then as you approach the East Ridge head steeply up right. Cut back left towards a prominent hole in the crest of the East Ridge, but before reaching it go up right then left and grovel onto a block on the ridge about 20 metres right of the hole. The gravel area at the top of the North Ridge is just to the right and the summit is easily reached from here.

167 East Ridge — Grade 2 *

| NM 395 953 | 2HRS 15 | INTRICATE | +150M |

Steep and quite fierce scrambling on a blunt ridge. The closeness of the sea gives it more of an 'up in the sky' feel than the other ridges.

Approach
From Kinloch take the back road towards the pier, turning right onto the Dibidil Track after a few hundred metres. Follow this for about 5km to its high point above Lochan Dubh. Head up right to go steeply up the prow south of Coire nan Grunnd, then from the col beyond walk steeply up to the first rocks of the ridge. This point is also easily reached by traversing south (and slightly down) from the first rocks of the North Ridge.

The Route
The rock starts with an overhanging prow. Pull onto this from the left, then ascend blocks on the crest, some of them lovely knobbly peridotite. Climb a squareish groove left of the crest, then continue in the same

line to reach grassy walking. The top tier is steep and intimidating, but can be sneaked up indirectly. Clamber up cracked blocks right of centre, then move up right behind a big pointed block. Go up a damp grassy groove to a platform, then climb an easy stepped arête. As the angle eases make an airy step across a jammed block over a prominent hole. This is avoidable but most scramblers will find it irresistible. A short distance further is the gravel area at the top of the North Ridge, with the summit an easy step away.

168 South Ridge — Grade 3 **

| ○ NM 394 949 | 🏃 3HRS | ⊿ BUTTRESS | ⊤ +150M |

Better scrambling than the well-known North Ridge but not quite as well positioned. Only Grade 2 if the three grooves and the vertical wall are avoided, but this is less good.

Approach
The obvious approach is from the coast path east of Dibidil Bothy, from where pathless walking leads up to the summit of Beinn nan Stac. The descent from this is an unpleasantly loose scramble at first, then more walking takes you down to the saddle and up the easy ridge ahead to the first rocks. A path goes off left here to avoid all difficulties.

The Route
Climb the first step on the left, then go right to the crest and up boulders. Ahead is a steep block with a pinnacle on its right. Climb a groove in the left side of the block (escaping left at half-height is Grade 2). Follow the continuation groove and its left arête to a platform, where a convenient jug allows the vertical wall ahead to be surmounted from a block halfway along. This is strenuous but easily avoided on the left. The ridge now eases to walking, then a fine long easy scramble up a blocky spur. About 50m below the summit this breaks up into outcrops, which are fun if tackled direct, a left-slanting V-groove making an excellent finish.

169 West Ridge — Grade 1

| ○ NM 392 952 | 🏃 2HRS 40 | ⊿ OUTCROPS | ⊤ +100M |

Most often followed in descent during a traverse of the main ridge, with any difficulties generally avoided, but a pleasant easy scramble if tackled direct.

Approach
Most people reach the Bealach an Oir by climbing something else first, but it can be reached from Kinloch by crossing the Bealach Bairc-mheall, losing about 100m height then traversing round the head of Atlantic Corrie (traces of path).

The Route
From Bealach an Oir (NM 385 953) take the path up eastwards, avoiding the lowest shattered rocks, then steep walking leads to higher rocks.

Where the path goes right keep ahead up blocks and steps on the crest, finishing right at the summit.

In descent it is easiest to keep left (looking out) on a well-used route, but a direct line is still quite reasonable.

Trollabhal 702m

A twin-topped peak with a lovely airy crest and lots of steep gabbro on its southern flank. The western top is the higher one.

 PAGE 324

 OS EXP 397

 VARIOUS

 GABBRO

170   East Ridge   Grade 1

| ◯ NM 380 952 | 🏃 2HRS 40 | ⊿ OUTCROPS | ⊤ +100M |

Walking at first, then enjoyable easy clambering to a superb sharp summit.

Approach
From Bealach an Oir (NM 385 953) go up the grassy spur to reach the rocks.

The Route
Clamber up blocks and short steps on the crest, all easily avoided if desired, usually on the right. Cross the East Top and follow the sharp arête to the higher West Top.

Approaching the summit of Trollabhal from the East Top (Route 170, Grade 1). Scrambler: George Sawicki. © Noel Williams

171 South Flank — Grade 1

| NM 378 950 | 3HRS | OUTCROPS | +150M |

Mostly rough walking but with some broken slabs to finish, the easiest way up or down the peak.

Approach
People generally get to Bealach an Fhuarain via one of the other peaks but it can be reached by a convoluted route from Kinloch. Go up to Bealach Bairc-mheall as for Route 165, cross this and descend around 100m to where traces of path traverse round Atlantic Corrie to reach the Bealach an Oir between Askival and Trollabhal. Cross this and traverse round south-westwards to the Bealach an Fhuarain. The same place can be reached more directly up Glen Dibidil.

The Route
From Bealach an Fhuarain (NM 378 948) go right of the first outcrop and up scree. Zigzag left then right through a broken rock band, then go up right of a steeper spur (which is Grade 2) to reach easy ground below the East Top. Follow the narrow arête to the higher West Top.

In Descent
This is used in descent on the usual version of the Main Ridge Traverse. From the East Top keep well left (looking out) until past the steep spur, then slant right down grass and rubble and zigzag through broken ground to a levelling (bits of path). Avoid the lowest outcrop down a gully on the left.

172 South Slabs — Grade 3 ✱✱

◇ NM 378 950   🏃 3HRS   ⊿ SLABS   ⊤ +150M

Superb rough slabs with the odd steeper section, shame it isn't longer. They are very clean and take hardly any drainage so are quick drying and little affected by rain.

Topping out on the South Flank of Trollabhal (Route 171, Grade 1).
Scrambler: George Sawicki. © Noel Williams

Approach
As for the previous route to Bealach an Fhuarain.

The Route
Go up the first minor outcrop direct to an easing. Walk a fair way left below steep slabs and pass under an overhanging prow. Go up left towards another steep wall and surmount it by a right-to-left ramp. Climb slabs above, heading for a vertical square tower. Dodge this on the right then work right up excellent cracked slabs to an airy step up on the right skyline. Keep ahead to finish up a superbly positioned cracked slab. Easy ground and a minor craglet lead to the East Top. Follow the narrow arête to the higher West Top.

173	**West Ridge**	**Grade 1** **
○ NM 374 954	4HRS 15	ARÊTE +50M

This lovely narrow ridge on excellent gabbro deserves more popularity, but because it's a long way from anywhere it gets few suitors. The good part is easily included as an out-and-back from the summit.

Approach
From Harris cross the bridge at NM 345 955 and head eastwards up pathless ground. This is grassy at first but becomes bouldery as it steepens. Carry on up the shoulder until it flattens out at about 600m. Soon after this it narrows into a fine arête.

The Route
Follow the crest direct, over several small pinnacles, as avoiding them is no easier. The fun continues all the way to the West Top, which is the true summit.

Ainshval   781m

A grassy summit ridge, but with lots of steep rock on the north and east flanks. The rhyolite is not as good as the gabbro of the peaks further north and east and is thoroughly nasty in the wet.

- PAGE 324
- OS EXP 397
- VARIOUS
- RHYOLITE

174	**Forgotten Ridge**	**Grade 2** *
○ NM 385 944	3HRS 10	SLABS & ARÊTE +400M

Ainshval's east ridge is a good line with excellent slabs to start. Higher up the ridge gets nice and sharp but is mainly walking.

Bealach an Fhuarain

Approach
Easily reached from the Bealach an Oir (NM 385 953) by heading southwards across the head of Glen Dibidil. The right-hand side of the foot of the ridge has two ribs with clean slabby right flanks.

The Route
Start up the left rib, following the angle of crest and slab to reach grass. Climb a spiky arête, then when a smooth clean slab appears off left cross below it and up another arête (crux). Link up slabby outcrops to reach the narrow ridge. This is a bit loose in places but easy and enjoyably airy. It steepens slightly before finishing suddenly right at the summit cairn.

175 North Ridge   Grade 2 or 3

○ NM 379 948	🚶 3HRS	◿ BUTTRESS	⊤ +230M

A route in two sections, the first quite hard, the second easier. Both are easily bypassed, and many of the Main Ridge aspirants miss out the lower buttress by scree to the right. In the wet this is a very sensible plan.

Approach
The lower buttress starts just above the Bealach an Fhuarain (NM 378 948), reached as for Route 171.

The Route
The buttress has a steep wall at the bottom. Follow a ramp up left below this and round onto the left face. Go up a grassy groove and the slab on its right to reach the crest. Move left up slabs and bypass the vertical rock band by a steep grassy groove on the left. Easy rock leads to a large overhang, passed on the left, then the ground gradually eases to walking.

There are several harder alternatives to this on the slabs to the right, all at least Moderate when dry and a very bad idea in the wet.

Walk up to the upper spur, which the path bypasses on the left. Tackled direct just right of centre this is a delicate and exposed Grade 3, but it is much easier to go up a short gully round to the left. Follow the airy crest above or an easier line to the right, not great rock but nice positions, to reach grass fairly close to the summit.

176	**Harris Face**		**Moderate**	
◯ NM 375 947	🏃 3HRS 30	⊿ BUTTRESS	⊤ +200M	

Lovely rock lower down, less so higher up. Unfortunately the crux is on the poorer rock.

Approach

This can be reached up Coire Fiachinis from Harris, but as few people base themselves there most will arrive by traversing westwards from the Bealach an Fhuarain. The quickest route slants upwards across unpleasant scree to reach a grassy saddle at the top of a stubby spur then descends the far side. Much nicer but longer is to descend the upper corrie to about the 400m contour then bear left along the foot of the slope until right of a scree shoot. The lower tier of the face is steep and shattered, but well right is a rib of rough gabbro (NM 374 945). From the top of this walk left along the shelf below the main face until just short of a stubby projecting spur with a grassy saddle at its top.

The Route

Climb the lowest rib, the rightmost of three, then use a dyke to break through a steeper band. Go up left then ascend a slab on the right. Climb another steep band delicately by a right-to-left diagonal. The spur now eases, heading for a steep tower right of a deep gully. This is the crux. Climb the left edge of the tower past a sharp pinnacle (an unlikely looking escape is possible from its top). Continue up the edge above the pinnacle until an airy traverse is possible to the crest. Breathe a sigh of relief and romp up the now much easier spur over a small pinnacle and up slabs until they peter out into the hillside. Moving left gains a few more outcrops and joins the North Ridge near its top, much better than slogging straight up the slope.

Sgùrr nan Gillean 764m

The ridge is a pleasant upland stroll above a steep east flank. There are also some enjoyable easy slabs low down on the south flank if coming up this way.

 PAGE 324
 OS EXP 397
 SOUTH-EAST
 RHYOLITE

177	**Dibidil Face**		**Grade 2**
◇ NM 385 930	🚶 3HRS 30	◁ OUTCROPS	⊥ +300M

Nice scrambling on volcanic breccia but a masochistic approach. The start is harder than it looks but it soon eases.

Approach

Directly above Dibidil Bothy a minor gully is central on the face, slanting up right directly below the apparent summit and well up left from the much larger dark gully lower down. Slog up to the upper gully, easiest further left. Right of the scree emerging from the gully are three ribs, the central of which has a slab topped with a vertical wall 10m up.

The Route

Scramble up to and climb the slab, then avoid the vertical wall on the right. Follow a rib up right to a grassy gully with steep broken rock up left and a clean rib on the right skyline. Climb the rib then go up left until you can string together outcrops to the top of the shoulder. Where this merges into the main mountain short easy rock steps lead to the summit ridge just south-east of the cairn.

Traverse of the Rùm Cuillin

The classic one day traverse of the island's main peaks will be many people's primary objective on a trip to Rùm. At around 22km and with nearly 2000m of ascent it is comparable to the Cuillin Ridge in terms of effort, although considerably easier in technical difficulty. Barkeval is usually omitted but can easily be added in via its north-west flank or as a detour from the Bealach Bairc-mheall (add 2km and 140m ascent).

🌐 PAGE 324
◁ OS EXP 397
↔ VARIOUS
⛰ VARIOUS IGNEOUS

178	**Main Ridge Traverse**	**Grade 1 to Moderate** ★★★
◇ NM 393 965	🚶 1HR 40 TO FIRST SCRAMBLING	⊥ +600M & -350M

Only the North Ridge of Askival is hard enough to attract a climbing grade, and all the harder parts can be bypassed (and usually are in descent). This reduces the standard to Grade 1, but misses many of the best bits. The traverse is perfectly feasible in the wet but if doing this note that the rock on Ainshval and Sgùrr nan Gillean has much poorer friction than that on the northern three summits. The Naismith time is around 8 hours but given the amount of scrambling involved most should allow a couple of hours longer.

The traverse is usually done north to south as this gives a less steep approach and means that you are going upwards at the Askival Pinnacle and the North Ridge of Ainshval, the hardest parts of the route. The trail back from Dibidil can seem a long drag at the end of the day though, and going the other way gets this out of the way early. This would let you include Trollabhal South Slabs but most would probably descend the easier route avoiding the Askival Pinnacle.

Approach
For the usual north-south traverse follow Route 160 into Coire Dubh, then either continue direct up to Bealach Bairc-mheall or slant up left before this (small path) to the small col behind Cnapan Breaca. Continue slanting up to reach the ridge at the stony area just before it rises to Hallival.

The Route
Carry on over Hallival and down its South Ridge, with some minor scrambling. Climb the North Ridge of Askival by either Route 165 (Moderate) or Route 166 (Grade 1), then descend the West Ridge by either Route 169 (Grade 1) or the path to its left.

From Bealach an Oir climb Trollabhal by its East Ridge, Route 170 (Grade 1), then from the West Summit return across the East Summit and descend the South Flank, Route 171 (Grade 1) to the Bealach an Fhuarain. Climb the North Ridge of Ainshval by Route 175, most people avoiding the lower section (Grade 3) by the scree to its right. Walking leads to Sgùrr nan Gillean, with a brief easy scramble over a minor summit on the way.

Descend well southwards, keeping well right until the angle eases, then swing left to reach the bothy at Dibidil. A good but occasionally boggy path leads back to Kinloch in about 8km (though it seems longer), gaining around 250m along the way.

Looking back to Askival (Route 178, Grade 1 to Moderate). © Noel Williams

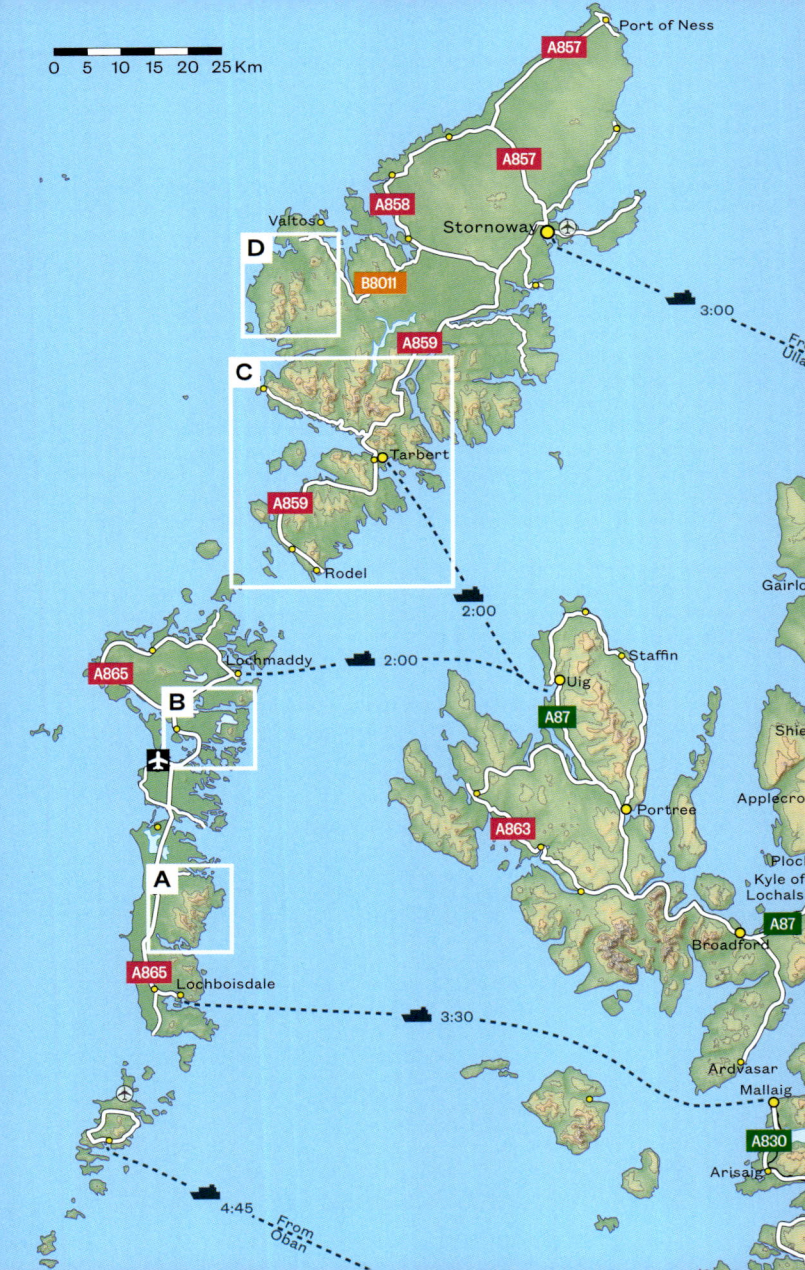

The Outer Hebrides

All the Outer Hebrides are rocky, as the Lewisian gneiss produces some of the roughest hills in the country, with rock outcropping all over the place. Much of it is easy-angled, but many of the steeper faces give superb scrambling. The wildly indented coastline of the islands means that the sea is everywhere, giving stunning views and an 'edge of the world' atmosphere.

Most of the scrambling is in two areas, the Uig Hills in West Lewis and the central knot of mountains in Harris, but there are also a few routes in South Harris, on the isolated peak of Eabhal in North Uist and in the Beinn Mhor group on South Uist. The Uig Hills are best accessed via the Ullapool to Stornaway ferry, the Harris routes from Skye via the Uig to Tarbert ferry and the Uist hills via either the Uig to Lochmaddy or Oban to Lochboisdale services. A ferry runs from Leverburgh to Berneray linking Harris and the Uists, and Calmac offer various 'Island Hopscotch' tickets which can be much cheaper than the standard fare. Bus services link Stornoway with Leverburgh via Tarbert, and Berneray with Lochmaddy and Lochboisdale, plus there is a minibus service from Stornoway to Uig (all Mon–Sat, information from Stornoway Bus Station 01851 704327, www.cne-siar.gov.uk).

All the island groups have different characters. Much of Lewis is blanketed in deep peat, but in the south-west corner the Uig Hills are as rocky as any scrambler could wish. They consist of two north–south ridges with rounded summits and steep sides, giving acres of slabby scrambling on excellent granite. There are many more possibilities than those described. Harris is not dissimilar, but the hills are higher and more crowded together, giving more of a big mountain feel. The Gillaval Dubh routes in particular are amongst the best in this guide. The Uist hills rise more suddenly from the surrounding bogland and the scrambling is mostly fairly minor.

Although only a few miles apart the east and west coasts often have totally different weather, so good route choice can pay dividends here. Finally it must be said that any visit to Lewis, Harris or Uist would be incomplete without a visit to at least one of the west coast's magnificent beaches, as beautiful as any in the world (just a pity about the water temperature!).

A.	South Uist	Routes 179–181	P.346
B.	North Uist	Route 182	P.352
C.	Harris	Routes 183–193	P.354
D.	West Lewis	Routes 194–199	P.368

South Uist

The long island of South Uist has a low west side fringed by splendid white beaches. The east side is a complete contrast, much wilder and rougher, with quite a remote feel. The rugged peaks of Beinn Mhòr and Hecla dominate the island and make a fine traverse with a little possible scrambling. The north flanks of both hills have bigger cliffs, with a reasonable scramble in Hecla's case, but although the Beinn Mhòr buttresses look dramatic they are very loose and vegetated. Many of the smaller hills are also very rocky, but it is hard to string the outcrops together into good scrambles.

1.	Beinn Mhòr	Route 179	P.347
2.	Beinn Corrdail	Route 180	P.347
3.	Hecla	Route 181	P.349

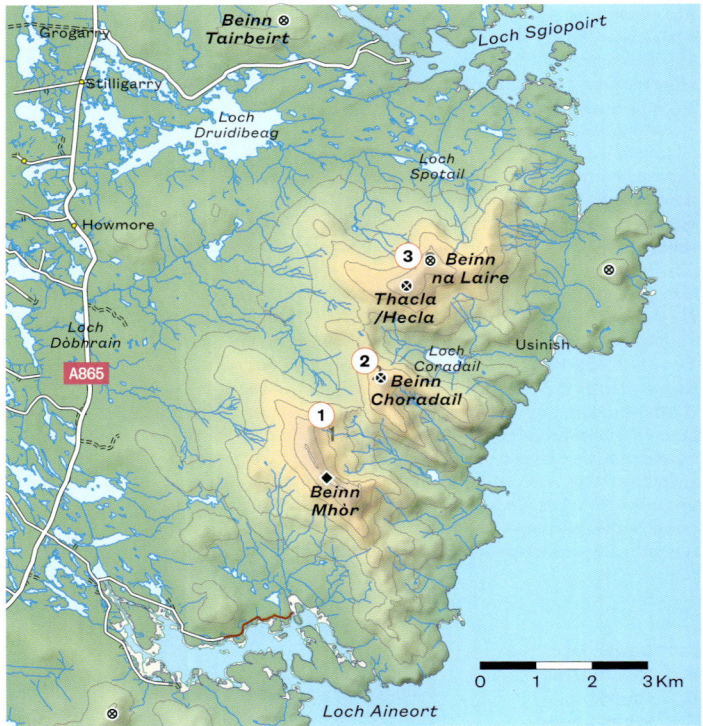

Beinn Mhòr   620m

The highest hill on South Uist, Beinn Mhòr has an enjoyably narrow summit ridge, with impressive buttresses falling northwards into Gleann Heileasdail. These are vegetated and frighteningly loose, although all have been climbed.

- PAGES 344 & 346
- OS LR 22
- NORTH-EAST
- GNEISS

179 North-East Ridge — Grade 1

NF 813 323 · 1HR 45 · OUTCROPS · +100M

A few minor outcrops make a pleasant way of gaining height.

Approach
Bealach Heileasdail (Hellisdale) will usually be reached by traversing Hecla and Beinn Choradail, but could be reached directly up Gleann Dorchaidh from the peat road starting at NF 767 346. At the west end of the bealach is a notch, with a steep wall on the left (looking up).

The Route
Climb a stepped rib on the right end of the wall to walking-angle slabs. At another steep wall climb the left arête. Minor outcrops then lead to an easy slabby spur. Follow this, then more outcrops higher up.

Beinn Choradail   527m

Although usually viewed as just an incident in the traverse of Beinn Mhòr and Hecla, Beinn Choradail is quite an individual peak. The north face is rocky but vegetated, while the face above Bealach Heileasdail is quite craggy too.

- PAGES 344 & 346
- OS LR 22
- NORTH-WEST
- GNEISS

180 North-West Ridge — Grade 2

NF 819 330 · 2HRS · BUTTRESS · +30M

Short but worthwhile. A steep start leads to exposed but easy steps.

Approach
Most will traverse Hecla first, descending to the saddle at the head of Gleann Uisinis, but a direct approach uses the peat road starting at NF 767 346 and goes up Gleann Dorchaidh. In either case go up the grassy north-west ridge to the twin buttresses just below the summit. Start at the right edge of the right-hand buttress, at a block, with a rocky gully to the right.

The Route

Climb a couple of steep steps, then move left onto the crest. Go up this, quite exposed at first, then the angle gradually eases to the summit.

North-West Ridge, Beinn Choradail (Route 180, Grade 2).
Scrambler: Peter McLeod. © Noel Williams

Hecla (Thacla) 606m

South Uist's second peak, Hecla, is largely grassy on its south flank, but the north side has three spurs with rocky ends. Coire Ruadail lies between the western two and has a rugged gneiss headwall leading up to Hecla's north-east top, Beinn na Laire. This is steep on its left, but a more amenable angle further right.

- PAGES 344 & 346
- OS LR 22
- NORTH
- GNEISS

---

181 Laire Rib Grade 2 or 3 ✱

NF 826 351 | 1HR 45 | OUTCROPS | +180M

A series of slabby ribs with steeper starts, the route inveigles its way through the steep sections to climb the enjoyable easy slabs beyond. There is one short (but good) Grade 3 section, easily avoided to make the route Grade 2.

Approach
From the road end at Loch Sgioport (NF 828 385, room for 3 cars) take the path running south around the coast. After 0.5km the track crosses a second bridge and you fork right on a boggier track and go up to an old house. Just before the building abandon the path and head southwards

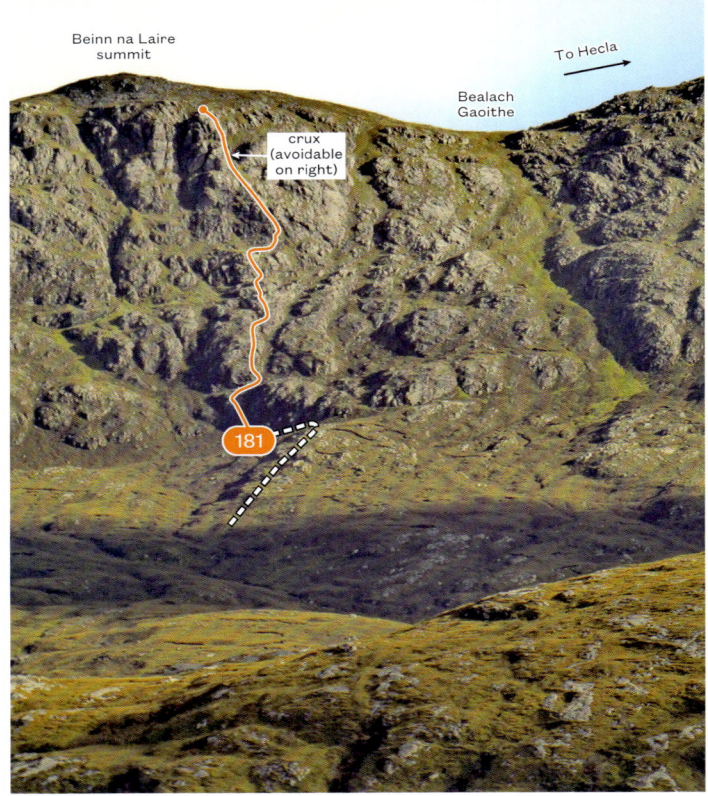

through lumpy ground. Keeping high over the first bump gets you slightly better ground, traversing right saves losing height, take your pick. Keep heading southwards across the bog, with occasional bits of deer path, to pass between Loch Fada and Loch Spotail. Now slant rightwards up easier ground into the east side of Coire Ruadail (called Coire Buidhe on the OS 1:25k map). The back left side of the corrie has a series of rock ribs, the described route being the right-hand one. A shallow spur leads up to the right-hand side of the face, ending below a line of steeper bluffs.

The Route
From the top of the shallow spur go left across a small stream and up a slabby rib below the main cliffs. Work up through steeper mossy rock and go up left to a cleaner rib. Climb this then move left and climb another rib, starting on steep jugs. Walking-angle slabs then lead to a terrace. Go up the right-hand edge of a steep buttress on the left, then follow the long slabby crest above. This eventually breaks up into separate outcrops, which lead to the half-height terrace.

Above the terrace climb the first outcrop by an easy right-to-left weakness. Gain the next outcrop from the right, then ascend more sustained rock on positive holds to another terrace. The slabs above are steep and mossy so move right a few metres and work rightwards up easier slabs. Climb cleaner rock on the left edge of a narrow gully to easy ground. Above are two steep outcrops separated by a grassy gully. The Grade 3 option climbs the steep right-hand edge of the left-hand buttress on excellent holds. Alternatively, go up the grassy gully for a few metres then traverse left across a slab onto the buttress above the steep section, making the route Grade 2. Either way, easy slabs lead to grassy ledges, then a rib of markedly looser rock leads to the top (easily avoided on the right). The summit of Beinn na Laire is just above.

Other scrambles nearby
The easternmost of the spurs, Beinn na h-Aire, has some scrambling on its north-west flank at NF 841 360. Scattered slabs can be linked up and provide an interesting start to a northern horseshoe of Hecla.

There is also a minor scramble up the west shoulder of Beinn Ruigh Choinnich (NF 804 197), and some slabs on the south flank of Easaval near Leac Sleamhuinn (NF 778 147) provide brief fun.

North Uist

Much of North Uist is very low and scattered with a maze of lochans – it would only take a minor rise in sea level to split it into a dozen islands. There are a number of small hills but by far the most prominent peak is Eaval, which is almost completely cut off from the rest of the island by a curving tidal loch.

1. Eaval   Route 182   P.352

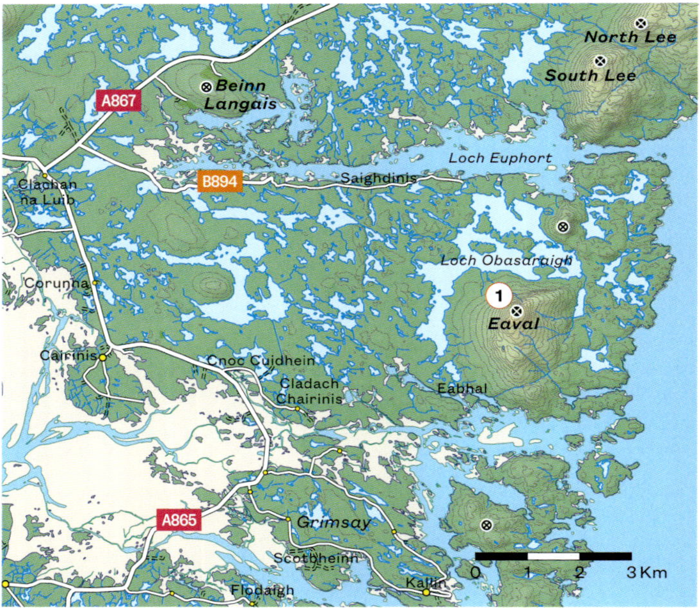

Eaval (Eabhal) — 347m

Eaval is one of the most distinctive peaks in the Hebrides, unrivalled by nearby summits and almost completely surrounded by water. Although it is pointed and very rocky the cliffs are fairly fragmented, with the clean rib below the summit on the north-west being the only really good line. The tremendous view over the 'waterscape' below is unique in Britain.

- ⊕ PAGES 344 & 352
- ⊿ OS LR 18 & 22
- ⇔ NORTH-WEST
- △ GNEISS

182   **The Route of all Eaval**   Grade 3

◯ NF 897 606   🚶 1HR 50   ◿ BUTTRESS   ⊤ +50M

A slabby rib of lovely rough gneiss, with an optional harder finish. Short but in a great position.

Approach
Park at the Loch Euphort (Saighdinis) road end (NF 891 631), take care not to block the turning space. Take a path eastwards past a cottage and a good path develops across the peat to the tidal outlet of Loch Obasaraigh (NF 897 630). At most (but not all!) states of the tide this is crossable on stepping stones, then the good path continues along the shore of Loch Obasaraigh to the small beaches at its east end. A rather wet path carries on up Eaval's north-east shoulder, skirting around minor outcrops. Above a minor saddle at 250m the path goes up left, while the spur ahead gives a short scramble (hardish Grade 1, not exposed). A much better scramble can be reached by descending the gully rightwards from the saddle until the ground opens out about 50m down. Follow the foot of the steeper ground up leftwards (looking out) for around 400 metres to reach the foot of a slabby rib, the cleanest and most continuous rock around, with a steeper cliff up left.

The Route
Climb the rib direct, sustained but escapable in several places. After 30m or so the angle eases and easy slabs lead up to the top of the rib, with the summit a brief clamber and short walk away. A harder finish can be added by traversing onto the steeper buttress on the left from the top of the rib, finishing up the left-hand of two left-slanting grooves (Diff).

Harris

Although Harris and Lewis are physically the same island, they have startlingly different characters. Harris is much hillier and more rugged, with An Cliseam rising to nearly 800m. North of the isthmus at Tarbert, North Harris consists of several north–south ridges with steep sides, many of which have areas of cliff, the most impressive being the huge overhanging pillar of Sròn Uladail. South Harris, on the other hand, has more isolated smaller hills with fewer scrambling possibilities, as well as having the lion's share of the beaches.

1.	Roineabhal	Routes 183–186	P.355
2.	Uamascleit	Route 187	P.358
3.	Beinn na Teanga	Route 188	P.359
4.	Gillaval Dubh	Routes 189–191	P.360
5.	An Cliseam (Clisham)	Route 192	P.363
6.	Huiseabhal Mòr	Route 193	P.366

Roineabhal   460m

A very rocky hill, mostly made of anorthosite (the commonest rock on the lunar surface), it hit the headlines in the early 2000s when it was reprieved from becoming the site of a superquarry. The deeply cut Coire Roineabhal on the north-east flank has lots of steep but broken rock on its headwall and slabs on its left side which give enjoyable scrambling. The most distinct route is on the left edge but a direct line up the middle has the best scrambling and the right edge is fun too. There is scope for another independent line right of centre, steeper at the top. Immediately right of the slabs is a short but excellent gabbro rib, Sandpiper Rib, easier than it looks. The corrie's far right edge also has an easy-angled rock spur at NB 045 866 that gives some brief Grade 1 fun. The summit has a fantastic view and is one of the best places in Britain for garnets.

- PAGES 344 & 354
- OS LR 18
- NORTH-WEST
- GABBRO, DIORITE & ANORTHOSITE

183   Left-Hand Slabs   Grade 2 *

⌖ NB 048 862	🚶 50MINS	◿ SLABS	↥ +150M

Very rough gabbro slabs, with lots of ledges and some steeper sections. There are lots of possible variations and some places are almost walking but you are committed to the general line. The slabs are much less steep than they look from below so exposure is minimal, but although the route is technically easy for the grade, it is serious. The bedrock is solid but there are lots of loose rocks sitting on the easy-angled sections.

Approach
There are several parking places around NB 059 851. Slant up northwards to reach a small stream (Abhainn Collam) and follow it up to a minor col. Continue slanting up north-westwards to traverse below steep craglets at around 180m and go round (slightly down) into Coire Roineabhal. The slabs are obvious up left. From the lowest point a plate of slabs slants up leftwards, separated from the main slab by a heathery runnel. Just up left from the lowest point are two heathery patches. Start at the larger left-hand one.

The Route
Go rightwards up a steeper section, keeping to the cleanest rock. Above this a series of ramps slant up from left to right, with two more steepish sections up and left. There is no best line, just follow the ramps up until you see a route through the steeper sections that you fancy, gradually working up left. Eventually the angle eases to mostly walking, but there are a couple of short steeper outcrops before the cliff finishes.

Left-Hand Slabs, Roineabhal (Route 183, Grade 2).
Scrambler: Iain Thow. © Paul Buchanan

184 Central Slabs — Grade 3 ★★

NB 047 862 | 50MINS | SLABS | +180M

The longest line on the slabs, including a couple of steep sections (taken direct by *An Àite Bòidheach*, Diff). As with the previous route, everything is much easier than it looks, but the situations are serious. The rock is excellent but with loose debris scattered on the easy-angled sections. There are lots of route options and both the steep walls can be avoided by detours right but you are committed to the slab until near the top.

Approach
As for Route 183 but start just right of the heathery runnel forming the left edge of the main slab, below a group of overlaps.

The Route
Go up direct, keeping to the cleanest rock. The angle eases after 20m or so, then steepens again at 50m into a nearly vertical wall. Move up right slightly, then slant leftwards across the wall on good holds. More slabs then lead to a line of overlaps at two-thirds height. Climb a vertical section just right of the overlaps on big rough steps, then go up to easy ground. Head rightwards up easy slabs to climb another short wall, then more slabs gradually ease to walking.

185 Right Edge — Grade 2 ★

NB 047 861 | 55MINS | SLABS | +120M

The easiest of the three routes, with much of it Grade 1 or walking, but still on serious ground. Nearly all on good rock, with less debris than on the rest of the slabs.

Approach
As for Route 183 but at the foot of the slabs walk rightwards up a heathery terrace to their right-hand edge. Walking-angle slabs just right provide an alternative, or there are more easy slabs further right, just left of a shallow grassy gully. The terrace ends at an open grassy area below a noxious-looking double gully. Start at the edge of the main slabs just left of this (or lower, as for the following route).

The Route
Go up the slabs to a slanting grass ledge. Move leftwards through a band of poorer mossy rock, then continue direct on clean slabs. At three-quarter height dodge a steep wall on the right and climb slightly steeper slabs above. Where these start to ease move rightwards to finish up a nicely positioned rib above the gully.

186 Sandpaper Rib — Grade 2 ★

NB 047 861 | 55MINS | SLABS | +120M

A clean rib of very rough gabbro, much easier than it looks. Would be worth another star if it was longer.

Approach
As for the previous route but start just down and right from the open grassy area, at the right edge of a steep wall at the foot of the rib. The easy slabs just left of the shallow grassy gully mentioned above provide a good preamble.

The Route
Climb steeply up rough gabbro steps, then move left onto the main slabs of the lower part of the rib. Go up these, mostly almost walking, until they steepen into a tower at half-height. Either climb this direct on good holds (intimidating but easier than it looks) or work up right to the skyline and a simple finish. The platform at the top is an excellent viewpoint, with the summit of Roineabhal about 15 minutes away.

Uamascleit 231m

A minor top overlooking West Loch Tarbert, accessible but with quite a remote feel.

 PAGES 344 & 354

 OS LR 14

 NORTH-EAST

GNEISS

187	**North-East Face**			Grade 3 *

⌖ NB 130 000	🏃 30MINS	◿ SLABS	⊤ +130M

This route avoids the steep lower slabs by an exposed traverse to reach easier ribs of excellent gneiss. Serious and exposed in its lower part, then escapable outcrops. The right-hand edge of the crag is a scrappy Diff (*Original Route*).

Approach
All approaches are rough and wet, but best is to follow the south shore of West Loch Tarbert from behind the school (NB 149 002). Where the steep shoreline falls back cut south-west across bogs to the cliff. Start at the left-hand end of the clean rock, left of the overhangs.

The Route
Go up an easy subsidiary slab left of the crag, then go right up heather to take a narrow exposed ledge horizontally right just above the main cliff. Climb a superb slabby rib and where this ends go up right to climb juggy slabs right of a steeper rib to a large shelf. An easy rib with a tiny overhang at the bottom leads to another shelf, then climb the next rib in a series of steps. Ahead is a steep slab of extreme roughness, then an easier slabby rib leads to the top.

Beinn na Teanga 440m

A minor top at the head of Glen Skeaudale, with rough spurs running south and south-east enclosing Gleann Lingeadail.

- 🌐 PAGES 344 & 354
- ✦ OS LR 14
- ✥ SOUTH-WEST
- ⌂ GNEISS

188	**Lingeadail Slabs**			Grade 1

⌖ NB 166 024	🏃 50MINS	◿ SLABS	⊤ +100M

Gently-angled slabs add interest to a wild hillwalk. Much harder when wet.

Approach
From the south end of the Laxadale track (NB 177 004) traverse up north-west past Loch Torsacleit. The slabs line the north-east side of the top end of Gleann Lingeadail. Start at the right-hand (lowest) end.

The Route
Slant left up the easy lower slabs to a heather shelf, aiming for a prominent stepped corner on the upper tier. Above the shelf climb more slabs bearing up left to a smaller shelf below the corner. Climb smooth slabs left of the corner and go up steps to its top. Clean ribs on the right make a good continuation.

Gillaval Dubh 417m

The north face of this hill consists of a row of six buttresses up to 250m high overlooking the Tarbert to Stornoway road, reached by a steep 15–20 minute walk. A, C and D Buttresses are all excellent scrambles on superb gneiss, E and F Buttresses are short and easy (F with a hard start, Grade 3), while B is horrible, cut by a series of steep greasy walls, forcing scramblers onto insecure vegetated ground. The ridges are nowhere near as steep as they look from the road and consist of alternating rock sections and grassy shelves, so you get plenty of breaks, but difficulties keep going right to the top. Some of the slabby parts are sustained, but the sections are usually avoidable and few are exposed. Usually there is plenty of choice of route, but there are no sideways escapes so once on a buttress you are committed to it. The slabby sections are clean so despite being north-facing they dry fairly quickly after showers, but after more sustained rain weeps develop and these take a few days to disappear.

- PAGES 344 & 354
- OS LR 14
- NORTH
- GNEISS

189   A Buttress   Grade 2 or 3 ✳

◯ NB 142 029   🚶 20MINS   ◿ BUTTRESS   ⊤ +250M

A broad buttress with much choice of route, grassy in places, but with some excellent slabby ribs.

Approach
From the bridge over the Skeaudale River (NB 138 034) go up south-east to the left-hand of the six buttresses (it forms the skyline from the bridge). There are a few isolated slabs low down, but start above these, on the left-hand side of the main buttress, just left of the lowest point, below a steep red wall about 6m up.

The Route
Go up left of the steep red wall. Easy rocks follow with the stepped blocky rib in the centre providing a good route. At the overhang go up left and climb the left-hand side of the tier. Continue up to a large projecting boulder, then go up right and climb stepped slabs. These are steep at the top (Grade 3), but easily dodged. Now choose between steep boulder problems on the left or easier ground to the right. Follow easy steps to a large shelf which slopes down into the gully on the right. Twin cracks on the right lead up a rib, then carry on up until the buttress peters out into open hillside. Go up right to the skyline and follow this up to finish up a superb juggy rib.

190   C Buttress   Grade 3 ✳✳✳

◯ NB 140 030   🚶 15MINS   ◿ BUTTRESS   ⊤ +250M

Sustained scrambling on perfect gneiss, intimidating but easier than it looks. Lots of minor grassy ledges, but they don't interfere with the flow.

Approach
From the bridge over the Skeaudale River (NB 138 034) go up south-east to the third buttress from the left. Start on the right, by the stream (often dry). There is a prominent little slab just right of the stream for an appetiser.

The Route
Go up slabs left of the stream to grass, then more slabs with a steeper move in the middle. Walking and easy rock now lead to a steeper buttress. Start centrally and go up to a stepped wall. Either follow a grassy ledge out right and slant up awkward slabby steps to easy ground, or go up left then swing right on a spike (Moderate) and go right to the same place. Go up left easily to grass on top of the buttress. The whole section is avoidable on the right. Go up to the next slabs and up the superb rib in the centre. Go up left to steeper rocks on the skyline and climb the left-hand of two grooves, then move left to a lovely friction slab. The steep tier ahead is easiest by its left edge, but the juggy middle is easier than it looks. The buttress now narrows and small steps lead to an imposing central crack (again, easier than it seems). The vertical wall above is dodged on the left, then broken slabs lead to the top.

C Buttress, Gillaval Dubh (Route 190, Grade 3).
Scrambler: Iain Thow. © Paul Buchanan

191 D Buttress — Grade 3 or Moderate ✶✶

◇ NB 139 030   🏃 15MINS   ◿ BUTTRESS   ⊤ +250M

Quite hard to start, but easier than it looks. Sustained and on excellent rock. Avoiding the steep section at one-third height makes the route Grade 3.

Approach
From the bridge over the Skeaudale River (NB 138 034) go up south-east to the fourth buttress from the left. Start at the largest area of slabs at the bottom left of the buttress.

The Route
Climb the slabs, steep but with good friction, to a heather terrace. Go up a slabby rib on the right, then up grass to a steeper buttress. Start up steps on the left and move into the centre as the angle eases. Climb steeper more awkward slabs (crux, with the remains of an old peg), then

go up left of a vertical wall to grass ledges. This section can be bypassed by taking a good ledge rightwards and climbing the right-hand edge of the buttress.

Go right up grass to the skyline, then climb steeper rocks centrally, up a nose and a mossy groove to easier ground. Follow easy slabs until a grassy gully comes in from the left and splits the buttress. Traverse left to climb a rib (possible at several levels, the avoidable bulge at the bottom is Difficult). Carry on up the slabby rib, passing right of two overhangs, until this gives out to grass. Boulders and a rib lead to a nose, passed on the right. The next rib is gained steeply from the right, then more slabs lead to the top, with an optional overlap on the left halfway up.

An Cliseam (Clisham) 799m

The highest peak in the Outer Hebrides, An Cliseam consists of a north-east facing horseshoe, with the summit on the southern arm. There is some scrambling on the ridge to Mulla-Fo-Dheas, mostly just boulders, but with some Grade 1 slabs just right of the skyline. The best scrambling, however, is on the headwall of Coire Dubh just south of this.

- PAGES 344 & 354
- OS LR 14
- SOUTH
- GNEISS

192 Coire Dubh Slabs — Grade 3 ✶✶

◯ NB 146 074　　🯁 1HR　　◿ SLABS　　⊤ +200M

The central weakness on the prominent slabs gives serious scrambling on superb gneiss. The lower rib and upper outcrops can be dodged but the main section is sustained and inescapable, so high in the grade.

The rib left of the slabs is Grade 2, with much variation possible. Avoid the overhangs at half-height by pink steps on the left.

Coire Dubh Slabs, An Cliseam (Route 192, Grade 3).
Scrambler: Peter Duggan. © Noel Williams

Approach
There is a small car park at the access road to the wind turbine (NB 144 044). Go up past the turbine then traverse northwards into Coire Dubh. The slabs are obvious, central on the back wall of the corrie. Below the right-hand edge is a broken rib. Start here, at a gritty slab below a short steep broken wall.

The Route
Climb the gritty slab and the left-hand edge of the steeper wall, then follow the rib and slabs above until they peter out. Go left and climb another rib to reach a rake slanting up left below the main sweep of cleaner steeper slabs - where there are two rock climbs. Follow the rake up left to a large grass patch, go up this and keep bearing left up broken steps below the cleaner slabs to reach grassy ledges leading off left.

Climb the slabs above by cracks left of a blank slab. On the right is a more crystalline slab. Climb this bearing left and crossing a small overlap to reach steeper slabs with a left-curving overlap. Climb steep cracks left of this, then go more easily up left to a reddish crystalline band. Climb this rightwards (serious), then go left up slabs to reach greyer smoother rock. Go direct up this to reach more broken ground.

Above this an optional square-cut rib on the right is tricky, but excellent, then easy ground with the odd problem leads to the skyline. A steep subsidiary rib on the left makes an interesting finish.

The optional square-cut rib (VDiff?), Coire Dubh Slabs, An Cliseam (Route 192, Grade 3). Scrambler: Gordon Rothero. © Noel Williams

Huiseabhal Mòr   489m

This ridge at the west end of the North Harris hills falls steeply into Glen Cravadale to the north. The face is very vegetated, but there is good scrambling at the west end, the best being the following route.

- ⊕ PAGES 344 & 354
- ◁ OS LR 13
- ✣ NORTH-EAST
- △ GRANITE

193	**Cravadale Rib**		Grade 3 ✱	
◇ NB 009 129	🏃 1HR	⊿ BUTTRESS	⊤ +60M	

A short but enjoyable granite scramble with great views, quite sustained. North facing and split by grassy ledges so slow to dry.

Approach
From the road end at Huisinis (parking at NA 993 121) take the path around northwards over the top of the first cliffs, then across a col to Loch na Cleabhaig. From the cottage just east of the loch go up left of the stream towards a prominent steep buttress on the skyline. Link easy-angled slabs to reach a shelf at the bottom of this.

The Route
Left of the small overhangs at the bottom are steep slabs, then left again is a grass shelf a few feet up. Pull up onto this and climb cracks above. At the top of the buttress these steepen, forcing a delicate traverse left

to the edge and up to a moss and heather shelf. This point can also be reached by climbing the right-hand edge of the buttress (Difficult), or by easier slabs further left.

Climb the right-hand edge of the steep buttress above on good holds, finishing up a thin crack, or the easier rib a few metres left. Easier slabs then lead to another shelf. Move left and climb the buttress above a small leaning wall to the top. A few more outcrops can be found up and left.

The parallel ridge 200 metres to the left has some easy scrambling (Grade 1). The rib left again is enjoyably slabby with plenty of route choice, starting up a subsidiary spur below and left (Grade 2).

Cravadale Rib, Huiseabhal Mòr (Route 193, Grade 3).
Scrambler: Paul Buchanan. © Iain Thow

West Lewis

Most of Lewis is fairly low, but south of the major indentation of Loch Roag the coast is dominated by the rocky Uig Hills, two lines of ice-scraped granite summits offering endless scope for scrambling and a few harder possibilities. Nearby are the Uig sea cliffs, with a vast number of rock climbs. In particular, many users of this guide might be interested in two excellent Diffs, *Sunset Rib* and *The Great Pretender.* The latter climbs a prominent pink pegmatite rib. The top of the sea cliffs also makes a very enjoyable evening stroll.

1.	Griomabhal	Route 194	P.369
2.	Teinneasabhal	Route 195	P.370
3.	Tathabhal	Routes 196–197	P.372
4.	Mealaisbhal	Route 198	P.375
5.	Suaineabhal	Route 199	P.378

Griomabhal 620m

This is the southernmost of the Uig Hills, with a real 'edge of the ocean' feel to it. The north face has the steep Teilasdail Slabs, home to the classic *Lochlann* (VS), but a few hundred metres east are easier angled broken slabs that make a good scramble. The west shoulder also has some pleasant walking-angle slabs that make an enjoyable way up from the sea, but the slightly steeper slabs a few hundred metres left of these are disappointing.

⊕ PAGES 344 & 368
⊲ OS LR 13
✥ NORTH
⌂ GRANITE

The easier Grade 2 options are shown with a dashed orange line

descend to reach main continuation

gap

194

194 Tealasdail Rib — Grade 2 or 3 ✱

| ⌖ NB 015 222 | 🯄 1HR 20 | ⟋ SLABS | ⟰ +150M |

Enjoyable granite slabs with the odd steeper step, quite broken but with some good sections. The best line is Grade 3 but zigzagging about can get it down to Grade 2.

Approach
From the road end at Mealasta (NA 993 234, limited parking) head south, with bits of path initially. Slant up into Gleann Tealasdail, either keeping

low to cross the stream between its gorge and the drop to the sea, or keeping high to stay above the gorge (more direct but less path). Go up to the hollow with the small Dubh Loch then up more steeply, either by keeping well right or by picking up an airy deer path slanting through the cliffs further left. Beyond the saddle is the large Loch Bhraighe Griomabhal, set in a very rocky bowl, and the route starts just above its southwestern tip, well left of the main Tealasdail Slabs. Start at the right-hand foot of a broad slabby rib.

The Route
Climb the first slabs, then move right and climb more slabs to steeper ground. Climb this by juggy blocks and flakes. Go up more slabs until they steepen, then either climb the steeper slabs on the left (Grade 3), or pull over the overlap in the middle on positive holds (an unlikely looking Grade 2), or avoid the step altogether on the right. Easy slabs then lead to an almost vertical wall, where you can climb either a steep crack on the right with big hidden holds or an easier slanting groove just left.

Traverse up left across a short slabby rib to reach a very overhanging wall on the left side of the buttress. Bridge up the groove right of this, then make an exposed traverse left between overlaps onto the front of the rib. Go up either via a shallow groove and a step right or by the slabs just right to reach easier slabs above all the overlaps. All this steep section can be bypassed on the right, traversing onto the rib as it eases, allowing an ascent at Grade 2. Nicely positioned easy scrambling then leads to grass on the edge of the buttress.

Move right onto the next rib, either straight across or descending slightly to its foot. Go up either via a delicate central groove with a small overlap (Grade 3, the overlap being easier than it looks), or by a stepped groove on the left edge (Grade 2). Easy slabs and a short wall lead to the top.

Teinneasabhal 497m

Sgorran Dubh Teinneasabhal, the craggy north-west face of Teinneasabhal, dominates the upper reaches of Gleann Raonasgail. The best climbing is on its Far South Buttress, but the sprawling North Buttress gives a good scramble.

- 🌐 PAGES 344 & 368
- OS LR 13
- WEST
- GRANITE

 North Buttress Grade 2

 NB 037 255  1HR 40  INTRICATE +300M

An intricate but logical line up a big face, mostly slabby but with some steeper sections. Many harder variations are possible. It is intimidating and parts of it would be difficult to escape from.

Approach
Follow the private vehicle track from NB 032 313 as far as Loch Mor na Clibhe (locked gate at the crossing of the Abhainn Stocaill). Stay on the track until 1km beyond the head of Loch Raonasgail. The face up left is split by a prominent central Y-gully. North Buttress is the broad face on its left, with preliminary slabs below. Go up to the right-hand base of these.

The Route
Start up the right-hand side of a short step at the foot of the slabs, then move left onto them and slant up right to the edge. Go up a slabby rib on the right-hand edge, then move left onto more slabs. Go rightwards up these to grass. Easy slabby ribs lead to more grass below the steep main face.

Walk 20 metres right to a clean rib on the skyline. Go up this, then steeper steps trending up right to grass. Move right again and climb another slabby rib, with a useful crack on the right at the steepest part. At steeper rock work up right across grooves to the right-hand edge, then go back up left above the steep section. Easier rock now leads up the centre of a broad spur to another steepening. Climb this by a groove full of spikes. Go up the right-hand arête of the next groove then follow the crest of the spur. Swing left onto a ramp below a steep wall, then go up right onto its top. Move left again and climb a series of short steps to the top. The summit is only a few metres away.

Tathabhal   515m

An exceptionally rocky hill, with the whole of the north and west faces giving scrambling, and occasionally harder routes. The clean rib at the right-hand end of the north face and the slabs and overlaps on the south-west corner are particularly good.

 PAGES 344 & 368
 OS LR 13
 SOUTH-WEST & NORTH
GRANITE

Loch Reonasgail

196 South-West Shoulder   Moderate ✱

| ⌖ NB 038 262 | 🚶 1HR 20 | ◢ INTRICATE | ↕ +300M |

A varied and sustained series of problems on clean granite, very reminiscent of Arran. Strenuous in places but not exposed. Most difficulties are avoidable.

Approach
Follow the vehicle track as for Route 195 until about 0.5km beyond the south end of Loch Reonasgail. Go steeply uphill to the lowest spur of

slabs descending from the cliffs up on the left. Go diagonally up left 20 metres to the next spur and start there.

The Route
Climb the left edge of the slabs until they finish, then transfer to the next set and follow these up right to a steep wall. Either make a precarious step left around this and go up or avoid it on the right. Gain the next slab from the left, then the next by a wide crack on the left and climb it direct. Climb a chimney in a nose, then the next nose by flakes. Another slab then leads to an apparent impasse.

Traverse right across big boulders into a slabby niche below vertical walls, then climb a strenuous chimney in the back (don't miss the very useful foothold out on the right arête!). Take the left fork of the chimney, then slant right up slabs to the right-hand edge of the cliff. Just before this go left up flakes to the crest.

Carry on up the crest, then big flakes lead up left to a gash running horizontally left. Go through this and up slabs. Follow more flakes up left and regain the crest. Go horizontally left below a huge block and up jugs behind it. The ridge now starts to break up into enormous blocks, giving problems of every conceivable grade. Generally work up left, with huge flakes, ramps and the odd strenuous crack providing plenty of entertainment. The easiest versions are generally on the right. The problems finally peter out only a few metres below the summit.

197 North-West Rib — Moderate **

◯ NB 043 268   🚶 1HR 30   ⊿ OUTCROPS   ⊤ +200M

A steep rib with some quite hard sections, occasionally exposed. Even better with a direct finish, but this is Very Difficult.

Approach
As for Route 195 to Loch Mòr na Clibhe, then cross the river at the foot of Loch Reonasgail and slant up south-east to the western edge of the saddle north of Tathabhal. The route is the almost continuous rib on the right-hand edge of the North Face. A few broken outcrops below it can

be bypassed or included to reach an overhanging block at the foot of the rib proper.

The Route
Gain the top of the initial face easily from the right, then go up a steep chimney on the left and follow steps up leftwards. Go up the right-hand side of the nose above to easy ground. Follow the crest up short steps, then move right onto an exposed arête above steep slabs. Follow this up right to a grass ledge, then go up a quartzy crack to a terrace.

Move left and go up a stepped arête, then climb the left arête of a wet V-groove (quite hard). A slabby arête leads to boulders, then climb a rib on the right. Easy slabs now lead to a more substantial buttress.

Thrutch up the obvious wide crack, then climb flakes and a slab above to a ledge below the final face. A slab and crack directly above are Very Difficult, so for a more consistent finish walk 10m up left, then go up the left edge and over a small overhang. Step up right to a delicate ramp, make a couple of moves up left on this, then make an airy move up right to the top.

Several additional options are nearby: *North-West Slabs* on Beannan a' Deas (NB 051 294) is an enjoyable Grade 3 ✶✶. Cracked grooves right of centre lead to a short corner and a left-slanting ramp. A direct finish is Diff. The separate rib above the foot of the loch (*Reservoir Rib*) is Grade 2. The *North Spur* of Beannan a' Tuath (NB 060 298) is a long Grade 2 and the *North-East Buttress* of Tarain (NB 053 279) is Grade 3, starting up a lovely sharp arête on the left.

Mealaisbhal   574m

The highest hill in Lewis, its northern spur has a steep vegetated cliff on its north side, named Creagan Tealasdale on the 1:25,000 OS map. The left-hand edge of the face is a broad slabby buttress of excellent granite.

🌐 PAGES 344 & 368
🧭 OS LR 13
✧ EAST
⛰ GRANITE

198 East Buttress   Grade 2/3 ✶✶

○ NB 032 280   🚶 1HR   ◿ BUTTRESS   ⊤ +300M

Open slabs, not exposed, with difficulties all avoidable. It is serious, however, and one steeper step borders on Grade 3.

Approach
Follow the vehicle track from NB 032 313 as for Route 195 as far as Loch Mòr na Clibhe (locked gate at the crossing of the Abhainn Stocaill). Go right and follow the south side of the loch, passing under the first slabs to more slabs forming the left edge of the main north face.

The Route
The slabs are easy at first, steepening briefly before a more serious bulge left of a square tower. Climb a crack just left of centre, then go right to left up a short steep wall on good holds. Climb another short wall on the right, then a nose at a pointed flake. Continue up the crest to a grassy shoulder, then small outcrops just left of the crest lead up to the top of the cliff. The last step has a flake-crack in its nose, giving an optional hard finish (Difficult).

East Buttress, Mealaisbhal (Route 198, Grade 2/3).
Scrambler: Suzy Devey. © Finlay Wild

Suaineabhal 429m

An isolated but accessible summit to the north-east of the main Uig group with a craggy west face. The views from the summit out over the sands of Traigh Uige are outstanding.

 PAGES 344 & 368
OS LR 13
WEST
GRANITE

Loch Suaineabhal

199	**West Slabs**		Grade 3 **	
◇ NB 071 305	🚶 15MINS	⟋ OUTCROPS	⊤ +250M	

Slabs to start, then steeper outcrops, all on excellent granite. Most parts are avoidable.

Approach
From the foot of Loch Suaineabhal (NB 064 310) cross the bridge and follow the loch shore round until below Suaineabhal. The first cliffs are steep, but 100 metres further on a slabby spur comes down close to the loch, with a cairn on a boulder at its foot.

The Route
Go up left of a prominent vertical crack, then up excellent slabs above. Pull over a small overhang on the right, then go up more slabs, with the rib becoming better defined. Where it ends walk left across a heathery hollow to another slabby rib. This is delicate at first, then easier up the line of a thin crack. Walk up to a steeper outcrop. The shattered crack in this is harder than it looks and better avoided on the left. Another steep tier is climbed by a groove with a hard start. Go up right to the next craglet and climb it by a knobbly groove. Broken steps above are still quite steep, then the ground eases to slabs. Above these follow a left-trending set of ribs to the top of the face. Minor problems can be found on the way to the summit.

Further south, on the west side of Sneihabhal (the summit south of Sròn ri Gaoith), there is a fun Grade 1 pinnacle (NB 074 286), while the outcrops east of it are Grade 2.

All Hebridean days ought to finish on a beach. This one is Traigh Mhangarstaidh below Mealaisbhal. © Iain Thow

Index of routes

Mainly listed by nearest mountain or crag

A' Chràileag	116
Allt Choire a' Chait	116
A' Ghlas-Bheinn	122
Allt Loch a' Chleirich	122
A' Mhaighdean	226
Bivouac Rib	227
Kids' Ridge	229
North-West Ridge	227
Red Slab	228
Ainshval	338
Forgotten Ridge	338
Harris Face	340
North Ridge	339
Am Faochagach	260
Cnoc na h-Iolaire	260
An Caisteal	102
South Face	103
An Cliseam (Clisham)	363
Coire Dubh Slabs	364
An Groban	211
Humpback Buttress	213
North-West Face	212
Right-Hand Slabs	214
An Ruadh-stac	149
Allt Loch Mòine a' Chriathair	150
Eastern Slabs	150
North-West Shoulder	151
An Teallach	246
Allt a' Ghiubhsachain	246
Corrag Bhuidhe Traverse	248
Ghiubhsachain Slabs	248
Sgùrr Ruadh	252
Aonach air Chrith	114
North Ridge	114
Arkle	302
South Rib	302
Askival	332
East Ridge	333
North Ridge, Askival Pinnacle	332
North Ridge, Easy Route	333
South Ridge	334
West Ridge	334
Baosbheinn	206
Oidhche Spur	206
Barkeval	326
Broad Buttress	327
Descent Spur	331
Honeycomb Arête	331
Narnia Arête	327
North-West Flank	326
Beinn a' Chàisgein Mòr	220
Grey Ridge	220
Sgùrr na Laocainn Right-Hand	222
Beinn a' Chapuill	110
East Slabs	110
Beinn a' Mhùinidh	199
Bonnaidh Donn, Route One	200
Beinn Àirigh Charr	235
Bell's Route	237
Square Buttress	235
Beinn Alligin	175
Backfire Ridge	176
Horns of Alligin	175
Na Fasreidhnean, Tom na Gruagaich	175
Beinn an Aodainn	93
East-North-East Ridge	95
South Face	94
Beinn an Eòin	275
South-West Flank, Sgòrr Deas	275
South-West Ridge, Sgòrr Tuath	277
Beinn Bhàn	144
A' Chìoch	145
Beinn Choradail	347
North-West Ridge	347
Beinn Damh	147
North-East Spur	148
Beinn Dearg	178
North Ridge, Càrn na Feola	179
South-West Face	178
Beinn Dearg Mòr	244
East Buttress	245
South-East Ridge	244
Beinn Eighe	190
Ceum Grannda	192
East Buttress, Coire Mhic Fhearchair	193
East Ridge, Stùc Coire an Laoigh	194
Lawson, Ling & Glover's Route	191
North Ridge, Spidean Coire nan Clach	194
Toll Bàn Headwall	195
The Black Carls	196
Beinn Fhada	121
Bealach an t-Sealgaire (Hunters' Pass)	122
Beinn Gharbh	83
North-West Face	85
Ursainn Slabs	84
Beinn Làir	231
Left Wing, Butterfly Buttress	233
North Summit Buttress	233
Tower Ridge	231
Beinn Liath Mhòr	163
Apex Buttress	165
Lochview Slabs	163
South-East Rib	165
Beinn Mhòr	347
North-East Ridge	347
Beinn Mhòr na Còigich – See Ben More Coigach	

Index

Beinn na Caillich	97
South-East Slabs	97
Beinn na Muice	132
South-West Slabs	133
Beinn na Teanga	359
Lingeadail Slabs	359
Beinn nam Bàn	252
Windy Ridge	252
Beinn Tharsuinn Chaol	230
Gorm Loch Mòr Spur	231
Ben Aden – See Beinn an Aodainn	
Ben Hope	316
Brown's (Myles's) Ridge	317
Petticoat Ridge	318
Ben Loyal	318
Sgor a' Chleirich Ridge	319
Sgor Chaonasaid Spine	319
Ben More Assynt	291
East Flank, Sail an Ruathair	294
South-East Slabs, Sail an Ruathair	293
South Ridge	292
South Slabs, Sail an Ruathair	292
Ben More Coigach	272
Isle Martin Buttress	273
West Ridge Direct	272
Ben Screavie	301
Allt Screavie	302
Ben Stack	299
North Flank	299
Bidean a' Choire Sheasgaich	136
North Face	136
Bidean an Eoin Deirg	139
North-East Ridge	139
Biod an Fhithich	126
Ankle Ridge	127
Càrn Eighe	130
Càrn Eighe Pinnacles	131
Càrn Eiteige	133
Creag a' Chaobh	133
Càrnan Bàn	223
Cakewalk (Maiden Buttress)	225
Doddle	226
Pocket Slab	223
South-East Face	224
Càrnan Cruithneachd	123
South-West Shoulder	124
Clisham – See An Cliseam	
Cnap Coire Loch Tuath	265
South Face	265
Cnoc a' Bhac Fhalaichte	88
Tarbet Slabs	88
Cona' Mheall	262
North-East Slab	264
South Ridge	263
Twisted Rib	263
Conival	290
South Ridge	290
Cranstackie	315
Dionard Rib	316
Creag Ghlas	135
East Buttress	136
Creag Mhòr Thollaidh	215
North-West Rib	217
Cùl Beag	281
Lurgainn Edge	283
Cùl Mòr	283
Pinnacle Ridge	285
Table Rib	284
Eaval (Eabhal)	352
The Route of all Eaval	353
Foinaven	304
Coire Duail Slabs	308
Ganu Mor Slabs	311
North Face, Cnoc Duail	308
Second Dionard Buttress	304
Twin Caves Ridge, A' Chèir Ghorm	306
Upper Slabs, Creag Urbhard	305
Forcan Ridge – See (The) Saddle	
Fuar Tholl	156
Leth Chreag	159
South Flank	157
Spare Rib	159
Summit Rib	160
Garbh Chìoch Mhòr	92
Coire nan Gall Slabs	93
Gillaval Dubh	360
A Buttress	361
C Buttress	361
D Buttress	362
Griomabhal	369
Tealasdail Rib	369
Hecla (Thacla)	349
Laire Rib	349
Huiseabhal Mòr	366
Cravadale Rib	366
Ladhar Bheinn	99
An Dìollaid	99
Liathach	180
Am Fasarinen Traverse	183
East Buttress, Am Fasarinen	185
East Ridge, Stùc a' Choire Dhuibh Bhig	187
North Ridge, Spidean a' Choire Leith	187
Northern Pinnacles	188
South Ridge, Mullach an Rathain	180
PC Buttress	187
Lurg Mhòr	138
Meall Mor Ridge	138
Maiden Pap	322

Entry	Page
North Flank	322
Maol Chean-dearg	151
East Shoulder	154
Ketchil Buttress	152
North Flank	156
Mealaisbhal	375
East Buttress	375
Meall Aundrary	207
North-West Buttress	207
Meall Ceann na Creige	172
West Spur	172
Meall Gorm	142
Long Buttress	142
Meall Mhèinnidh	234
North-East Face	234
Meall na Teanga	73
Central Buttress, Meall Dubh	74
Right-Hand Buttress, Meall Dubh	74
Meall nan Ceapraichean	266
West Face	267
Meall nan Eun	104
Cannonade	107
Morven	323
North-East Ribs	323
Mullach Coire Mhic Fhearchair	242
East Ridge	242
Mullach Fraoch-choire	117
South Ridge	117
Quinag	294
East Buttress, Sàil Gharbh	294
Roineabhal	355
Central Slabs	357
Left-hand Slabs	355
Right Edge	357
Sandpaper Rib	357
Ruadh-stac Beag	197
Long Stroll Slab	197
Overlooking Rib	199
Rùm Cuillin	342
Main Ridge Traverse	342
Saddle, The	111
Forcan Ridge	112
Seana Bhraigh	268
An Sgùrr Ridge	268
Corriemulzie Rib	269
Sgorr Ruadh	161
Academy Ridge, Lower Slabs	162
Raeburn's Buttress	163
Sgùrr a' Chaorachain	143
Cioch Indirect	144
Sgùrr an Eilein Ghiubhais	89
Right-Hand Rib	90
Sgùrr an t-Searraich	119
South Ribs	121
Sgùrr Dubh	166
North-West Slabs	167
Sgùrr Dubh Gorge	168
Sgùrr Mhuidhe	83
North-East Flank	83
Sgùrr Mòr	255
North Spur	255
Sgùrr na Ciste Duibhe	118
North Buttress	118
Sgùrr na Lapaich	131
East Ridge	131
Sgùrr na Sgine	113
North-East Ridge	113
Sgùrr nan Clach Geala	253
Slanting Buttress	253
Sgùrr nan Coireachan	79
Riabhaich Slabs	80
Sgùrr nan Conbhairean	115
North-East Spur	115
Sgùrr nan Gillean	341
Dibidil Face	342
Sgùrr nan Spainteach	117
North Buttress	118
Sìthean Mòr	210
North Face	211
Slioch	201
North-West Buttress	202
Sròn a' Choire Ghairbh	76
South Face, Sean Mheall	77
Stac Pollaidh	277
East-West Traverse	278
Stob a' Chearcaill	100
North-East Ridge	100
Suaineabhal	378
West Slabs	378
Suilven	287
Ridge Traverse	287
Tathabhal	372
North-West Rib	374
South-West Shoulder	372
Teinneasabhal	370
North Buttress	370
Thacla – See Hecla	
Toll Creagach	130
Toll Creagach Slab	130
Trollabhal	335
East Ridge	335
South Flank	336
South Slabs	337
West Ridge	338
Uamascleit	358
North-East Face	359
Ullapool Gorges	258
Allt a' Bhraighe	258
Allt a' Gharbhain	258
Allt Leacachain	259
Allt na h-Ighine	259
Ardcharnich Gorge	258

Wildlife: Further Reading

Stewart Angus, *The Outer Hebrides, Moor and Machair* (Cambridge and Harris: White Horse Press, 2001).

J Morton Boyd & IL Boyd, *The Hebrides (Collins New Naturalist)* (London: Collins, 1990).

F Fraser Darling & J Morton Boyd, *The Highlands and Islands (Collins New Naturalist)* (London: Collins, 1964).

PA Evans, IM Evans & GP Rothero, *Flora of Assynt* (Published privately, 2002).

Mark Wrightham & Nick Kempe (Eds.), *Hostile Habitats: Scotland's Mountain Environment* (2nd Edition: Scottish Mountaineering Press, 2019).

John A Love, *Rum: A Landscape Without Figures* (Birlinn, 2001).

Chris Lowe, *Torridon, the Nature of the Place* (Shieldaig, Ross-shire: Wester Ross Net, 2000).

Magnus Magnusson, *Rum: Nature's Island* (Edinburgh: Luath, 1997).

RJ Pankhurst & JM Mullin, *Flora of the Outer Hebrides* (London: The Natural History Museum, 1994).

DA Pearman, CD Preston, GP Rothero & KJ Walker, *The Flora of Rum: An Atlantic Island Reserve* (Published Privately, 2008).

Michael Scott, *Mountain Flowers: British Wildlife Collection No.4* (Bloomsbury, 2016).

Alan R Walker, *Identify Mountain Flowers of Britain and Ireland*, www.alanrwalker.com/mountain-flowers, [retrieved 15 April 2022].

Scottish Mountaineering Club

Established in 1889, the Scottish Mountaineering Club is at the forefront of climbing and mountaineering in Scotland. We want our guidebooks, covering hillwalking, scrambling and climbing, to be the first book you reach for when you head for the cliffs, hills and outcrops of Scotland.

www.smc.org.uk/publications

Scottish Mountaineering Press

The Scottish Mountaineering Press exists to promote and share Scotland's natural wonders. We do this by embracing the creativity and art born out of an explorer spirit. Whether it's poetry, photography or prose, our publications capture the moments when nature stuns us into silence and stops us in our tracks.

www.scottishmountaineeringpress.com

Scottish Mountaineering Trust

All profits from Scottish Mountaineering Press books go to help fund the Scottish Mountaineering Trust, a charity that provides grants to projects and organisations that promote recreation, knowledge and safety in the mountains, especially the mountains of Scotland.

www.thesmt.org.uk